VOLUME 28   NUMBER 2   2022

Queer Fire: Liberation and Abolition

Edited by Marquis Bey and Jesse A. Goldberg

QUEER AS IN ABOLITION NOW!

Marquis Bey and Jesse A. Goldberg

This special issue of *GLQ* begins and stays with this conviction as its premise and conclusion, one that is both heightened by and exceeds the boundaries of the present moment of crisis that is the COVID-19 pandemic: Prison abolition is a project of queer liberation and queer liberation is an abolitionist project. No ifs, ands, or buts.

The occasion for the topic of this special issue—queerness and abolition, inflected, necessarily, through one another—began in coalition. We, the editors, forged this special issue in conversation, in intellectual and political community both within and in excess of academic spaces. Such collective struggle is characteristic of the kind of ethos we hope the entries in this issue exude: one that articulates the radical tenor of abolition and queerness, where abolition is not affixed to certain "bad" institutions but is a pervasive call for the eradication of carcerality; where queerness is not merely a non-het, non-cis "identity" but a political posture subversive of normativity, hegemony, and power.

Indeed, the pandemic has highlighted the necropolitical mechanics of jails and prisons. According to a recent study published in *JAMA* (Saloner et al. 2020), "The COVID-19 case rate for prisoners was 5.5 times higher than the US population case rate"—and that is based on data that the researchers acknowledge likely undercounted both cases and deaths. While there is much to be written about COVID-19 and the prison-industrial complex (PIC), what we emphasize here is the way that this fact of higher case and death rates among the incarcerated indexes the fundamental functions of carceral institutions: containment and elimination.

In the face of this, activists around the globe are connecting the biopolitics of the pandemic to issues of climate justice, racial justice, gender justice, and disability justice that span a *longue durée* of racial capitalism made possible by extractive genocidal colonialism and chattel slavery.[1] We hear the phrases "abolition now" and "defund the police" uttered more frequently and in more main-

GLQ 28:2
DOI 10.1215/10642684-9608091
© 2022 by Duke University Press

stream venues than at any previous time during the twenty-first century. With renewed energy drawing on a radical politics that has always been present in queer life, we see more public debates about excluding cops from Pride marches.

It is in this context of attending to simultaneously the heightened precarities of the immediate now and the accumulating histories of both retrenched hegemony and lived refusals of the terms of order that we offer "Queer Fire: Liberation and Abolition." This issue is aimed at dislodging the comfortable logic of "the most vulnerable," or "the most affected," or "the disproportionately impacted" that often governs common discourse about the PIC in regard to various modes of difference, including along the axes of gender and sexuality as they intersect with race, ethnicity, and disability. This issue is an attempt to push analyses of queer liberation and abolition past the observations that prisons disproportionately or especially harm queer people toward seriously, rigorously imagining and working toward liberatory futures without prisons, police, or the tyranny of colonial gender systems.

The carceral epistemology of the prison not only is similar to but also is, itself, a carceral epistemology of gender, as scholarship and activism beyond liberal mainstream spaces has been arguing for decades (Stanley and Spade 2012: 119–21). "Queer Fire" pivots from Judith Butler's (2004: 1) insightful conditional, "if gender is a kind of doing," and asks, "What if gender is a kind of prison?" Thus, the issue takes seriously the question of gender abolition and the often-unspoken gender of (carceral) abolition. Abolition and queerness, taken together, name the eradication of the current terms of order imposed by racial capitalism as an ongoing settler-colonial structure. As a capitalist and settler-colonial structure, the terms of order that queerness and abolition undermine must end, full stop. Alexandre Martins and Caia Coelho, in this issue, make such an all-encompassing argument in their essay, "Notes on the (Im)possibilities of an Anti-colonial Queer Abolition of the (Carceral) World." Collaboratively writing from and about Brazilian anti-colonial queer politics, they elaborate a definition of "the world" as a construct of colonialism. From there, they envision both the end of prisons and police *and*, in a forceful and committed sense, the end of gender, sexuality, class, and race as structures of "the world" as such.

While Martins and Coelho's essay is unique in its explicit "abolition as a form of apocalypse" tenor, this spirit of setting queer fire to the current world—a present that is, according to José Esteban Muñoz (2009: 1), a "prison house"—in the process of building a new one is central to all of the articles in this issue. That is, if we understand the World to be a construct of colonialism, the essays in this issue collectively demonstrate how there are always worlds within the World; there is building happening at the same time that razing is required. Abolition is always two-sided in this way, not dissimilar to the queer futurity that is then and there on the horizon and also here and now in moments of relation.

S.M. Rodriguez's "Queers against Corrective Development: LGBTSTGNC Anti-violence Organizing in Gentrifying Times" begins the issue by arguing that gentrification is a carceral mechanism. At the same time, by zeroing in on the "myth of the lesbian gentrifier" and attending to the simultaneous criminalization of race, gender, disability, and sexuality, gentrification emerges as a site where anti-carceral and queer analysis must necessarily meet, ultimately arriving in an elaboration of how queer-of-color organizers in Brooklyn, New York, model the queerness of abolitionist politics. Stephen Dillon's "'I Must Become a Menace to My Enemies': Black Feminism, Vengeance, and the Futures of Abolition" continues Rodriguez's place- and space-conscious analysis by turning to the transnational scope of June Jordan's poetry. Dillon examines Jordan's mobilization of "black feminist vengeance" as a form of violence to open space for new ways of thinking. Far from offering an easy, reductive map of oppression and liberation, for Dillon,

> Even as Jordan is "the history of rape," she is also the history of gendered violence against other women of color around the world. In her terms, she is the enemy of Iraqi women, of Palestinian women, of Nicaraguan women, of Guatemalan women, of indigenous women. And so, Jordan must become not only an enemy to the police . . . but also an enemy to the enemy that she is as well. Being an enemy is not ontological, but epistemological.

This insight resonates with the anti-colonial energies of Martins and Coelho's essay.

In their essay, Martins and Coelho analyze the distinctions between "hegemonic" and "minor" LGBT movements in Brazil, arguing for the necessity of anti-carceral queer politics that do not look to punishment apparatuses for queer justice. Just as their anti-colonial analysis echoes Dillon's readings of Jordan, their unflinching critique of carceral LGBT political movements dovetails with Alison Reed's "'We're Here! We're Queer! Fuck the Banks!': On the Affective Lives of Abolition," which "takes up the spatial and symbolic relationship between the Pride parade and the prison industrial complex" in order to "demonstrate the urgency of queer abolitionist constellations of affect." In so doing, Reed analyzes the affective terrain of organizing spaces, protest marches, and jail programming while staying with the messy difficulties of doing abolition work and building queer kinship within institutional spaces that are imbricated in carcerality.

Like Reed's reflections on her own navigation through carceral institutional spaces as an abolitionist, Lorenzo Triburgo and Sarah Van Dyck carefully attend to the ethics of making queer art that represents the lives of incarcerated people in their essay, "Representational Refusal and the Embodiment of Gender Abolition." Through imagistic modes of representation attempting to, paradoxically, image non- and un-representability, they meditate on their creation of prison abolitionist photographs that subvert connections between queerness, deviance, and criminality. Jaden Janak directly continues these threads on art and the politics of (trans) visibility from Triburgo and Van Dyck's essay, while taking up again the focus on space and place that Rodriguez, Dillon, Martins and Coelho, and Reed sustain, in "(Trans)gendering Abolition: Black Trans Geographies, Art, and the Problem of Visibility." Moving through autobiography, documentary film, and recorded music, Janak highlights the importance of art as a medium through which to consider the process of making Black trans (abolitionist) geographies.

Closing the issue is "A Trans Way of Seeing," an essay collaboratively authored by Kitty Rotolo and Nadja Eisenberg-Guyot, who are physically separated by the walls of jails and prisons. The essay meditates intimately, lovingly, and rigorously on trans identity, affinity, and community across prison walls. As they reflect on their kinship via a trans and abolitionist mutuality, the authors theorize transness in excess of a specific corporeal form and affix it to and as a modality of relation: transness becomes an abolitionist posture that brings people together on the grounds of how they resist, commune, practice, and struggle in coalition with the project of dismantling violence. Their theorizing of a trans way of seeing inflects the desire to destroy the Colonial World with the affects of love and leaves us with the provocation to continue envisioning freedom.

It turns out, the fundamental affect at the heart of queer fire, and thus a condition of possibility for forging the possible out of what the World deems impossible, may very well be abolitionist love.

Notes

We deeply appreciate the labor of Liz Beasley and the advice and encouragement of C. Riley Snorton, Jennifer DeVere Brody, and Marcia Ochoa throughout this editorial process. We also deeply appreciate the labor of the workers at Duke University Press, the publisher of *GLQ*, and continue to call on the Press to recognize the results of their employees' 2021 unionization election.

1. Throughout her work Ruth Wilson Gilmore explains how the drawing of such connections is how "abolition geographies" are built; this is especially clear in Gilmore 2018.

The numerous writers whose works are collected in *Captive Genders: Trans Embodiment and the Prison Industrial Complex* (Stanley and Smith 2016) illustrate various analytic frameworks for understanding prison abolition as a queer politic specifically attendant to gender liberation as a horizon of trans politics. Angela Davis, throughout her work but especially in *Are Prisons Obsolete?* (2003) (chap. 4), as well as Beth Richie (2012) and Mariame Kaba (2021), explains clearly and definitively that prisons and police are enactors of, and therefore can never be tools for eliminating, gender violence. Liat Ben-Moshe (2020) expands analysis of carcerality through engagement with disability studies and activism. And a recent symposium in the journal *Antipode* titled "Abolition Ecologies" offers a number of ways of thinking about abolition as an ecological project—including an essay by Laurel Mei-Singh (2021) that critically and productively reflects on the struggles and possibilities for building abolitionist futures on a rapidly warming planet in partnership with indigenous communities.

References

Ben-Moshe, Liat. 2020. *Decarcerating Disability: Deinstitutionalization and Prison Abolition.* Minneapolis: University of Minnesota Press.

Butler, Judith. 2004. *Undoing Gender.* New York: Routledge.

Davis, Angela. 2003. *Are Prisons Obsolete?* New York: Seven Stories.

Gilmore, Ruth Wilson. 2018. "Making Abolition Geography in California's Central Valley." *Funambulist* 21, December 20. https://thefunambulist.net/magazine/21 -space-activism/interview-making-abolition-geography-california-central-valley-ruth -wilson-gilmore.

Kaba, Mariame. 2021. *We Do This 'til We Free Us: Abolitionist Organizing and Transforming Justice.* Chicago: Haymarket.

Mei-Singh, Laurel. 2021. "Accompaniment through Carceral Geographies: Abolitionist Research Partnerships with Indigenous Communities." *Antipode: A Journal of Radical Geography* 53, no. 1: 74–94.

Muñoz, José Esteban. 2009. *Cruising Utopia: The Then and There of Queer Futurity.* New York: New York University Press.

Richie, Beth E. 2012. *Arrested Justice: Black Women, Violence, and America's Prison Nation.* New York: New York University Press.

Saloner, Brendan, Kalind Parish, Julie A. Ward, Grace DiLaura, and Sharon Dolovich. 2020. "COVID-19 Cases and Deaths in Federal and State Prisons." *JAMA* 324, no. 6: 602. https://jamanetwork.com/journals/jama/fullarticle/2768249.

Stanley, Eric A., and Nat Smith, eds. 2016. *Captive Genders: Trans Embodiment and the Prison Industrial Complex.* Oakland, CA: AK Press.

Stanley, Eric A., and Dean Spade. 2012. "Queering Prison Abolition, Now?" *American Quarterly* 64, no. 1: 115–27.

QUEERS AGAINST CORRECTIVE DEVELOPMENT

LGBTSTGNC Anti-violence Organizing in Gentrifying Times

S.M. Rodriguez

$\mathcal{I}$n January 2016 the nearly condemned property next door to me in Brooklyn, New York, sold for $150,000. In the following year, we watched our neighbor, affectionately called "Hell Yeah" by the block, as he was forcibly evicted. The owner did nothing to update or renovate the property but instead focused on the riddance of the Black "squatters" and waited until the tide of gentrification traveled eastward, from Bed-Stuy to us in Ocean Hill, enough to make even an unlivable property valuable. In 2018 he sold it for $1,090,000.

My landlords, a European couple of Swedish and German descent, celebrated the removal of my neighbors, while other residents mourned that Hell Yeah's beloved cat wasn't safely retrieved from the basement before the full-gut renovations began. Seemingly sparing no expense on the renovation, the new white landlord next door remarked to the Chinese construction laborer that he intended to rent out each of the three floors at $3,000/month (only a few years ago, most people would have laughed at the thought of paying $1,300 for even a three-bedroom). In 2019 my Swedish landlord laughed when he heard this. Dismissively, he exclaimed, "Yeah right, not yet. Maybe if we can get a few more cafés up." He passed over my and my partner's dismay.

In this moment we see the owning class, the police, the prospective business, the new high-income resident—the gentrifying bodies—clearly. They collaborate to settle in and develop an idle land. Long-term residents wear racialization as a mark for removal. Displacement will occur through pricing us out or, like the neighbor who has been transformed into "squatter," through criminalizing whoever remains.

However unexpected the bald-faced admission was, the relationship

GLQ 28:2
DOI 10.1215/10642684-9608105
© 2022 by Duke University Press

between café culture and economic dispossession is furtive and historical. The earliest coffee shops mushroomed during the height of imperialism (Ellis 2004). A false marker of civility within uneven rule, European cities boldly featured the African delight that is coffee, acquired through the power and wealth accumulated by imperial expansion. Markman Ellis (2004) remarks that such grandeur and elegance surrounded the café, that building a café was often one of the "first things Ottoman rulers did in newly conquered cities." The English attributed coffee to the "Oriental," the Muslims whose settling of East Africa predated their own. In this way, perpetual colonization thrives with the usurpation of ownership over cultural goods and practices, the naturalization of the new belonging.

The café provides the opportunity to consume the exoticized Black culture; materialized, coffee becomes a simulacrum of the colonized other. Brooklyn is just one "perpetually colonial place" offering a taste of Blackness (Shange 2019). The many cafés with brand-new, commissioned murals or imitation graffiti with "Spread Love, It's the Brooklyn Way" (the famous Biggie lyric) host newcomers who don't remember the just-before—the recent history erased like the paint from the brick that told us whose cousin/sibling/child died from gun violence on the block. Their names and faces washed off, laundered as so much of the state-enabled violence that created this Black death world.

And still, most of us do not remember the name of the Lenape who thrived here in the long-ago, despite the very street name *Rockaway* and the neighborhood *Canarsie*. Instead, the "native" New Yorker is created through notice of who is displaced in the wake of shorter waves of settling forces. These waves, in turn, force migration.

The new café that appeared on my block whistled to its desired clientele through the honky-tonk tunes loudly played and the success at hiring an all-white staff in a deeply segregated, all-Black neighborhood. The 2010 census recorded 1.4 percent of Ocean Hill residents as white. The patrons always come from Bushwick, the neighborhood to the northeast, and hurry past any resident shuffling up or down the stairs of the Rockaway subway station. There's a subtle hostility underlying this new business, not merely in the averted eyes, the absence of greeting potential patrons of African descent. It is within all that is being communicated to each other, in exchanges beyond the interpersonal; we sense it, but it is never spoken. It is instead communicated in policy, through the expansion of surveillance and securitization as well as the quality-of-life ordinances that rely on police discretion for regulation of racially marked people despite "race-neutral" language.[1] In this article, I demonstrate that gentrification is thus a process that is facilitated by, and also facilitates, mechanisms of the carceral state, and so we must include gentrification as an axis of our analyses of the prison-industrial complex and visions of abolition.

Corrective Development

New York State entered a period of rapid prison expansion between the 1970s, when there were twenty-one "correctional facilities," including work camps and institutions for the "mentally ill or retarded,"[2] and the 1990s, when the state reached sixty-five prisons (Lawrence and Travis 2004). At the juncture of this phase's settling and the neoliberal and punitive ideologies of Mayors Rudy Giuliani and Michael Bloomberg, Brooklyn began to experience gentrification. That is, we see the displacement of the working-class population by higher classes, through a nexus of policy changes, increased policing, housing renovations exclusively accessible to the rich, and replacement of local, small businesses. Gentrification includes housing development, which prices out "unwanted people" or coerces people into moving out through aggravated landlord neglect (Crosby 2020; Ponder 2016) and racially targeted buyouts (Gibson 2015). It is aided by hyperpolicing, in which state terror methods increase stops and tickets (Kaplan-Lyman 2012; Robinson 2020) as well as arrests, assaults, and homicides against marginalized people (Rodriguez, Ben-Moshe and Rakes 2020). Importantly, hyperpolicing is also upheld by newcomers (often collectively called gentrifiers and, more recently, Karens) who knowingly or unknowingly deploy the forces of state terror to satisfy their personal senses of order and control in the area (Robinson 2020).

Gentrification therefore relies on "corrective development": the forced movement of Black mad, poor, and/or queer bodies from a target geography to less desired areas by use of corrective violence. Corrective violence is structural and systematic, encompassing the utilization and tacit approval of regularized violence against oppressed peoples as well as the violent enforcement of social immobility by protecting poverty in one of the richest states in the richest country of the world.

I offer the term *corrective development* to combat the idea of gentrification as a passive occurrence in which higher-income people happen to find the hood interesting, trendy, or convenient. Instead, it is imperative that we acknowledge the underlying violence and how the power to dispossess is wielded. In this article, I also offer a snapshot of the abolitionist (anti-corrections) work that queer people of color in Brooklyn have mobilized to empower the community against corrective violence. Ultimately, I offer this language and analysis of corrective development so that we understand the entanglements of queerphobia, racism, ableism, and disposability that queer transformative justice moves to abolish in Brooklyn.

Ejection, Invitation, Correction

To usher in trendy cafés and other profitable, gentrifying bodies, neighborhoods need both sides of correction; the punitive removal of racialized, poor, disabled people is met with the invitation of the desired resident. While the removal relies on police violence that criminalizes, brutalizes, and kills residents, the invitation, on the other hand, arrives through white investments: suddenly the city lends a regular sanitation effort, there is access to fresh or freshly prepared foods. The state makes available certain quality-of-life investments that would have transformed life for previous residents.

Gentrification "develops" racialized areas for the colonial settling of those with high racial capital. Roderick Ferguson (2018) argues that the "one-dimensional queer" is a manifestation of this highly valued subject, as high marks on (white) gay equality indexes begin to positively indicate the economic potential of the successful, creative (one-dimensional) city. Racial capitalism, within a neoliberal framework, creates surplus out of the unassimilable (Gilmore 2007). Surplus bodies, in turn, are capitalized on, through their rebirth as carceral objects. Within "idle" lands recently marked for neoliberal development, carcerality serves as an opportunity to expand employment. Those within productive, assimilated classes gain access to opportunities for violence work, which proliferate with the passage of new punitive governmental policies that increase the presence and technologies of law enforcement. Simultaneously, a neoliberal rationality encourages a market to regulate human life (and death) and to work alongside the government to demarcate the safe citizen from the deviant.[3] Development, therefore, equally relies on carceral tactics of surveillance, threat, and punishment as it does the projection of innovation, freedom, and "progressive" potential to achieve neighborhood corrections.

Corrections in the United States most often describes the institution that holds custody of criminalized people, purportedly to reform or reorient them from nonnormative behaviors through labeling, isolation, and constraint. Federal and state governments' corrections departments warehouse people with the retributive and/or incapacitating aim to neutralize the populations that cannot be incorporated into the "normate" (Garland-Thomson 2017). This includes a disproportionate representation of people of color, disabled and neurodivergent people, queer people, and the indigent. Therefore, in my use of the term *corrections*, I point to two intentions: (1) forced assimilation of the unproductive body into the normate social body or, if found impossible, (2) the removal of this body from the public to correct the "balance" of the social environment.[4]

Foundational to corrective violence is the pathologization of difference. Sanism and criminalization interplay to manage the threat of different people and ways of being (Ben-Moshe 2020). The perception of deviance is entrenched in the idea of an altered or sickened state of mind, therefore attaching psychiatrized meaning on to the queer body. These imaginative, ableist attachments then justify various attempts at neutralizing the deviance. One may witness such attempts in forced medicalization and (carceral) institutionalization in psychiatric hospitals (Ben-Moshe, Chapman, and Carey 2014; Appleman 2018; Ben-Moshe 2020), as well as jails or prisons (Black 2008; Davis 2003). However, as the "one-dimensional queer" enjoys the cultural and state process of normalization through homonationalism, the multidimensional suffer the brunt of anti-queer pathologization and, in turn, corrective violence (Puar 2007).

Other forms of corrective violence include social exclusion, brutalizing, and killing, which all exist in concomitant anti-queer manifestations, by our state, our neighbors, and our loved ones. These tactics are meant to invoke deterrence—"retribution's specter" (Gilmore 2007: 14)—and symbolically communicate to others that the form of deviance chosen or embraced is indeed unacceptable in the society. The state also undertakes corrective violence to shift surplus bodies (the unwanted, unproductive, unassimilable) geographically, ushering them out of the desired urban or suburban location and "depositing them somewhere else" (14). The "somewhere else," strikingly, is often a distant and isolated rural location, removed from community and kin. In many ways, carceral violence is used to correct certain people and spaces, in service of protecting desired people and spaces (Rodriguez, Ben-Moshe, and Rakes 2020).

Within queer theory, we have the opportunity to put forward a more expansive understanding of corrections, so that its applicability extends outside the prison or the jail. We can look into aspects of society imprisoned by similar logics: ones that "correct" (cure, reform, or fix) deviance through coercive and violent practices. One of the most well-articulated in academic literature is corrective rape—a practice of weaponizing sexual assault to instill a lasting fear into queer people with the aim of limiting their future expressions to heterosexuality and gender conformity (Morrissey 2013; Moffett 2006). Importantly, corrective rape has always been acknowledged to exist at the intersection of queerness and Blackness, so much so that authors in South Africa often limit its definition explicitly to intraracial violence (Morrissey 2013). Within ostensibly democratic countries, particularly those with recent histories of overt white supremacist political domination, such as South Africa or the United States, racially or ethnically minoritized people become the most susceptible to extra-legal punishment (Kynoch 2016). As is the case of all violent criminalized action, the vast majority of it is intraracial, occurring within one racial group, rather than between groups. Corrective rape is one hate-based extension of the nationalist violence used to coerce a population into coherence. Mirroring the state's mandate for conformity, it is just one form of violence that is unironically utilized to "teach" or "convince" a perceived "offender" of social deviance to fall in line (Moffett 2006). It is time to more comprehensively account for "corrective" violence.

Gender-Based, Hate, and State Violence as Mutually Constitutive Corrective Violence

Corrective violence articulates itself through various institutional bodies and cultural exchanges. If we queer the gender-based violence (GBV) framework, that is, if we think of GBV not as violence against women but rather as attacks in service of gender correction, which disproportionately targets femininity (Haynes and DeShong 2017; West 2013), then we are more likely to see how anti-LGBT hate violence, intimate partner violence (IPV), and state violence all represent corrective violence.

S.M. Rodriguez, Liat Ben-Moshe, and H. Rakes (2020) offer an intersectional view of state violence as corrective control, particularly of homicide in encounters with police, in which racial criminal pathologization relies on gendering Black and queer bodies as other. This other gender is cast as perpetually invulnerable to violence, despite being constantly subjected to it and disproportionately likely to experience early death (5). Following Cathy Cohen's (1997) expansion of queer politics beyond those who identify with sexual marginalization or deviance, we can situate the police killings of even Black cismen like Michael Brown in the realm of gender correction. Such killings are the manifestation of hegemonic—or structurally authorized[5]—masculine domination of marginalized or subordinate masculinities. In this case, it is the white male state's correction of the imagined unruly Black subject's masculinity.

The "gender-deviant," queer body, especially those of Black transwomen, has been at the forefront of this conversation owing to increased vulnerability to corrective violence. The National Coalition of Anti-Violence Programs has shown through regularly collected reports on anti-queer violence that it is not atypical that the majority if not all IPV-related deaths in the queer community are of transwomen of color (NCAVP 2013, 2014, 2015, 2016). Similarly, the majority of people who suffer fatal victimization from anti-queer hate violence in a given year are transwomen of color (GLAAD 2018; NCAVP 2013, 2014, 2015, 2016).

This corrective violence manifests sexually and is reinforced interpersonally and structurally. An interlocutor in Brandon Andrew Robinson's *Coming Out to the Streets* (2020), "Justice," explains the circumstances surrounding a rape that she suffered. Not only did police not "protect" her, but they told her that the incident was not important because they believed she engaged in sex work to make a living (which, to them, justified the rape). Notably, they also regularly harassed her before and after the incident for what is colloquially referred to as "walking while trans."

Justice's identity as a Black transwoman increases her likelihood of bias-motivated harm, IPV,[6] and gender policing by both the state's official violence workers as well as those protected by the state, such as Justice's rapist. With a sample of 27,715 respondents, the 2015 U.S. Transgender Survey (USTS) found that 72 percent of respondents who had engaged in sex work had been sexually assaulted in their lifetime (James et al. 2016). The majority of respondents—sex working or not—did not feel safe or comfortable calling the police if they needed help. More than half (58 percent) of transwomen had been mistreated by the police—many of whom experienced further assault. When we narrow our look into USTS data on Black transwomen in sex work, the figure becomes more striking, as 90 percent report experiencing harassment and sexual and nonsexual physical assault by the police. Therefore, cases like Justice's demonstrate not arbitrary police discrimination or mistreatment but systematic and perpetual violence work in service of correcting the deviance associated with queer sexual exchanges (Dalton 2007) and Black gender expansiveness (Robinson 2020).

As mutually constitutive correctives, state violence and gender violence are appropriated or exacerbated in gentrifying times. For example, gender-based state violence increased in the crackdown of Australian "beat spaces," when plainclothes police officers would perform a caricaturized mimicry of presumed gay male femininity (Dalton 2007). The pursuit of correcting "homocriminality" rose in the context of protecting normative straight, white publics during rapid cultural and social change (Dalton 2007). This corrective pursuit followed the logic of "cleaning up" the streets by removing the "filth" of homosexual sex, a logic bolstered by the association of excrement with the bathrooms that were frequented for sexual interaction. In the former "lavender scare," this police action may have been a part of a "Pervert Elimination Campaign" (Robinson 2020). Today, in New York City, however, this is part of the neoliberal limitation of public "contact spaces" that used to nurture queer life and expression before gentrification (Delany 1999; Ferguson 2018). The contact spaces of the old, multidimensional city were meant not just for sex but also for self-invention, self-exploration, and the invention of new communities by those who have been expelled from their bio-family homes (Ferguson 2018: 94).

Relatedly, Katie Hail-Jares, Catherine Paquette, and Margot Le Neuveu (2017) demonstrate the detrimental effects of forced local migration due to neo-liberal shifts in city policy. Civilian hate violence can occur when people, unaccustomed to the rules of particular blocks, unintentionally encounter a queer or trans space. This is especially likely if the encounter involves sex work or sexual exchange (Oselin and Cobbina 2017). The collapse of formerly distinct neighborhoods can force displaced folks into new blocks with differently established cultures or politics (Hail-Jares, Paquette, and Le Neuveu 2017). In Brooklyn, we see this as gentrification haunts from west to east, pushing Black residents to move their livelihoods to the furthest neighborhoods east, such as East New York.

As a community organizer, I have seen how hate violence occurs when community members begin to scapegoat queer people for the changes to the neighborhood. There is a prevalent myth of the "lesbian gentrifier," in which *lesbian* always signifies white woman.[7] The tension is heightened as the cautionary tale, "Park Slope was first gentrified by the lesbians," circulates and provides a target for anxieties caused by racial capitalism. This perception has its basis in urban developers' strategic deployment of the image of a "one-dimensional queer": the white, working-professional gay whose simplified creativity is one, perhaps, of a musical interest or software development, rather than a political commitment to creating a new, radical community-oriented culture (Ferguson 2018). The image of the gay, white elite signals a "meritocratic norm" (Florida 2012) in place of a repressive or backward norm. Unlike queer people of color, this gay subject ushers in new capital and the migration of an elite creative class (i.e., "techies") who—as individuals and as businesses—constitute highly coveted gentrifying bodies (Ferguson 2018). This presence becomes a representation of a racialized otherness, even when non-white queer people were always in the neighborhood, even among the truly Indigenous who once prospered on and with the land (Barker 2017).

Lastly, gentrification causes economic and housing insecurity, which can instigate intimate partner violence. Navigating multiple valences of structural violence, trans and gender-nonconforming people are already at increased risk of experiencing IPV. In the national survey collected by Richard S. Henry and colleagues (2018), 71.8 percent of trans and gender-nonconforming respondents reported experiencing at least one form of IPV in their lifetime. Police often shield those who enact hate violence and GBV, as they are guided by their own subjectivities, which may also hold anti-queer biases (Richie 2012; Mogul, Ritchie, and Whitlock 2011). Police are disproportionately likely to commit gender-based violence, both in the home through domestic disputes (Valentine, Oehme, and Martin 2012) and against queer and trans people who attempt to seek their help (NCAVP 2013, 2014, 2015, and 2016). Data overwhelmingly suggest that police officers in the United States do not respond satisfactorily to 911 calls for domestic disputes, thereby enabling violence (Mogul, Ritchie, and Whitlock 2011: 119). Additionally, many 911 calls made by LGBTQ people end up with the police physically assaulting the queer caller (NCAVP 2016, James et al. 2016).

Importantly, both phenomena of police violence and GBV affect multiply marginalized groups, whether cis Black or immigrant women or queer femmes. As Saidiya Hartman (2020) remarked in an interview with Catherine Damman, Black femme life is in part defined by an "incredible vulnerability to violence and to abuse." This is due to the underlying corrective impulse to maintain a cis-hetero-patriarchal social order, which views acts of gender subversion as particularly threatening. In this way, GBV epitomizes the spirit of policing. Only through acknowledgment of these interconnections are we able to exact abolitionist work.

Therefore, corrective violence is not only a distinctly gendered phenomenon but one that queer-of-color activism is particularly well suited to address. The root of such work must be anti-corrective, so that abolition does not just eliminate physical institutions (jails and prisons) but also transforms the cultural institutions that lie at the foundation of our most harmful impulses. So while distinct campaigns such as #NoNewJails reflect abolitionist organizing, abolition itself "is constituted by so many acts long overlapping, dispersed across geographies and historical moments, that reveal the underside of the New World and its descendant forms—the police, jail, prison, criminal court, detention center, reservation, plantation, and 'border'" (D. Rodríguez 2019: 1577). It is also constituted by movements against penal attitudes (Berger, Kaba, and Stein 2017; Pepinsky 1994) and the "carceral enclosures" that contain our corrective logics (Ben-Moshe 2020: 111).

Grassroots Anti-violence Activism

Arriving home one fourth of July, my wife and I noticed two lovers, both women, fighting. I note that it was an American holiday not for reverence for the date but because holidays often accompany spikes in interpersonal violence. The lovers were noticeably intoxicated, especially the "stud," as they walked from one party to a family BBQ in the neighborhood. An argument ensued because the femme lover did not want to go to the stud's family's BBQ; she wanted to stay home. At some point, the argument escalated and became physical. At the point of my arrival, the femme had been pushed into the street while attempting to use a parallel-parked-car as a buffer between her and her lover. She narrowly missed an oncoming car, speeding above the twenty-five-mile-per-hour limit for the city.

It took forty-five minutes and the twice unintentional shedding of blood to de-escalate the situation. Forty-five minutes on a New York City block is enough time to encounter an entire small town's worth of people. No one helped. No one stopped outside the café. My partner and I only succeeded in moving them away from the café's doorstep because the country music served as a clear indicator that all of us were in danger of police violence at any moment. The back-and-forth of insults, the mutual cycles of aggression and self-pity, the little failures and successes to defuse finally—they remind me of the imperative of Black-led, queer, abolitionist organizing in Brooklyn.

According to Ejeris Dixon (2020: 19), transformative justice works when neighbors execute "bold, small experiments" to practice community accountability and reduce or eliminate interpersonal violence. Ejeris, the founding coordinator of the Safe OUTside the System Collective (SOS), believes in the power of community-based strategies for intervening in violence. This belief is grounded in a history of coordinated anti-violence movements that began largely in the 1970s, coinciding with the advent of mass incarceration and the growth of the carceral state (Pleck 1987). Transformative justice describes a system of responses to violence that relies on community and civil leadership, especially of those most impacted by violence, to identify and transform the root causes of violence (Kim 2018).

The SOS Collective is the creation of lesbian, gay, bisexual, two-spirit, transgender, and gender-nonconforming (LGBTSTGNC) abolitionists of color who have committed to fighting state and hate violence without the use of the police.[8] Its fifteen-year history of enacting abolitionist anti-violence organizing has only grown stronger and more strategic through the rapid, forced displacement of Central Brooklyn's working-class people of African descent. The SOS Collective employs transformative justice (TJ) responses, acknowledging that interpersonal violence thrives in the context of structural violence: the poverty, ableism, racism, and heterosexism embedded within coloniality exacerbate interpersonal division. Transformative justice also allows practitioners to recognize that the retributive justice system, or regime of punishment that we currently endure, provides counter-deterrent measures that actually further entrench cultures of violence (Bazemore and Umbreit 1995).

Therefore, community accountability organizers experiment and employ anti-violence tools in which the state doesn't invest. Empowering community members with verbal violence de-escalation strategies is one such "bold, small experiment." The SOS Collective regularly offers trainings and grounds this work as the foundation of its many community offerings. For example, the Safe Party Toolkit (ALP 2016) teaches how to minimize the likelihood of violent encounters during social gatherings.[9] Community Security for protests and events provides a buffer between protestors and state agents or counter-protestors. There are workshops for safety planning when surviving IPV. All of these community engagements stimulate the propagation of learned anti-violence in Brooklyn.

Verbal de-escalation is the centerpiece of it all. The larger community organizing center, the Audre Lorde Project (ALP), to which the collective belongs, regularly offers verbal de-escalation training and security training for free to its thousands of members and allies. Developed in conversation with other Black community organizations such as the Malcolm X Grassroots Project, the antiviolence strategies let community members identify their own core skills. Violence de-escalation can occur with humor, with empathy, with elder authority or youth leadership, and so forth. What fits each de-escalator is learned and personalized, and the idea is that each trained individual would feel not only personally responsible for intervening in violence but also empowered to do so safely.

Trainings focus mostly on the how of engagement: how do you communicate antiviolence with your posture or tone; how do you avoid attracting violence workers (police); how do you deliver a calming message? How do you offer a follow-up that supports those who may be harmed in the interaction (or, especially in IPV situations, both parties, as healing and support is especially necessary to transform situations of sustained engagement)?

In my de-escalation of the fight between the lovers, I knew my best traits to engage were sincerity, sternness, and empathy. (I am not particularly funny, physically imposing, or elderly). Instead of flatly assuming a mimicry of a patriarchal power dynamic, I listened to the stud express anguish that her lover had hit and scratched her; I heard the femme describe her frustration with this arbitrary and forceful detention. I expressed sympathy for their pains and doubled-down on the need to never push or strike each other. In the breaks between the agitation—the calm openings—I stressed the urgency of separation for the day.

In the moments taken over by the chaos of anger, all that could be done was an attempt to create buffers between the two parties. We swiped the femme lover into the subway station, hoping that the physical bars would facilitate separation. In the Rockaway subway station, where the stillness of the (dependable) train delay required everyone to witness the commotion rather than "keep it moving," it was ultimately the sustained, outside attention and my and my wife's unrelenting company that abated the tension. I collected both of their phone numbers so that I could verify that they were safe and separate that night and refer them to a caring check-in from someone in the collective.

Those who undergo safety training also learn how to identify violence. While some forms of violence are easily spotted, others are subtle, especially when in your own peer group, romantic relationship, or social structure. The violence of the state can be especially veiled. This remains true regardless of how obvious the effects are: the unavailability of fresh food in my food desert, the early death of my people, the school-to-prison pipeline. Every training offers a theoretical and speculative introduction, which offers us not only a deeper grounding in the work but also ownership over the *why* to engage.

The SOS Collective expanded the definition of violence during the Community Freestyle "Space Violence" in 2014, under the leadership of Ejeris's successor, Che Johnson-Long. The annual Community Freestyle is an event that provides an opportunity for the neighborhood to come together and learn from member-led facilitators, "riff off each other" (exchange thoughts in a casual or even poetic manner), and develop new relationships. Freestyles connect people intergenerationally and without regard to gender identity or sexual orientation, as allies are welcome. The "Space Violence" event featured four workshops, in two sessions where members could choose which to attend based on the relevance in their lives or what they desire to learn. The workshops focused on "being a supportive community member in a new neighborhood," "creating safe spaces," and "know your rights," with the last topic discussed in two sessions—one about encounters with police, the other about encounters with landlords. The event closed out with an open mic session.

This conceptual expansion transforms the collective members from passive victims of displacement to active participants in combatting neighborhood correction, a form of violence experienced by the majority of those involved in the anti-violence movement. Incorporating gentrification into the purview of the anti-violence collective allows for the work to extend into housing security organizing. This proves particularly necessary, given the problematic assumption that queer people are themselves a sign of gentrification or a new racialization of the neighborhood. The "Space Violence" framework also allows us to highlight the connections between the forms of violence that both queer people of color and straight men experience in Brooklyn at the hands of the state. It is this connection making that encourages the involvement of Black cisgender-owned businesses in intervening in anti-trans violence on the block. In fact, when SOS started the Safe Neighborhood Campaign (SNC), the majority of businesses involved were owned by Black cismen.

How Space Violence Compromises Grassroots Activism

The Safe Neighborhood Campaign's central tenet is that anti-violence is a communal responsibility, and local businesses are crucial entities nurturing and cultivating community. A fuller reduction of "the bystander effect" requires the participation of the businesses that often serve as the backdrop to violent public encounters. Therefore, the SNC initially set out to train business owners, managers, and employees to become "safe spaces" that would provide safe harbor to queer people experiencing harassment, threat, or assault on nearby streets. The imagined network of businesses would provide a geographical web that would cover the relatively small area of Central Brooklyn neighborhoods (predominantly Bed-Stuy and Crown Heights). This collaboration invites two major accomplishments: it halts some of the street-based removal of queer and trans people by cops, and it increases business flow into Black-owned businesses by queer patrons who want to support the livelihood of their neighbors. The mutuality affirms Black lives locally and forges connections between queer and straight community members.

The initial work of a Safe Space training as conceived by the SNC is, like de-escalation trainings, to identify the why's of engagement. Why not just call the cops? Why bother do anything at all? We are able to do this with a "methodology of connection" that grounds us in the "historical present tense" (D. Rodríguez 2019: 1576) necessary for the abolitionist imagination. That is, we engage the overlaps between our struggles more furiously than the disconnects, and we stress it while highlighting the continued marginalization and state of "normalized misery" that those of African descent endure, regardless of sexuality (D. Rodríguez 2010: 8). This, in fact, puts us in a similarly queer position—outside, contrary to, or disruptive of assumptions of what Americanness supposedly proffers. It also radically reframes the deviant label applied to Black trans people and the supposed "invulnerability" of the Black (queer) body (Rodriguez, Ben-Moshe, Rakes 2020).

By 2018 the SNC included not just "brick-and-mortar" businesses but also virtual businesses, cultural workers, and others who may be more transient (working from home or in shared work spaces). This transition was due not only to the desire to expand the network but also to the striking decline in Black-owned physical spaces in Central Brooklyn. For example, in 2014 Che Johnson-Long, Ceci Piñeda, and I trained a small café in Bed-Stuy owned by an enthusiastic, young Black (straight) woman. The training took four hours and especially attended to the ways in which certain forms of structural violence—racism, nativism, homophobia, and transphobia—are connected. We ran through tactics of de-escalation, what to do when you hear antagonistic language yelled outside (deployments of *faggot* or rape threats, for example), and role-played some strategies that she could use since she owned a private space. I remember leaving an eager and engaged business owner. I remember holding our cyphers—casual, topic-based political consciousness raising events—in the space to support her business. I remember her rent rising in the following year and community members going out of their way to buy goods from her location. I remember her going out of business and losing her economic livelihood anyway. This has happened to the majority of spaces that we trained in the first half of the 2010s.

Therefore, gentrification limits the number of safe spaces available in a neighborhood for queer people of African descent. The rising cost of rent, both residential and commercial, means that not only are the old faces gone (elders and lifelong residents—who are often more likely to say something or intentionally witness a hostile exchange) but also the longtime, local business owners who develop personal relationships with residents, straight or queer. The high turnover, in a practical sense, makes on-the-ground training campaigns unsustainable. As soon as we trained a business, it closed down. As soon as it closed down, a new sign is erected, often something in French or Italian, with another class of clientele in mind. The new spaces transformed Black people into an indistinguishable, undesirable mass, even when purporting queer friendliness, like the new café on my block, which hosts "RuPaul Drag Nights" for an all-white audience.

When I attempted the de-escalation in front of the café, the range of tactics that I could use were limited. The white-only nature of the café "renovated" it from a potential safe space that could aid in the intervention into hostile territory that could invite violence workers at any moment. The proprietors of the safe spaces who were trained between 2010 and 2016 were trained with connection in mind: the violence we face is the violence you face. The violence has a different angle, but the makeup remains. On the other hand, places that rely on "space violence" articulate that they are not only okay with our removal through housing displacement, but that when we—suited in various amalgamations of racialized, queer, and disabled codes—become a nuisance, they are okay with our removal through criminalization and corrections.

Conclusion

In conclusion, *corrective development* describes the marriage of coercive logic with the clearing and resettling of our hometown by populations of greater racial capital. The regulatory desire to "clean up" a neighborhood is intimately linked to the white, heterosexist imagination that positions the queer and Black body as inherently sullied and sullying. The streets that have been known as queer spaces are refashioned or repurposed for state-corporate commercial endeavors, which elites and the state then rely on the police to "clean up" or "perpetually surveil" (Dalton 2007). This is well known in certain New York (Manhattan) spaces such as the Christopher Street Piers (Struening 2016). It is less well known that areas of Brooklyn, especially Coney Island and the Promenade, underwent this process (Ryan 2019). Today we see the same patrolling of Riis Beach—just the queer side—that invites police harassment and brutality for the desire of commodifying the land (Carber 2016; Sayers 2021).

The mandate to "clean up the streets" also leaves some to suffer quality-of-life policing, which enables expansive measures to consign racialized people to the cyclical reality of labeling. Whether poor in real terms of income, or assumed poor through the lens of racial capitalism, this labeling allows those in power to assign criminality and deviant potential. The criminalized class then "requires" additional surveillance, which produces regularized punishments (especially through fines and jailing). These punishments accumulate and produce a "high crime area," which then justifies increased policing. This cycle exists while securitization funds snowball and state violence workers take over our streets, our schools, our subways.

The queer praxis currently combatting corrective development embraces abolitionist methods to create and sustain life in this increasingly panoptic, punitive area. Our transformative methods decrease the likelihood of encountering the violence workers of the state and the institutions of corrections that liberal leadership seeks to multiply.[10] Queer abolitionist community organizing also cultivates messages and methods to encourage and empower us to engage in anti-violence practices that can actively create the safety that we seek as a multiply marginalized community.

Queer community organizing that centers transformative justice and community accountability holds the potential to radically reimagine our sense of deservingness. A collective struggle against the state and structural space violence of gentrification amplifies the message that everyone deserves bodily integrity, livable shelter, a clean environment, food, and community. What does penal abolition mean to SOS and ALP? It means ridding the community not only of institutions of violence and corrections but also of the perpetual punishment of African bodies in the United States. It means enabling life-affirming institutions and practices that rehumanize us after slavery and colonization. This is abolition, reimagined by queer collectivity in Brooklyn, New York.

Notes

1. See Michelle Alexander's *New Jim Crow* ([2010] 2020) for an elaboration of colorblind racism in the US criminal legal system.

2. The New York State Department of Corrections published the booklet *100 Years of Progress* in 1970, boasting the centralized governance of the twenty-one facilities, which featured unprecedented diversity of its officials and responsive medical care. The facilities included "four conservation work camps for young men, an institution for the mentally retarded male offenders and one for mentally retarded female offenders, two hospitals for mentally ill offenders, six maximum security facilities for men and four medium security facilities for men, three female correctional facilities." See NYSDOC 1970.

3. The violent tactics of the goon squad, at the employ of "elite corporate institutions using powers traditionally reserved by the state to clean up the streets," serve as a strong example of private investment in state terroristic policing during neoliberal times (Kaplan-Lyman 2012).

4. For example, an explicit admission of this project was made by the sheriff of Kenosha, who argued for the warehousing of the Black population before they have time for wanton reproduction, which would serve the "greater good." See Radcliffe 2020.

5. Raewyn Connell offers an introduction into these many layers of masculinities with the 1995 text *Masculinities*. She posits that the structural violence of racism and poverty excludes Black male masculinity from the hegemon.

6. With a sample of 27,715 respondents, the 2015 U.S. Transgender Survey (USTS) found that the majority (54 percent) of trans and gender-nonconforming adults had experienced intimate partner violence in their lifetime (James et al. 2016).

7. This narrative is commonly held and communicated. It is also found within academia, including in Tamar Rothenberg's (1995) concluding remarks. The reductive point that is made is that clusters of lesbians (implying white women) moved to Park Slope as a network that eventually led to white domination of the space. The displacement is marked by the most recent census data that shows Park Slope is nearly 70 percent white, 36.9 percent whiter than the rest of New York City in total.

8. SOS is also the organizing body to which I have dedicated nearly the last decade. I offer this analysis after engaging in sustained grassroots efforts ("experiments") that have helped de-escalate violence, safety plan, keep people out of jail, and protect LGBTSTGNC people while assembling.

9. The Safe Party Toolkit is available free for anyone (ALP 2016).

10. In 2019 the administration of New York City's mayor Bill de Blasio allocated $8.7 billion dollars to build four "modern," borough-based jails to replace Rikers Island by 2026. With no firm deadline to actually close Rikers facilities, activists fear that by 2026, a new administration will retain Rikers and utilize new jails to expand incarceration. See Brown et al. 2020.

References

Alexander, Michelle. (2010) 2020. *The New Jim Crow: Mass Incarceration in the Age of Colorblindness*. New York: New Press.

ALP (Audre Lorde Project). 2016. "Safe Party Toolkit." Updated February 18, 2016. drive.google.com/file/d/0BxlqoamGVS6lMV9oSy0zNGlYNEE/view?resourcekey =0-nWxnYp4Kqx7Yyy-U5w1S_Q.

Appleman, Laura I. 2018. "Deviancy, Dependency, and Disability: The Forgotten History of Eugenics and Mass Incarceration." *Duke Law Journal* 68, no. 3: 417–78.

Barker, Joanne, ed. 2017. *Critically Sovereign: Indigenous Gender, Sexuality, and Feminist Studies*. Durham, NC: Duke University Press.

Bazemore, Gordon, and Mark Umbreit. 1995. "Rethinking the Sanctioning Function in Juvenile Court: Retributive or Restorative Responses to Youth Crime." *Crime and Delinquency* 41, no. 3: 296–316.

Black, Lee. 2008. "Forced Medication of Prison Inmates." *AMA Journal of Ethics* 10, no. 2: 106–9.

Ben-Moshe, L. 2020. *Decarcerating Disability: Deinstitutionalization and Prison Abolition*. Minneapolis: University of Minnesota Press.

Ben-Moshe, Liat, Chris Chapman, and Allison Carey. 2014. *Disability Incarcerated: Imprisonment and Disability in the United States and Canada*. New York: Palgrave Macmillan.

Berger, Dan, Mariame Kaba, and David Stein. 2017. "What Abolitionists Do." *Jacobin*, August 24. jacobinmag.com/2017/08/prison-abolition-reform-mass-incarceration.

Brown, Osha Oneeka Daya, Lee Doane, Sterling Fleming, Hakim Trent, Jeremy Valerio, and No New Jails NYC. 2020. "$11 Billion for What?! Incarcerated Organizers with No New Jails NYC Explain How to Shut Down Rikers without Building New Jails." *City University of New York Law Review* 23, no. 1: 1–24.

Carber, Frank. 2016. "NYC Gay Man Tackled, Arrested by Police on LGBT-Friendly Beach." *Metro Weekly*, July 7. www.metroweekly.com/2016/07/nyc-man-tackled -police-gay-beach/.

Cohen, Cathy. 1997. "Punks, Bulldaggers, and Welfare Queens: The Radical Potential of Queer Politics?" *GLQ* 3, no. 4: 437–65.

Connell, Raewyn. 1995. *Masculinities*. Berkeley: University of California Press.

Crosby, Andrew. 2020. "Financialized Gentrification, Demoviction, and Landlord Tactics to Demobilize Tenant Organizing." *Geoforum* 108: 184–93.

Dalton, Derek. 2007. "Policing Outlawed Desire: 'Homocriminality' in Beat Spaces in Australia." *Law and Critique* 18, no. 3: 375–405.

Davis, Angela. 2003. *Are Prisons Obsolete?* New York: Seven Stories.

Delany, Samuel R. 1999. *Times Square Red, Times Square Blue*. New York: New York University Press.

Dixon, Ejeris. 2020. "Building Community Safety." In *Beyond Survival: Strategies and*

Stories from the Transformative Justice Movement, edited by Ejeris Dixon and Leah Lakhsmi Piepzna-Samarasinha, 15–26. Chico, CA: AK.

Ellis, Markman. 2004. *The Coffee House: A Cultural History.* London: Orion House.

Ferguson, Roderick A. 2018. *One-Dimensional Queer.* Cambridge: Polity.

Florida, Richard. 2012. *The Rise of the Creative Class: Revisited.* 10th anniversary ed. New York: Basic Books.

Garland-Thomson, Ruth. 2017. *Extraordinary Bodies: Figuring Physical Disability in American Culture and Literature.* New York: Columbia University Press.

Gibson, David-William. 2015. *The Edge Becomes the Center: An Oral History of Gentrification in the Twenty-First Century.* N.p.: Abrams Press.

Gilmore, Ruth Wilson. 2007. *Golden Gulag: Prisons, Surplus, Crisis, and Opposition in Globalizing California.* Berkeley: University of California Press.

GLAAD. 2018. "GLAAD Calls for Increased and Accurate Media Coverage of Transgender Murders." October 20. glaad.org/blog/glaad-calls-increased-and-accurate-media-coverage-transgender-murders-0.

Hail-Jares, Katie, Catherine Paquette, and Margot Le Neveu. 2017. "Meeting the New Neighbors." In *Challenging Perspectives on Street-Based Sex Work*, edited by Katie Hail-Jares, Corey S. Shdaimah, and Chrysanthis S. Leon, 51–77. Philadelphia: Temple University Press.

Hartman, Saidiya. 2020. "Saidiya Hartman on Insurgent Histories and the Abolitionist Imaginary," interview by Catherine Damman. *Artforum*, July 14. www.artforum.com/interviews/saidiya-hartman-83579.

Haynes, Tonya, and Halimah DeShong. 2017. "Queering Feminist Approaches to Gender-Based Violence in the Anglophone Caribbean." *Social and Economic Studies* 66, nos. 1–2: 105–31.

Henry, Richard S., Paul B. Perrin, B. Ethan Coston, and Jenna M. Calton. 2018. "Intimate Partner Violence and Mental Health among Transgender/Gender Nonconforming Adults." *Journal of Interpersonal Violence*, May 21. doi.org/10.1177/0886260518775148.

James, Sandy E., John L. Herman, S. Rankin, Mara Keisling, Lisa Mottet, and Ma'ayan Anafi. 2016. *The Report of the 2015 U.S. Transgender Survey.* Washington, DC: National Center for Transgender Equality. https://transequality.org/sites/default/files/docs/usts/USTS-Full-Report-Dec17.pdf.

Kaplan-Lyman, Jeremy. 2012. "A Punitive Bind: Policing, Poverty, and Neoliberalism in New York City." *Yale Human Rights and Development Law Journal* 15, no. 1: 177–222.

Kim, Mimi E. 2018. "From Carceral Feminism to Transformative Justice: Women-of-Color Feminism and Alternatives to Incarceration." *Journal of Ethnic and Cultural Diversity in Social Work* 27, no. 3: 219–33.

Kynoch, Gary. 2016. "Apartheid's Afterlives: Violence, Policing, and the South African State." *Journal of Southern African Studies* 42, no. 1: 65–78. doi.org/10.1080/03057070.2016.1087167.

Lawrence, Sarah, and Jeremy Travis. 2004. *The New Landscape of Imprisonment: Mapping America's Prison Expansion*. Research Report, April. Washington, DC: Urban Institute Justice Policy Center.

Moffett, Helen. 2006. "'These Women, They Force Us to Rape Them': Rape as Narrative of Social Control in Post-apartheid South Africa." *Journal of Southern African Studies* 32, no. 1: 122–44.

Mogul, Joey L., Andrea J. Ritchie, and Kay Whitlock. 2011. *Queer (in)Justice: The Criminalization of LGBT People in the United States*. Boston: Beacon.

Morrissey, Megan E. 2013. "Rape as a Weapon of Hate: Discursive Constructions and Material Consequences of Black Lesbianism in South Africa." *Women's Studies in Communication* 36, no. 1: 72–91.

NCAVP (National Coalition of Anti-Violence Programs). 2013. *Lesbian, Gay, Bisexual, Transgender, Queer, and HIV-Affected Hate and Intimate Partner Violence in 2012: A Report from the National Coalition of Anti-Violence Programs*. https://avp.org/wp-content/uploads/2017/04/ncavp_2012_ipvreport.final_.pdf.

NCAVP. 2014. *Lesbian, Gay, Bisexual, Transgender, Queer, and HIV-Affected Hate and Intimate Partner Violence in 2013: A Report from the National Coalition of Anti-Violence Programs*. https://avp.org/wp-content/uploads/2017/04/2013_ncavp _hvreport_final.pdf.

NCAVP. 2015. *Lesbian, Gay, Bisexual, Transgender, Queer, and HIV-Affected Hate and Intimate Partner Violence in 2014: A Report from the National Coalition of Anti-Violence Programs*. https://avp.org/wp-content/uploads/2017/04/2014_IPV_Report _Final_w-Bookmarks_10_28.pdf.

NCAVP. 2016. *Lesbian, Gay, Bisexual, Transgender, Queer, and HIV-Affected Hate and Intimate Partner Violence in 2015: A Report from the National Coalition of Anti-Violence Programs*. https://avp.org/wp-content/uploads/2017/04/2015_ncavp _lgbtqipvreport.pdf.

NYSDOC (New York State Department of Corrections). 1970. *100 Years of Progress*. New York Correction History Society. www.correctionhistory.org/auburn&osborne/miskell /100yearsnysdocs/1970-NYS-Correction-100-Years-of-Progress-Part-1.html.

Oselin, S. A., and Jennifer E. Cobbina. 2017. "Holding Their Own: Female Sex Workers' Perceptions of Safety Strategies." In *Challenging Perspectives on Street-Based Sex Work*, edited by Katie Hail-Jares, Corey S. Shdaimah, and Chrysanthis S. Leon, 78–99. Philadelphia: Temple University Press.

Pepinsky, Hal. 1994. "Penal Abolition as a Human Birthright." *Humanity and Society* 18, no. 4: 19–34.

Pleck, Elizabeth Hafkin. 1987. *Domestic Tyranny: The Making of American Social Policy against Family Violence from Colonial Times to the Present*. New York: Oxford University Press.

Ponder, Emily. 2016. "Gentrification and the Right to Housing: How Hip Becomes a Human Rights Violation." *Southwestern Journal of International Law* 22: 359–83.

Puar, Jasbir. 2007. *Terrorist Assemblages: Homonationalism in Queer Times.* Durham, NC: Duke University Press.

Radcliffe, JR. 2020. "Kenosha County Sheriff's 2018 Comments That Some People 'Aren't Worth Saving' Resurface after Violence." *Milwaukee Journal Sentinel*, August 27. www.jsonline.com/story/news/2020/08/27/kenosha-county-sheriff-2018-statement -under-new-scrutiny/5645279002/.

Richie, Beth. 2012. *Arrested Justice: Black Women, Violence, and America's Prison Nation.* New York: New York University Press.

Robinson, Brandon Andrew. 2020. *Coming Out to the Streets.* Berkeley: University of California Press.

Rodríguez, Dylan. 2010. "The Disorientation of the Teaching Act Abolition as Pedagogical Position." *Radical Teacher: A Socialist, Feminist and Anti-racist Journal on the Theory and Practice of Teaching* 1, no. 88: 7–19.

Rodríguez, Dylan. 2019. "Abolition as Praxis of Human Being: A Foreword." *Harvard Law Review* 132: 1575–1612.

Rodriguez, S.M. 2019. *The Economies of Queer Inclusion: Transnational Organizing for LGBTI Rights in Uganda.* Lanham, MD: Lexington Books.

Rodriguez, S.M., Liat Ben-Moshe, and H. Rakes. 2020. "Carceral Protectionism and the Perpetually (In)vulnerable." *Criminology and Criminal Justice* 20, no. 5: 537–50. doi.org/10.1177/1748895820947450.

Rothenberg, Tamar. 1995. "'And She Told Two Friends': Lesbians Creating Urban Social Space." In *Mapping Desire: Geographies of Sexualities*, edited by David Bell and Gill Valentine, 165–81. London: Routledge.

Ryan, Hugh. 2019. *When Brooklyn Was Queer: A History.* New York: St. Martin's.

Sayers, Jah Elyse. 2021. "Black Queer Times at Riis: Making Place in a Queer Afrofuturist Tense." *Wagadu: A Transnational Journal of Women and Gender Studies* 21.

Shange, Savannah. 2019. *Progressive Dystopia: Abolition, Antiblackness, and Schooling in San Francisco.* Durham, NC: Duke University Press.

Struening, Karen. 2016. "Walking while Wearing a Dress: Prostitution Loitering Ordinances and the Policing of Christopher Street." *Stanford Journal of Criminal Law and Policy* 3, no. 16: 16–18.

Valentine, Colby, Karen Oehme, and Annelise Martin. 2012. "Correctional Officers and Domestic Violence: Experiences and Attitudes." *Journal of Family Violence* 27, no. 6: 531–45.

West, James. 2013. "Rethinking Representations of Sexual and Gender-Based Violence: A Case Study of the Liberian Truth and Reconciliation Commission." *Journal of International Women's Studies* 14, no. 4: 109–23.

"I MUST BECOME A MENACE TO MY ENEMIES"

Black Feminism, Vengeance, and the Futures of Abolition

Stephen Dillon

I have been the problem everyone seeks to eliminate.
—June Jordan, "Poem about My Rights"

$\mathcal{I}$n her classic 1978 "Poem about My Rights," the poet and essayist June Jordan (Jordan 2005: 311) outlines the relationship between US imperial violence around the world and her "terrorized incarceration" within antiblack, heteropatriarchal violence on the street, in her home, on the beach, in the woods, and throughout the contours of her thinking. Jordan begins by writing that she would like to take a walk to clear her head so she may consider these very topics. But as she writes, she can't go outside without changing "my clothes my shoes my body posture my gender identity my age my status as a woman alone in the evening." She does not have the space to retreat into the world to think about god, or children, or stars, or silence, or thought itself—"I could not go and I could not think and I could not stay there alone as I need to be" (309). Jordan declares, "I am the history of rape / I am the history of the rejection of what I am" and that her thought, mobility, and desire are shaped by this possessive temporality in which the past captures the present within a hauntological regime that mimics the carceral (311; Derrida 2006; Childs 2009). She can't think about thinking because she is thinking about how not to be destroyed by the past, present, and future of the world.

But Jordan also can't think because thought appears to arrive at an impasse. The conditions for thought are absent because "they fucked me over" because "I am wrong." But from this space of absence—from the void of thought—she goes on to connect the terror that shapes her subjectivity, body, and mind to apartheid

GLQ 28:2
DOI 10.1215/10642684-9608119
© 2022 by Duke University Press

in South Africa, the legal politics of sexual violence in France, the Central Intelligence Agency (CIA) and Federal Bureau of Investigation (FBI) around the world, and the intimate racist, patriarchal regulations of her parents who made clear that she had the "wrong" hair, body, gender, teeth, and skin (309).

Even as the forces of the world seek to manage, contain, and break her desire to go outside, think, and be, Jordan refuses to "consent" to the decimation of her ability to dream, love, and fight for a vision of collective liberation. As she proclaims, "Wrong is not my name" (311). The poem ends with a declaration that apprehends the antagonism at the heart of her militant black feminist politics: "My simple and daily and nightly self-determination may very well cost you your life" (312). Throughout her larger body of poetry, Jordan articulates a vision of revolutionary queer, black feminist politics that embraces the use of physical and emotional violence against those she calls her enemies. Jordan deploys violence as a methodology to break through the stranglehold on thought. For example, in her "Poem about Police Violence," she asks, "What you think would happen if every time they kill a black boy we kill a cop," while in "I Must Become a Menace to My Enemies," she embraces the destruction and death of "lawandorder jerkoffs of the first terrorist degree" who should be "cauterized from earth . . . completely" (232).

If antiblack, heteropatriarchal violence makes certain forms of thought impossible, then Jordan smashes "a hammer to his head" to open up other ways of knowing the present, past, and future (309). As she struggles to name the unspeakable violence of patriarchy, white supremacy, imperialism, war, antiblackness, apartheid, and racial capitalism—to reckon with their crushing and pervasive presence throughout the banality of her life and all life—she also imagines a new, unknowable world made possible by black feminist vengeance—"How many of my brothers and my sisters will they kill before I teach myself retaliation? Shall we pick a number?" (231). Imagining black feminist violence is a tactic Jordan deploys to feel past the terror of the past-as-present and imagine unknown collective becomings. She embraces "the impressive terror I must be" and imagines blossoming "bloody on an afternoon surrounded by my comrades singing terrible revenge in merciless accelerating rhythms" (230). Even as her poetics envisions love, compassion, tenderness, and coalition across a variety of modes of difference as central to a revolutionary queer black feminist politics, they simultaneously embrace revenge, vengeance, death, and scorching the earth of her enemies.

In what follows I examine Jordan's poetic invocations of black feminist violence as well as her theory of racialized state violence. I argue that Jordan uses violence in her poetry to envision ways of feeling and being that make the present impossible and unimaginable and thus make possible new ways of knowing and becoming. As Sara Clarke Kaplan (2007: 112) argues, the deployment of violence by black women can "destabilize the . . . positioning of the slave at the boundary of the human." In other words, imagining black feminist vengeance can rewrite the order of things in the name of a future that flashes by in our present as affect even as it escapes our knowing as epistemology. It can undo an epistemological as well as infrastructural order of what Sylvia Wynter (2003) calls "Man" and Audre Lorde (1984: 36) calls the "white fathers." For my purposes in this essay, Jordan's poetic incantations of violence undo the epistemological as well as infrastructural foundations of "the afterlife of slavery" as they manifest in the mundane and spectacular—from the regulations of the patriarchal parent to the restrictions on thought in an antiblack, heteropatriarchal world, as well as the terror of a country covered in cages and always at war (Hartman 2007: 6; James 2007).

In this essay, I am not concerned with answering questions about the strategies and tactics we should utilize as we work to end racial capitalism and its technologies of control, incorporation, capture, and death. There is much to theorize about a thrilling and growing body of literature on transformative (nonviolent) justice that aims to abolish incarceration and the assemblage of forces that make the racial and gendered terror of the prison possible.[1] At the same time, there is a long and rich conversation about the use of violence and non-violence in leftist social movements in the United States and globally that has been, and continues to be, worthy of vigorous debate but is beyond the scope of my project in this essay.[2] In short, my goal does not include the politics of prescription. I am instead interested in Jordan's thought on violence as a yet unexamined genealogy of queer black feminist thought and abolitionist politics. My mode of engagement with Jordan's poetry is inspired by Barbara Christian's (1987: 52) argument in "The Race for Theory":

> For people of color have always theorized—but in forms quite different from the Western form of abstract logic. . . . How else have we managed to survive with such spiritedness the assault on our bodies, social institutions, countries, our very humanity? My folk, in other words, have always been a race for theory—though more in the form of the hieroglyph, a written figure which is both sensual and abstract, both beautiful and communicative. In my own work I try to illuminate and explain these hieroglyphs, which is, I think, an activity quite different from the creating of the hieroglyphs themselves.

Christian encourages us to be in sensual relation with our writing and the ephemera with which we work. Similarly, the choreographer Sarah Lass encourages theorists to perform a duet in our writing as opposed to maintaining a subject/object relation.[3] In this way, we may practice a mode of critique that refuses mastery and instead stays with the questions and the absence of an answer (Tompkins 2016). As I work with Jordan's poetry, I seek to undo a separation between the method-ological categories of primary and secondary texts. I engage Jordan as a poet, his-torian, critic, and theorist. Dylan Rodríguez (2021: 20–22) calls for such a project as a method for undoing the "white academic raciality" institutionalized in our ways of reading, writing, and citing in which we should be "experimentally rigor-ous and rigorously experimental."

To understand why Jordan turns to violence in her poetry, it is important to understand her theory of US state violence as it seems to expand exponentially in the ruins of the radical and revolutionary movements of the 1960s and early 1970s. After outlining her theory of violence, I consider how she theorizes life and death within the long arc of antiblack, white supremacist empire. I examine these two subjects before returning to her black feminist vengeance in the final section of the essay. This turn to violence in Jordan's thinking indexes a black feminist methodology for breaking open alternative forms of thought that exceed the present in all its repetitious, circuitous, and novel forms of capture.

A Black Feminist Theory of State Violence

Jordan's massive, forty-year body of poetry consistently seeks to reckon with forms of post-1960s US necropolitical state violence that includes bombings, war, star-vation, welfare, police violence, colonization, incarceration, sexual violence, and occupation across Lebanon, Nicaragua, Palestine, Iraq, Boston, Detroit, and New York. As Barbara Ransby and Barbara Smith argue, this global valence to black feminism was central to its politics in the 1970s. As Ransby says to Smith in an interview, "So this idea that a woman of color or Third World feminism was one that was inherently global and anti-imperialist even in choosing the terms and issues, it broke out of a very narrow, exceptionalist view of things" (Jones, Eubanks, and Smith 2014: 57). In *Black Feminism Reimagined* Jennifer Nash (2019) argues for a return to this intimacy between a transnational, anti-imperialist politics and US-based black feminist (academic) politics. Nash argues for reading intersection-ality and transnationalism together to unleash intimacies between women of color as well as ways of knowing that are often treated as discrete by systems of dis-ciplinarity. Nash examines black feminism as an affective project that functions alongside and inside its historical, theoretical, institutional, spiritual, creative, and, we could add, activist operations (3). She argues that the feeling of defensiveness prevents black feminism and black feminists from taking flight to unexpected and currently unknown possibilities. Staying on guard can prevent other modes of thought, flourishing, and attack. By letting go of defensiveness, black feminism may open up new ways to imagine living otherwise as well as "being done and undone through relationality" (107).

Nash turns to Jordan's essays and poetry to highlight the possibilities of this politics. As she writes,

> [Jordan] tracks both the persistence of structures of domination and their shifting meanings across national borders, their salience for producing conditions of subordination, and their insufficiency for producing intimacies and connections. It is an account that sits at the intersections of transnationalism and intersectionality, reflecting both on the interlocking nature of structures of domination and on their shifting meanings across national borders. It asks what, for example, black womanhood means when we inhabit it in the context of US global supremacy. (108)

Nash wants to hold on to the distinctions between formations of power like anti-blackness, settler-colonialism, imperialism, and white supremacy while also feeling and knowing their intimacies (109). Jordan demonstrates this analysis across hundreds of poems where she makes connections across time, space, and scale—here, there, then, now, elsewhere, you, me, us, body, nation, world. As I argue later, this accounting of the politics of scale, time, place, discreteness, and intimacy incites Jordan's turn to thinking vengeance. We can see her practice Nash's call for an intimacy between transnationalism and black feminism when, after describing how the law in France protects men who rape in "Poem about My Rights," Jordan writes, "Which is exactly like South Africa penetrating into Namibia penetrating into Angola." Jordan highlights the imperialism of rape and the rape of imperialism while also holding on to questions of difference, scale, and particularity. For her, dispersed but connected global regimes of racial and gendered violence animate differently similar outcomes. In short, Jordan's poetry "imagines difference without separability" (Silva 2007: 42). The logic that makes racialized sexual assault possible also fuels the CIA-orchestrated murders of Kwame Nkrumah and Patrice Lumumba (Jordan 2005: 310). It animates "my mom and dad," the FBI, Exxon, social workers, and "the problems of white America in general" (310). What is this force that animates life and death from the intimately banal to the world at large?

In Jordan's work, racialized, gendered (state) power and its effects on social and psychic life is animated by a logic of elimination. Elimination may look like your mother telling you to get braces and a nose job, to sit up straight and smile, to stay quiet, to be this and not something else. It may also look like the assassination of a democratically elected, socialist leader, or the fire and force of imperial warfare. According to Jordan, the aim is similar—eradicate errant life. Life as it is, and in its incalculable becomings, poses a problem, and regimes of violence and regulation (state, familial, interpersonal, and institutional) emerge to eliminate what is wrong. Or, as she articulates, she is a problem, and "everyone" seeks to end what is fugitive from, and before, normativity because "I was wrong I was wrong again to be me being me where I was / wrong / to be who I am" (309). Jordan describes what Marquis Bey (2020: 17) calls a "primordial mutiny to which regulation responds." Those with the wrong nationality, age, sex, skin, gender, ability, clothing, and thought are eliminated by "limitless / armies against whatever I want to do with my mind / and my body and my soul and / whether it's about walking out at night / or whether it's about the love I feel" (311). A force emerges to kill the love she feels because her love threatens an order that is always working to perfect its modes of capture, but this normative order never fully arrives. Its totality is a wish undone by countless practices of fugitivity, refusal, disobedience, sabotage, resistance, or mundane practices of disregard. It can take the form of the parent, the cop, the soldier, the administrator, the teacher, or even that most pernicious mode of capture called "the self." But critically, the "armies against whatever I want to do" do not statically exist in some timeless space of repressive power. Elimination emerges anew as life blooms into previously unknown forms of fugitivity. To put it plainly, slave catchers came into being to capture people who were already on the run. Running away was prior to capture (Pargas 2018; Diouf 2014; Franklin and Schweninger 2000). In Jordan's work, what is wrong was loved before it was named as such.

After her consent is claimed without her consent—because freedom as it is requires violence—Jordan declares "I am not wrong" and that "my name is my own my own my own" (Reddy 2011; Jordan 2005: 311). Jordan doesn't want freedom in its historical or contemporary form—not if freedom means rape and war and cutting up your nose and staying quiet and millions starving and occupying someone else's home. Simply, liberal freedom is a subordination born of violation, and Jordan refuses it in its totality. This conception of scale and freedom—from your teeth to the stars—is helpfully elucidated by Denise Ferreira da Silva.

In *Toward a Global Idea of Race* Silva (2007) argues that modern subjects emerge between two "moments of violence"—engulfment and murder. Elimination can take either form. Elimination is the logic, while engulfment and murder are its methodologies. Engulfment is a partial negation that arises from the productive and "violent act of naming" (29). Naming functions as violence when representation requires something be left behind in order to be seen, to live, to be loved. In this way, naming can take the form of "soul murder" (Painter 1995). We may think here of Hortense Spillers's (1987: 65) declaration, "I am a marked women but not everybody knows my name." Being named can mimic a type of ontological capture in which "telegraphic coding" made "excess in time, over time" appears to make possession close to total so that "coming clean" from the inside feels impossible (65). Jordan refuses this form of engulfment when she declares with repetition, "wrong is not my name." The *my* and *I* repeated countless times in the poem are of a different order than the *I* seen by the racial state or the patriarchal parent or the administrator. For example, if thinking "by myself" alone in the woods is forcibly denied to Jordan, then she cannot think along the lines of the Western philosophical tradition in which "by myself" is a fictionalized but forceful coherent locus of self-determined epistemological and identitarian stability (Carter 2020: 178; Silva 2007: 21–35). In her oeuvre, Jordan's *I* is a collective assemblage of people, animals, plants, temporalities, violence, laws, dreams, and affects. But this conception of the human, of "My" and "I," is "wrong" because it is wrong "to be who I am." And Jordan doesn't want to be "right" (Jordan 2005: 309).

Engulfment colludes with but is distinct from murder, which is "total annihilation" (Silva 2007: 29). As Silva writes, "As the others of Europe gaze on the horizon of death, facing certain obliteration, the racial keeps the transparent 'I' . . . alone before the horizon of life" (30). For Silva, engulfment and murder function on a continuum of racialized, gendered management. This is also how they function as a broader logic of elimination in Jordan's poetry. For example, being named an American citizen (engulfment) goes hand in hand with the creation of death worlds that span time and place (murder). For Jordan, the fantasy of American freedom requires the targeted mass killing and slow deaths of people of color around the world. Jodi Melamed (2011) describes this as the twin tactics of "represent and destroy" under racial capitalism. Representation functions as a form of biopolitical management. When it fails, destruction takes over.

The examples are countless, but, to briefly take one up: in the period of the poems discussed in this essay, Richard Nixon's "black capitalism" occurred simultaneously with COINTELPRO, the secret program in which the FBI used torture, beatings, spying, assassination, and incarceration to try and end radical and revolutionary resistance in the 1960s and 1970s (Ferguson 2012: 54–75; Churchill 2001). Both were forms of counterinsurgency that sought to undo the anticapitalist, black, Native, and third world liberation movements of the period.

Engulfment was the invitation to join racial capitalism, while murder was its constitutive underside. This is why Jordan repeats over and over that "wrong is not my name"—she refuses the logic of engulfment as well as the logic of annihilation. At the end of the poem, she tells the reader that her most mundane, basic resistance to everything described in the poem may "cost you your life" (Jordan 2005: 312). Jordan will not be named, and she will not be eliminated.

The Unthinkable Impasse of Thought

Jordan's uncompromising resistance to antiblack, heteropatriarchal violence is intimately connected to her theory of her complicity with imperial violence. In a number of poems, she appears categorically haunted by the breadth and depth of US state violence. Language and thought collapse in the presence of this haunting. In "Apologies to Lebanon" the refrain "I didn't know and no one told me and what could I do or say, anyway?" repeats between graphic descriptions of violence:

> They blew up your homes and demolished the grocery
> stores and blocked the Red Cross and took away doctors
> to jail and they cluster-bombed girls and boys
> whose bodies
> swelled purple and black into twice the size
> and tore the buttocks from a four month old baby
> and then
> they said this was brilliant
> military accomplishment and this was done
> they said in the name of self-defense they said
> that is the noblest concept
> of mankind isn't that obvious?
> They said something about never again and then
> they made close to one million human beings homeless
> in less than three weeks and they killed or maimed
> 40,000 of your men and your women and your children
> But I didn't know and no one told me and what could I do or say, anyway?
>   (381)

One of the last stanzas of the poem describes engulfment and murder: "Yes, I did not know it was money I earned as a poet that paid for the bombs and planes and tanks that they used to massacre your family." Money and bombs, engulfment and murder, complicity inside of resistance. The poem ends simply, "I'm sorry. I really am sorry" (382). Of course, the apology is intended to be incompatible with the violence to which it responds. And yet, the question "what could I do or say" remains. What to do in the face of such horror? What to do in the face of the logic of elimination, when engulfment and murder appear as an unceasing totality? What to do in relation to the indigenous girl in "Poem for Guatemala" who had her tongue cut out, was raped, and whipped on a tree and covered in flies. And then the worms. And then the dogs. And then the buzzards. And then the laughter of the soldiers. And then the handshakes and speeches about freedom and democracy from the White House. What to do? And how to think?

Jordan's struggle with thought also concerns how to think with such horror. Language, thought, and reason crumble at the scene of the "guerilla girl with no arms," but Jordan says she is "learning new syllables of revolution" from these scenes at which thought becomes impossible. She watches as "You go with no arms into the mountains hunting revenge" (369). Jordan's black feminist vengeance is animated by third world anti-imperialist politics that seeks to right wrongs to which there is no redemption. It's not recovery or restitution Jordan is after. It's not the absolution of her guilt in the bloody politics of vengeance. It's something that often vibrates at the edges of her poems—a somewhere else where these scenes don't happen and couldn't happen, where they are impossible and inconceivable. But they happen and happen and happen and happen and keep happening. How to end an unceasing past that refuses to heed to the imagined merciful progress of historical time? How to end the terror of the coming future before it rises?

A through line in so many of Jordan's poems about racialized state violence is its undaunting, ceaseless nature. This is described in the first section of her poem "The Bombing of Baghdad," about the first US war on the people of Iraq.

> began and did not terminate for 42 days
> and 42 nights relentless minute after minute
> more than 110,000 times
> we bombed Iraq we bombed Baghdad
> we bombed Basra/we bombed military
> installations we bombed the national museum
> we bombed schools we bombed air raid
> shelters we bombed water we bombed
> electricity we bombed hospitals we
> bombed streets we bombed highways
> we bombed everything that moved/we

> bombed everything that did not move we
> > bombed Baghdad
> > a city of 5.5 million people
> we bombed radio towers we bombed
> > telephone poles we bombed mosques
> > we bombed runways we bombed tanks
> > we bombed trucks we bombed cars we bombed bridges
> > we bombed the darkness
> > we bombed the sunlight we bombed them and we
> > bombed them and we cluster bombed the citizens
> > of Iraq and we sulfur bombed the citizens of Iraq and we
> > complemented these bombings/these "sorties" with
> > Tomahawk cruise missiles which we shot
> > repeatedly by the thousands upon thousands
> > into Iraq (535–36)

In this passage, Jordan theorizes racialized state violence as a machinic force detached from reason and thought itself. *Machinic* is a helpful term, as it describes how something new emerged in the relation between bomb, body, school, sunlight, air, dark, highway, telephone pole, mosque, street, water, duration (forty-two days), intensity (110,000 times). It helps clarify the implications of the repetition occurring throughout the poem. In *A Thousand Plateaus* Gilles Deleuze and Félix Guattari (1987: 398) write that the weapon can be known only through its consequences. Jordan's refusal of the weapon comes not from what it is, but from what it does and who executes the doing. The weapon's consequences are determined by its machinic relationality—"It is always the assemblage that constitutes the weapons system" (399). Darkness, sunlight, road, people, water, what moved, and what stayed still. She repeats, but with variation, so we know the essence and the breadth of racial violence.

Critically, these machinic assemblages inaugurate new figures of violence and power. In Deleuze and Guattari's example, "the stirrup, in turn, occasioned a new figure of the man-horse assemblage, entailing a new type of lance and new weapons" (399). If the stirrup gave rise to a new methodology of violence in the form of the lance moving at the speed of a horse, then the bomb does something that should be unimaginable. The poem describes a total attack on life itself. Jordan is alerting us to something terrifyingly new in the twentieth century—the bombing of light and dark and water and 5.5 million people. For Jordan, we can most clearly know the racial state when we attempt to comprehend it as a force that bombs the setting sun. And what does one do when the darkness is bombed, when an indigenous girl's arms are torn off, and black children are shot, kidnapped, caged, and malnourished? What to do when, as Christina Sharpe (2016: 7) argues, black death is necessary for our very notions of democracy, justice, and the stolen ground so many of us stand on?

Jordan does not ask us to understand state violence, or racialized state power more broadly, through the discourses used to justify its operation—freedom, safety, security, preemption, equality, peace, and justice. She does not try to understand the logic of state violence and then argue an alternative value system or advocate a softer form of state power. She does not argue for new laws or the abolition of existing laws. State violence is thus not open to the logics of positivism, liberal sentiment, compromise, reform, or what Frantz Fanon (1963: 61) calls "reasoning faculties." When she repeats "we bombed, we bombed, we bombed, we bombed, we bombed," she detaches racialized state violence from logic and instead highlights its repetitious and unremitting nature. The crushing totality of the past makes the present uninhabitable and the future feel like the past returned once again. Even as "we bombed" is a statement about the past, it is also a vision of the future, one that understands the future (and the present) as what Silva (2007: 28) calls a "horizon of death." The state deploys racialized violence and preemptive action (war, assassination, sterilization, incarceration, policing, administrative violence, and surveillance) to make its "imagined future come to pass" (Martin 2007: 67). The racial state is at war with the present in the name of a future where it has a future. For Jordan, the future of the social order meant race would continue to collude with gender, class, and sexuality in the unequal distribution of life, death, and dying. Her poetry shows what the future holds because it already happened—in the past that was the future that already arrived. The racial state, as Jordan makes clear, will not heed our pleas, tears, petitions, or requests. She knows what the racial state will keep doing because she knows what it does in all its repetitious, circuitous violence. What to do when now feels like then and the coming dawn of tomorrow looks like the dead weight of centuries past?

Becoming Menace, Becoming Otherwise

In the final pages of *Black Feminism Reimagined* Nash (2019: 118) turns to Jordan's "Poem about My Rights" to argue that it embodies the "potential peril" of viewing oneself as "bound up with others." Nash highlights the menace embodied by Jordan's conception of the self as a collective becoming of relationality with difference. This becoming threatens a liberal conception of the self that anchors racial capitalism, heteropatriarchy, settler-colonialism, and imperialism. Nash also observes that Jordan's vision of collectivity and mutuality animates her turn in the final lines of the poem to "forceful" resistance (119). As it is beyond the contours of her project, Nash sets this forceful resistance aside to argue for new ways of engaging the law and the state. One of my goals in this essay has been to sit with Jordan's many calls for black feminist vengeance and to consider their implications for our political imaginaries. If, according to Nash, letting go of defensiveness opens up new possibilities, then following Jordan as she goes on epistemological attack may open up other currently unthinkable ways of being, knowing, and feeling.

For example, in her essay "Killing Rage: Militant Resistance," bells hooks (1995: 8) describes a series of mundane, routine racist experiences on the way to the airport that lead her to "long to murder" an anonymous white man sitting next to her. hooks argues that swallowing black rage is central to maintaining white supremacy because it prevents the "militancy that is necessary for transformative revolutionary action" (19). She writes that rage can create clarity in our political analyses and that it can guide "courageous action" (16). Like letting go of defensiveness, rage can open up alternative possibilities that exceed the limitations of the current order of things. Yet Jordan not only unleashes her fury—she also imagines violence as central to black feminist freedom and thus freedom absolute. Jordan's (2005: 230–32) call for black feminist vengeance is most pronounced in the poem "I Must Become a Menace to My Enemies."

> I will no longer lightly walk behind
> a one of you who fear me:
> Be afraid.
> I plan to give you reasons for your jumpy fits
> and facial tics
> I will not walk politely on the pavements anymore
> and this is dedicated in particular
> to those who hear my footsteps
> or the insubstantial rattling of my grocery
> cart
> then turn around
> see me
> and hurry on
> away from this impressive terror I must be:
> I plan to blossom bloody on an afternoon

surrounded by my comrades singing
terrible revenge in merciless
accelerating
rhythms

. . .

How many of my brothers and my sisters
will they kill
before I teach myself
retaliation?
Shall we pick a number?
South Africa for instance:
do we agree that more than ten thousand
in less than a year but that less than
five thousand slaughtered in more than six
months will
WHAT IS THE MATTER WITH ME?
I must become a menace to my enemies.
And if I
if I ever let you slide
who should be extirpated from my universe
who should be cauterized from earth
completely
(lawandorder jerkoffs of the first the
terrorist degree)
then let my body fail my soul
in its bedeviled lecheries
And if I
if I ever let love go
because the hatred and the whisperings
become a phantom dictate I o-
bey in lieu of impulse and realities
(the blossoming flamingos of my
wild mimosa trees)
then let love freeze me
out.
I must become
I must become a menace to my enemies.

Jordan will no longer tolerate living inside the name *wrong*. She will no longer alter comportment and gait and desire to prevent "jumpy fits" of passersby. Her call to clear the earth of her enemies is animated by a "killing rage," and this rage is clarifying. It reminds her to stay with a love that manifests as a merciless collective rhythm in which abolition looks like a universe absent any whisper from "lawandorder jerkoffs." Unlike hooks's, Jordan's rage is not targeted at an individual. An anonymous white man never appears in her work. *Jerkoffs* is plural and the *you* remains unnamed—it's a collective *you*, a *you* that has built an unlivable world for so many, a *you* that sustains that world, a *you* that must vanish. This *you* is also a *they* that has slaughtered thousands in South Africa and elsewhere and there and here and then and now and tomorrow. Yet, while Jordan wants to abolish terror from the universe, she also embraces her own terror—a terror that terrorizes her enemies—"be afraid." In other words, she embraces her monstrosity—"the terror I must be." And more so, she wants this terror to expand into a collective blossom that opens on to a place she does not name.

Critically, the collective blossom of menace is non-identitarian. If Jordan experiences subjection from a multiplicity of directions, she refuses to imagine resistance within given rubrics like "woman" or "American" or "bisexual." Instead she is love and terror and blood and rhythm and flowers and water and sun and song and her comrades. As Spillers (1987) argues, refusing to join the ranks of femaleness and the human on the terms antiblackness demands opens up an insurgent ground in which a different story may be written. This story does not escape annihilation only to end at engulfment. Spillers is "less interested in joining the ranks of gendered femaleness" and instead wants to deploy the terror of an "insurgent" force against the terror of antiblackness (80). If there is no gender and sexual difference without racial violence, then for Spillers one must become "good at being a marksman and ducking" (Spillers et al. 2007: 301; Snorton 2017; Gil-Peterson 2018).

Spillers (2007) narrates her writing as an attack—"a way to be in battle" and go to "war with a whole repertoire of violent behavior that was performed in a very genteel way." Like Jordan, Spillers made central to this battle creating a new vocabulary that could come close to apprehending the previously indescribable because "language broke down" (301). A new language was needed to escape the crushing present, to take flight to somewhere previously unspeakable and unknown. This is why Jordan's concept of menace is not restricted to the concrete outcome of revenge; or restoring a degraded manhood to patriarchal pride; or rebuilding a fallen, errant America; or even reconstructing a stolen claim to the human. She doesn't want something previously held that has been lost. She wants the unimaginably new. Jordan wants to become a menace—a bloody blossom of accelerating rhythms called vengeance. This story is not restricted by staying quiet for someone else's comfort or imagining freedom on the terrain of the individual who lives in a future with a transformed notion of justice. Jordan doesn't want transformation— she wants to cauterize the earth of "lawandorder jerkoffs."

We can place Jordan's call here within the longer arc of what Kellie Carter Jackson (2019: 17) calls "black abolitionist thought." In *Force and Freedom: Black Abolitionists and the Politics of Violence,* Jackson outlines the half-century-long debate among abolitionists in the nineteenth century about the ethics and morals of using violence against the terror of slavery. If, as the abolitionist Peter Paul Simmons argued, "the northern freedom is nothing but a nickname for northern slavery," then freedom given or taken on terms acceptable to a white supremacist state was nothing but unlivable (33). Many black and some white abolitionists saw the use of force as a means to open up other possibilities left unattainable by moral suasion or William Lloyd Garrison's nonviolent "nonresistance." And so, many abolitionists sent out the warning and the call, "So, people of the South, people of the North! Men and brethren, choose ye, which method of emancipation you prefer—Nat Turner or John Brown" (7). Jackson also highlights the centrality of black women in the broader turn toward insurgent, abolitionist violence in the mid-nineteenth century. As Maria Stewart, the first black woman to lecture on women's rights and a contributor to the *Liberator,* declared in an 1835 rallying cry, "Far be it from me to recommend to you, either kill, burn, or destroy. But improve yourselves, express yourselves, rise!" (29). Jackson argues that black women were critical to John Brown's vision and tactics, and so we may see Brown as one of many fires set by black women's insurgent knowledge and practice against racial terror. She writes that black women cannot be "separated from the telling and sanctioning of political violence . . . the silent and silenced partners of Harpers Ferry were predominantly black women, including Anna Murray Douglass, the wife of Frederick Douglass, who for over a month hosted Brown while he sought refuge from his activities in Missouri" (117). And so, Jordan's many calls for vengeance are part of a much longer genealogy of black women arguing for the use of violence against racial terror.

It's important to be clear about what and who the enemy is in Jordan's work. There is no easy ontological or identitarian distinction between the "native" and "settler" (to borrow Fanon's [1963] language) or oppressor and oppressed. The *you* never bears an ontological or identitarian distinction. This is clear when she continually references her own complicity as a black woman in the United States with imperialist regimes that manufacture racialized death, writing, "And in the aftermath of carnage / perpetrated in my name / how should I dare to offer you my hand / how shall I negotiate the implications/of my shame?" (Jordan 2005: 538). Even as Jordan is "the history of rape," she is also the history of gendered violence against other women of color around the world. In her terms, she is the enemy of Iraqi women, of Palestinian women, of Nicaraguan women, of Guatemalan women, of indigenous women. And so, Jordan must become not only an enemy to the police and the "lawandorder jerkoffs of the first the terrorist degree" but also an enemy to the enemy that she is as well. Being an enemy is not ontological, but epistemological. For Jordan, epistemology is the structuring animus of state violence. It is also the methodology of becoming menace.

For example, in "The Bombing of Baghdad" Jordan argues, "All who believed some must die / they were already dead" (537). All who believe in the liberatory power of "F-15s/F-16s/ 'Apache' helicopters/ / B-52 bombers/smart bombs/ dumb bombs/napalm/artillery/ /battleships/nuclear warheads" were "already dead" (538). One believes "some must die." We see her struggling with her own beliefs in "I Must Become a Menace to My Enemies" when she alerts us to the violence and terror that has become so normal that we no longer notice it. Jordan begins counting how many deaths are tolerable before she learns to retaliate. Is ten thousand a year acceptable? Five thousand? How many indigenous girls? How many black children? How many black women? How many trans women of color? How much life stolen before it becomes unbearable? Jordan interrupts this line of thought—the calculation of life in market terms—and instead asks, "WHAT IS THE MATTER WITH ME?" One way of thinking draws her toward rationalizing mass death through a market logic of counting, and she catches herself, to come back to ways of loving life and terrorizing those who terrorize. She repeats similar questions over the course of her career—Who am I? What is the matter with me? How much more can I take? Why am I not doing more? What do I do with the knowledge I have? "What kind of people are we?" (392). These questions repeated over her life are a way to draw her away from legitimating the banality of racialized mass death and back to a vengeful politics in defense of life.

The enemy is an idea, and it lives inside all of us. The costs of this possession are devastating. In "Necropolitics," Achille Mbembe (2003: 40) writes that there exist "new and unique forms of social existence in which vast populations are subjected to conditions of life conferring upon them the status of living dead." On the one hand, Jordan's poetry outlines this process in great detail and breadth. And yet Jordan also locates death elsewhere. Those who imagine they are alive—and who may be legally, civically, and socially alive—are also possessed by death. Believing in the idea kills you—all who believe are already dead. When

Jordan writes "WHAT IS THE MATTER WITH ME?," she is holding on to life because to believe in necropolitical regimes means that one submits to death and becomes death. Those responsible for the uneven distribution of death and dying are already dead, even in their terrifying social aliveness. And the dead, for Jordan, cannot be reasoned with. They inhabit another world, one she wants to raze from the universe in the name of making new forms of life possible as well as expanding the livability of existing forms of life.

For Jordan, there are other ways to think, feel, and become that could leave death in the shadows of life instead of at its center. Jordan doesn't want life as life is currently produced. And, critically, she sees thinking with violence—thinking as menace, as a hammer, as a killer of cops who kill children, as a blooming bloody blossom, as death come for the rapist, as vengeance rattling the racist state—as a means to open up new forms of thought. Along these lines, Judith Butler argues that we do not need to relinquish hatred and aggression to the affective terrain of fascists. We can channel these destructive feelings and affective orientations against state violence—"one form of destruction against another" (Butler 2020: 180; Stanley 2018). According to Butler, hating state violence is a method for opening up alternative futures.

In other words, vengeance, in Jordan's articulation, leads somewhere else, toward new forms of desire and becoming. Jordan makes clear that almost all who are politically alive are still dying premature deaths. This is why Jordan's merciless revenge is articulated in unison with her "comrades." Jordan offers us a vengeful coalition—a differential coalescing of all who are "wrong"—grounded in a black feminist theory of the state that is queer in Cathy Cohen (1997) and Beth Richie's (2012) understanding of the term. Fred Moten (Moten and Harney 2013: 140–41) describes this coalition when he says in an interview, "The coalition emerges out of your recognition that it's fucked up for you, in the same way that we've recognized it fucked up for us. I don't need your help. I just need you to realize that this shit is killing you, too, however much more softly, you stupid motherfucker, you know?" In other words, those who are alive are dead and dying although in different ways, at different speeds, and with different outcomes. For Jordan, the goal is to create a merciless, collective rhythm of vengeance that ends a present in which almost everyone doesn't have a future.

Notes

I'm grateful for Sara Clarke Kaplan and the participants in the "Black Feminist Afterlives and the Proliferation of the (Im)possibility" symposium at UCSD as well as Nicole Fleetwood, Che Gossett, and the organizers and participants of "Abolitionist Imperatives" at Rutgers for feedback on earlier versions of this essay. I also thank Britt Rusert for participating in a workshop at the Center for Humanistic Inquiry at Amherst College as well as Marquis Bey, Jesse Goldberg, and two anonymous reviewers for their feedback and insight. This essay was completed while I was a fellow the at the CHI.

1. For more on transformative justice, see Dixon and Piepzna-Samarasinha 2020; Brown 2020; Kaba and Hassan 2019; Kaba 2021; Simmons and Moore 2019; Levine and Meiners 2020.
2. A small sampling of literature important to debates in the United States includes Berger 2005; Burton-Rose 2010; Butler 2020; Dillon 2018; Fanon 1963; Churchill 2017; Gelderloos 2007; Gelderloos 2015; Carter 2020; Umoja 2013; Williams 2013; Cobb 2015.
3. Sarah Lass, personal email to the author, March 9, 2021.

References

Berger, Dan. 2005. *Outlaws of America: The Weather Underground and the Politics of Solidarity.* Oakland, CA: AK.

Bey, Marquis. 2020. *Anarcho-Blackness: Notes toward a Black Anarchism.* Oakland, CA: AK.

Brown, Adrienne Marie. 2020. *We Will Not Cancel Us: And Other Dreams of Transformative Justice.* Oakland, CA: AK.

Burton-Rose, Daniel. 2010. *Guerrilla USA: The George Jackson Brigade and the Anticapitalist Underground of the 1970s.* Berkeley: University of California Press.

Butler, Judith. 2020. *The Force of Non-violence.* London: Verso.

Carter, J. Kameron. 2020. "Other Worlds, Nowhere (or, The Sacred Otherwise)." In *Otherwise Worlds: Against Settler Colonialism and Anti-Blackness*, edited by Tiffany Lethabo King, Jenell Navarro, and Andrea Smith, 158–209. Durham, NC: Duke University Press.

Childs, Dennis. 2009. "'You Ain't Seen Nothin' Yet': *Beloved*, the American Chain Gang, and the Middle Passage Remix." *American Quarterly* 61, no. 2: 271–97.

Christian, Barbara. 1987. "The Race for Theory." *Cultural Critique* 6: 51–63.

Churchill, Ward. 2001. *The COINTELPRO Papers: Documents from the FBI's Secret Wars against Dissent in the United States.* Boston: South End.

Churchill, Ward. 2017. *Pacifism as Pathology: Reflections on the Role of Armed Struggle in North America.* Oakland, CA: PM.

Cobb, Charles, Jr. 2015. *This Nonviolent Stuff'll Get You Killed: How Guns Made the Civil Rights Movement Possible.* Durham, NC: Duke University Press.

Cohen, Cathy J. 1997. "Punks, Bulldaggers, and Welfare Queens: The Radical Potential of Queer Politics?" *GLQ* 3, no. 4: 437–65.

Deleuze, Gilles, and Félix Guattari. 1987. *A Thousand Plateaus: Capitalism and Schizophrenia.* Minneapolis: University of Minnesota Press.

Derrida, Jacques. 2006. *Specters of Marx: The State of the Debt, the Work of Mourning, and the New International.* New York: Routledge.

Dillon, Stephen. 2018. *Fugitive Life: The Queer Politics of the Prison State.* Durham, NC: Duke University Press.

Diouf, Sylviane A. 2014. *Slavery's Exiles: The Story of the American Maroons.* New York: New York University Press.

Dixon, Ejeris, and Leah Lakshmi Piepzna-Samarasinha, eds. 2020. *Beyond Survival: Strategies and Stories from the Transformative Justice Movement.* Oakland, CA: AK.

Fanon, Frantz. 1963. *The Wretched of the Earth.* New York: Grove.

Ferguson, Roderick. 2012. *The Reorder of Things: The University and Its Pedagogies of Minority Difference.* Minneapolis: University of Minnesota Press.

Franklin, John Hope, and Loren Schweninger. 2000. *Runaway Slaves: Rebels on the Plantation.* Oxford: Oxford University Press.

Gelderloos, Peter. 2007. *How Nonviolence Protects the State.* Boston: South End.

Gelderloos, Peter. 2015. *The Failure of Nonviolence.* Seattle: Left Bank Books.

Gil-Peterson, Jules. 2018. *Histories of the Transgender Child.* Minneapolis: University of Minnesota Press.

Hartman, Saidiya. 2007. *Lose Your Mother: A Journey along the Atlantic Slave Route.* New York: Farrar, Straus and Giroux.

hooks, bell. 1995. *Killing Rage: Ending Racism.* New York: Henry Holt.

Jackson, Kellie Carter. 2019. *Force and Freedom: Black Abolitionists and the Politics of Violence.* Philadelphia: University of Pennsylvania Press.

James, Joy, ed. 2007. *Warfare in the American Homeland: Policing and Prison in a Penal Democracy.* Durham, NC: Duke University Press.

Jones, Alethia, Virginia Eubanks, and Barbara Smith, eds. 2014. *Ain't Gonna Let Nobody Turn Me Around: Forty Years of Movement Building with Barbara Smith.* Albany: State University of New York Press.

Jordan, June. 2005. *Directed by Desire: The Collected Poems of June Jordan.* Port Townsend, WA: Copper Canyon.

Kaba, Mariame. 2021. *We Do This 'til We Free Us: Abolitionist Organizing and Transforming Justice.* Chicago: Haymarket Books.

Kaba, Mariame, and Shira Hassan, eds. 2019. *Fumbling towards Repair: A Workbook for Community Accountability Facilitators*. Chicago: Project NIA.

Kaplan, Sara Clarke. 2007. "Love and Violence/Maternity and Death: Black Feminism and the Politics of Reading (Un)representability." *Black Women, Gender, and Families* 1, no. 1: 94–124.

Levine, Judith, and Erica Meiners. 2020. *The Feminist and the Sex Offender: Confronting Sexual Harm, Ending State Violence*. London: Verso.

Lorde, Audre. 1984. *Sister Outsider: Essays and Speeches*. Berkeley, CA: Crossing.

Martin, Randy. 2007. *An Empire of Indifference: American War and the Financial Logic of Risk Management*. Durham, NC: Duke University Press.

Mbembe, Achille. 2003. "Necropolitics." *Public Culture* 15, no. 1: 11–40.

Melamed, Jodi. 2011. *Represent and Destroy: Rationalizing Violence in the New Racial Capitalism*. Minneapolis: University of Minnesota.

Moten, Fred, and Stefano Harney. 2013. *The Undercommons: Fugitive Planning and Black Study*. New York: Minor Compositions.

Nash, Jennifer. 2019. *Black Feminism Reimagined: After Intersectionality*. Durham, NC: Duke University Press.

Painter, Nell Irvin. 1995. *Soul Murder and Slavery*. Waco, TX: Baylor University Press.

Pargas, Damian Alan, ed. 2018. *Fugitive Slaves and Spaces of Freedom in North America*. Gainesville: University Press of Florida.

Reddy, Chandan. 2011. *Freedom with Violence: Race, Sexuality, and the U.S. State*. Durham, NC: Duke University Press.

Richie, Beth. 2012. *Arrested Justice: Black Women, Violence, and America's Prison Nation*. New York: New York University Press.

Rodríguez, Dylan. 2021. *White Reconstruction: Domestic Warfare and the Logics of Genocide*. New York: Fordham University Press.

Sharpe, Christina. 2016. *In the Wake: On Blackness and Being*. Durham, NC: Duke University Press.

Silva, Denise Ferreira da. 2007. *Toward a Global Idea of Race*. Minneapolis: University of Minnesota Press.

Simmons, Aishah Shahidah, and Darnell L. Moore, eds. 2019. *Love with Accountability: Digging up the Roots of Child Sexual Abuse*. Oakland, CA: AK.

Snorton, C. Riley. 2017. *Black on Both Sides: A Racial History of Trans Identity*. Minneapolis: University of Minnesota Press.

Spillers, Hortense. 1987. "Mama's Baby, Papa's Maybe: An American Grammar Book." *Diacritics* 17, no. 2: 64–81.

Spillers, Hortense, Saidiya Hartman, Farah Jasmine Griffin, Shelly Eversley, and Jennifer L. Morgan. 2007. "'Whatcha Gonna Do?': Revisiting 'Mama's Baby, Papa's Maybe: An American Grammar Book': A Conversation with Hortense Spillers, Saidiya Hartman, Farah Jasmine Griffin, Shelly Eversley, and Jennifer L. Morgan." *Women's Studies Quarterly* 35, nos. 1–2: 299–309.

Stanley, Eric. 2018. "The Affective Commons: Gay Shame, Queer Hate, and Other Collective Feelings." *GLQ* 24, no. 4: 489–508.

Tompkins, Kyla Wazana. 2016. "We Aren't Here to Learn What We Already Know." *Los Angeles Review of Books*, September 13. avidly.lareviewofbooks.org/2016/09/13/we-arent-here-to-learn-what-we-know-we-already-know/.

Umoja, Akinyele. 2013. *We Will Shoot Back: Armed Resistance in the Mississippi Freedom Movement*. New York: New York University Press.

Williams, Robert F. 2013. *Negroes with Guns*. Eastford, CT: Martino Fine Books.

Wynter, Sylvia. 2003. "Unsettling the Coloniality of Being/Power/Truth/Freedom: Towards the Human, after Man, Its Overrepresentation—An Argument." *CR: The New Centennial Review* 3, no. 3: 257–337.

NOTES ON THE (IM)POSSIBILITIES OF AN ANTI-COLONIAL QUEER ABOLITION OF THE (CARCERAL) WORLD

Alexandre Martins and Caia Maria Coelho

*T*his world must be abolished. Anti-colonial, queer abolition is a project of ending the world as we know it (Silva 2007), structured through the categories of race, gender, sexuality, and class. From our Ladin Amefrican[1] formation, we reflect on the relationships and implications between queer movements, anti-colonial struggles, and abolitionist horizons.

World is here understood as a set of collectivities organized according to the colonial interests of imperialist societies (for example, in the division of South America between Europeans in the Treaty of Madrid). In this sense, this world is a colonial symbol of difference and hierarchy between man and his others (Wynter 2003). Since its beginning, the racial order (Silva 2007) has spread violence and punishment and imposed normative genders and sexualities, the only ones thought possible in this world. Rather than tackling the sense of collectivity in itself, we aim to dismantle the organization of collectivities as thought by colonialism. Abolishing the world means, therefore, reclaiming other meanings of collectivity.

Departing from this history of intertwined relationships between carceral, racial, sexual, and gender norms, we present, in the first section, the limits of the safety promised by the law and the criminal justice "cystem."[2] In an analysis of contemporary LGBT strategies in Brazil, in the second section we critique a trend in LGBT politics that aligns itself with carcerality. In the third section, we argue for an anti-colonial, queer abolition of the (carceral) world as a set of practices and imaginaries beyond punishment, raciality, sexuality, and gender. We

GLQ 28:2
DOI 10.1215/10642684-9608133
© 2022 by Duke University Press

speculate toward other ways of making the world as a sharp critique of carceral LGBT politics. As building the end of carcerality and of the world as we know it requires imagining beyond the limits of this world's possibilities, in the last section we reflect on the production of other forms of life and politics beyond (colonial) humanity.

Brazilian Queers and the Penal Cystem: A Genealogy

The limit is the (modern) World.
—Castiel Vitorino Brasileiro, *Ancestralidade Sodomita Espiritualidade Travesti*

The limiting of possibilities of ways of living via restrictive taxonomies of these categories has been an essential function of colonialism from its beginning. Sexual colonization became possible through a kind of violent translation or, in Édouard Glissant's ([1990] 2010) terms, the reduction of the opacity of Indigenous peoples to Western globalizing transparency. In other words, when the density of a certain reality suffers a subtraction of its own matter, it becomes accessible. For example, the opacity of the *tibiras* Tupinambás in Brazil and the *kyrypy-meno* Guayaki in Paraguay was reduced to transparency; the *tibiras* and the *kyrypy-meno* were translated by Jesuit chroniclers and missionaries as sinful and diabolic sodomites and addicts and as such compulsorily introduced to colonial society. To dominate and exploit those lives, it was necessary, paradoxically, to make them possible to be understood within the Church's and European laws. Meanwhile, Indigenous peoples were forcibly incorporated, and, as they were redefined in unequal power relations, their self-enunciating opportunities were restricted.

On these Abya Yala lands invaded by the same colonizers who later named them Brazil, criminalization and punishment practices along the lines of gender, race, class, and sex (in embryonic form) landed with the Portuguese caravels. Since the first years of colonization, Jesuit missionaries sought to regulate Indigenous collectivity, evangelizing the Native peoples and teaching European values and paradigms against "nudity, polygamy, weddings between relatives, lust, sodomy" (Fernandes 2017: 79–80).

As anti-colonial feminism has shown, the imposition of a world structured through the mandates of (European) man and his norms of masculinity and femininity has led to the subjugation and annihilation of other relationships, sexual practices, and experiences that here existed (Wynter 2003; Lugones 2008; Rojas 2017). These violent processes were not only cultural, but brutally physical as well. In *Existe Índio gay?* (2017), Estevão Rafael Fernandes reports, through Pietro Martire d'Anghiera's work "Decades of New World," the incident when, in 1513 Panama, the Spanish nobleman Casco Núñez de Balboa killed the brother of the Quaraca leader and forty of their companions for being "dressed as women."

The colonial process framed Native and Black peoples in general and their own constructions in particular as subhuman, irrational, savage, and, ultimately, as queer to the colonial world. It would be, thus, negligent to tell the stories of Brazilian queer struggles apart from a history of (im)possibilities imposed by a colonial world and its gendered, sexualized, racialized, and carceral forms.[3] As Pedro Paulo Gomes Pereira (2019: 409) writes on the convergences of queer and decolonial analytics, "Queer bodies are constituted according to colonial difference. There is no way to separate abject bodies and dissident sexuality from geographic location, from language, from history, and from culture." Therefore, it is not possible to separate queer bodies from the project of destroying the forms of life of Indigenous and Black people in Ladin Amefrica. Precisely when this world came into being, the other worlds ended, and the resistance and reimagining of other horizons were ignited.

In the colonial period (1500–1822), the violent process of colonization and "heterosexualization" far exceeded the purview of the Portuguese criminal law condemning to fire those whose practices could be framed as sodomy (Rojas 2017). However, sodomy—"highly sinful and heretical acts, offenses that encapsulated a host of nonprocreative sexual practices condemned by the Catholic Church" (Aidoo 2018: 31)—is a category particularly relevant to our exposure of colonial promises made by judicial institutions, represented by the Holy Inquisition for centuries. The real extension and enforcement of these anti-sodomy laws were always produced by gender, race, class, and sexual positions. Analyzing "confessions and denunciations" of enslaved men raped by their landlords, Lamonte Aidoo (2018: 33) states that "many slaves were aware of the severity of sin and thought that their confession might provide some sort of protection for themselves or punishment for their masters, but most were mistaken." Notwithstanding the low credibility of their narratives, victims of sexual violence relied on Christian dogma to seek punishment of the rapists by legal means, believing in the severity of the sin and that their report could also bring protection for themselves. However, "in the case of the rape of a male slave by his master, the sin accrued to the victim rather than the perpetrator" (36).

The Inquisition decreed that every Catholic had the obligation to report crimes against the Church. This created an atmosphere of distrust that permeated many areas of life in the colony, including sodomy practices, stimulating much espionage and many reports (Aidoo 2018). Furthermore, a farmer accused of sodomy could lose one-third of his farm to his accuser. Sodomy laws also inaugurated tense historical relations between families and sinners/criminal sodomites, especially when sodomy was associated with lèse-majesté, which condemned descendants of several generations to infamy and banishment from public office.

In addition to sodomy laws, multiple forms of extermination of other possibilities of subjectivity and relationships that flourished in the Americas (Perra 2014) were daily reproduced. Diffuse practices of policing gender and sex encompassed many informal and privatized ways of punishing dissident practices. In the middle of the eighteenth century, the Portuguese crown published a set of laws called the "Directory of Indians," which created sexually segregated schools, instituted the use of Portuguese, and prohibited nudity, leisure/loitering, and collective housing. This represented, above all, the forceful imposition of European values over Indigenous life and the incorporation of Native peoples into colonial society, transforming the "barbarians" into "vassals" and the collective into individuals through interventions on the conditions of private life (Fernandes 2017). Through these forms of control, not only sex was regulated but also marriage, race, work, kinship, and education. Given this reality, the maintenance of the colonial cystem must be thought of as linked to the control of sexualities (Fernandes 2016).

Since Brazilian independence (1822) and the implementation of its first penal code (1830)—which was influenced by legal processes from revolutionary France—sodomy practices have been decriminalized. Some of the lives that, until the eighteenth century were "defined" by the law and the Church as "sodomites," started to be addressed as "homosexuals" during the nineteenth century, a period under the strong influence of growing European scientism. The world would speak of homosexuality as a social pathology and investigate its causes, symptoms, and possibilities of treatment and cure without ceasing to consider it a sin or a crime within the criminal justice cystem. To Aidoo (2018: 161), that "period of scientific discourse shows the convergence of national, racial, and sexual anxieties that attempted to create a hierarchy of sexualities (as they did with race), with heterosexuality, particularly white male heterosexuality, being the only possible and real sexuality."

Since then, although gender and sexual dissident practices have never been formally criminalized again, anti-queer punishment has been enacted through the articulation of multiple tactics outside the sodomy statutes. Notably, poor and Black queers, travestis,[4] and gender-nonconforming people have been the main targets of the pathologization and criminalization of Brazilian sexual and gender dissidents. In the words of João Silvério Trevisan ([1986] 2000: 56):

There are no anti-homosexual laws in Brazil, either in the Constitution or in the Penal Code. . . . But, when they want to put their best foot forward, the police make raids and the diverse representatives of the order humiliate homosexuals, more constantly than we think, in public and private places. Indirect reasons ("indecent assault," "vagrancy," or "drug use") are created to trigger repression that is due to the basic authoritarianism of the Brazilian social organization and one of its most genuine reflexes: sexism.

Over the course of the nineteenth century, among the multiple changes in Brazilian society, the "scientific" shift in all aspects of life would provide new "justifications for the actions of the civilization of the Indians" (Fernandes 2017: 133, 134), which included torture and arrests, the militarization of Indigenous villages, and the creation of prisons to discipline Indigenous peoples (147–48). As for the Amefrican population, Brazil was the last Western territory to officially abolish slavery (in 1888) but since then has kept and updated many forms of its afterlives. This process was ideologically justified by the "racial exceptionalism" discourse, disproved by the reality hidden under the myth of "racial democracy" (Aidoo 2018: 27). The people in "Brazilian" lands were racially complex because of forced Indigenous assimilation and the rape of enslaved women by their white lords, but racial complexity was narrated to the world as proof of equality and of the absence of racism in Brazil. Thus racism by denial operates (Gonzalez 1988).

The construction of this territory as a nation took place continuously as a white *heteronación* (Curiel 2013) where the *ciscolonial* (vergueiro 2019) world and its violence have been maintained throughout the ongoing genocide of Native peoples and multiple forms of subordination of Black people. Up to this day, the others of the white supremacist, cis-heteronormative nation have been targets of persecution and punishment for their gender and sexual practices.

The scientific shift, essential to the emergence of notions of homosexuality (in the nineteenth century) and transsexuality (in the twentieth century), displaced former practices of punishment of queer bodies. Psychoanalysis, psychiatry, and criminology, then, started to play important roles in controlling and punishing sexual dissidents. Homosexuality and transsexuality, supposed mental diseases, were "treated" in asylums where the method of cure by torture involved shock treatment and induced comas—practices that reduced these bodies to exploitable territories. Some psychoanalytic notions crystalized by European science, especially regarding sexual difference, continue to be spread around the world in clinical practice, so much so that—even in the twenty-first century—"in the dominant medical and psychological discourse, the trans body" can be considered "a colony . . . A place of immense wealth and culture that surpassed the imagination of the Empire. A place of extraction and annihilation of life" (Preciado 2020: 46–47).

To understand the relationship between queer bodies and the criminal system in the twentieth century, we must consider the military regime in Brazil, which ruled between 1964 and 1985. The dictatorship reinforced anti-queer discourses of a virile *heteronación*, defense of the "family," and "morals and good customs," as well as criminalized those framed as subversive—such as communists, homosexuals, or other "degenerated" subjects. In the armed forces, practices of "pederasty" became a crime in the 1969 Military Penal Code (until a 2015 Supreme Court decision ruled it unconstitutional).

In 1968 during the military regime, Queen Elizabeth II from the United Kingdom visited São Paulo. To "better receive Her Majesty," its mayor ordered the social cleansing of travestis and homosexuals from the center of the city, including murder, arrest, and other forms of police violence. During the next decades, even after redemocratization, similar initiatives were used to persecute gender and sexual dissidents, especially travestis, across the country. Mainstream newspapers reported on the dangerousness of the travestis (Ocanha 2014), and the police arrested them for merely walking in public places.

In the 1970s public spaces of homosexual sociability expanded in large urban centers like Rio de Janeiro and São Paulo. While these homosexual networks were being consolidated, they faced harsh military repression. This was the basis for the emergence of Brazilian homosexual activism in 1978 in São Paulo with the founding of the Somos Homosexual Affirmation Group's newspaper, *Lampião da esquina Lamp in the Corner*, and in the next years the Lesbian-Feminist Action Group. A decade later in 1992, to fight against police repression and the AIDS epidemic, travestis who had already acted on other fronts (like sex work social movements and feminist spaces) founded the Associação de Travestis e Liberados, or Astral Travestis and Liberateds Association, the first political group of non-cis people in the country.

Even among lesbian and gay cis people repressed by the police under the military dictatorship, there was a desire to be integrated into society and protected by the law. Therefore, many of them sought to differentiate themselves from travestis. Interestingly enough, João Antônio Mascarenhas, founder of *Lampião de esquina* and the Triângulo Rosa Group Pink Triangle, tried to distance the "good" homosexuals from the "criminal" travestis by lobbying (unsuccessfully) for the inclusion of the term *sexual orientation* in the constitutional article prohibiting discrimination by "origin, race, color, and age" that would be enacted in 1988. In his speech at the National Constituent Assembly, aware of the selectiveness of that institution that punishes only some social groups seen as dangerous and/or abnormal, Mascarenhas argued that some should be accorded protection under the law. "There is, according to him, 'the common homosexual and the travesti, that are in many cases prostitutes and end up getting involved with petty theft or drugs.' The image predominantly attributed to the homosexual actually corresponded to the travesti and this approximation would disturb the organized movement" (Câmara 2002: 57).

The denial of Mascarenhas's plea to include the term *sexual orientation* in the constitution's antidiscrimination article, as well as his strategy of differentiating homosexuals from travestis to accomplish such ambition, demonstrate some of the limits in pursuing promises of protection under the law—both on the part of legislative institutions and the hegemonic LGBT movement. Who are those to be protected by law? What are the limits of protection and juridical punishment within gender, sexual, class, and racial norms?

LGBT phobia, racism, and the criminal justice cystem are part of the same paradigms presented by the colonial world as possible. These paradigms, which by definition impose habits, identities, and ways of thinking and reacting (Latour 2013), also establish the solution to the colonial world's problems by limiting the possibilities of life within this world. In a critique of these possibilities, we move toward "an altered state of perception, another imaginary, that would disorient us from the givens of the political present" (Butler 2021).

Queer Penalties and Carceral LGBT Activisms

Neoliberal, contemporary, hegemonic, Brazilian LGBT activisms have been articulating punitive and carceral instruments to counter violence and produce justice by criminalizing and punishing the other. Relying on the politics of the possibilities of this colonial political game, most LGBT activists keep betting on the criminal justice cystem as a form of protection even in a conjuncture of an ascending Far Right movement and an openly white supremist and cis-heterosexist government. In this section, we aim at delineating the reliance on safety promises of penal institutions as a feature of both Bolsonaro politics and much of the Left. Before arguing so, we present a brief history of carcerality in Brazilian LGBT politics.

In 1980 when more than seven hundred travestis and homosexuals were detained in one night, the first queer protest against police raids occurred in downtown São Paulo. To counter the regular association between homosexuality and criminality, and in deep articulation with other antiauthoritarian movements such as Black liberation, the "homosexual" movement made as its top priority the struggles against police violence and queer and trans imprisonment. A lesbian rebellion at Ferro's Bar in São Paulo in 1983 became known as the Brazilian Stonewall. In the "First Homosexual Conference" ("Encontro Brasileiro de homossexuais"), the end of prisons was up for debate during discussions of incarcerated homosexuals. Reforms were explicitly associated with the end of prisons in the long run.

Since those first years, much has changed in Brazilian LGBT movements.[5] We briefly categorize two faces of the relationships enacted between the LGBT movement and the criminal cystem: (1) critiques of the cis-heterosexism of the punishment cystem and (2) claims for the penal cystem to repress LGBT phobia.

The hegemonic LGBT movement's struggles for de facto decriminalization of queer people progressively became partially reforming ones. From the 1980s to the beginning of the 2000s, there was frequent criticism of LGBT phobia among the police, with a focus on tactics to change and limit criminal laws such as those of "morals and good customs." In the 2000s the tone of critics toward the penal cystem changed. At the "LGBT National Conferences" ("Encontros Nacionais"), the violence of the penal cystem would be pointed out only by trans and travesti discourses on the ongoing construction of travestis and sex workers as criminals (Martins 2020). The horizons of anti-queer violence struggles have been hegemonically reduced to partial reforms of the penal cystem through measures such as human rights training for police officers and the creation of LGBT prison cells.

Critiques of penal cystem violence were displaced at the same time as the rise of mass incarceration in Brazil from the mid-1990s. The ongoing criminalization of trans and gender-nonconforming people, in particular Black and poor travestis, has been an important feature of the contemporary expansion of state violence. Not only would the police continue to be "the great perpetrator of crimes. . . against our [travestis and trans] communities" (vergueiro 2015: 149), but also the Brazilian judiciary would maintain the discourse of travestis as "people affected/ prompted to crime," since they would inherently occupy a place of abjection, as one could apprehend from contemporary judicial sentences (Serra 2018).

The hegemonic LGBT movement has been largely engaged in the expansion and legitimization of the criminal justice cystem by calling for the criminalization of violence against LGBT people. Between 1980 and 1986, the first attempts to criminalize discrimination by sexual orientation were made by a group of white middle-class gay leaders, but not until 1999 would a bill be proposed for the criminalization of homophobia. In the mid-2000s, the enunciation of homophobic and transphobic practices as crimes became a central strategy in hegemonic LGBT activism. Henceforth, crime frameworks would take root in Brazilian

LGBT politics, as if it were impossible to counter violence without criminal law (Martins 2020).

The criminalization strategy remained central to these movements while the Far Right expanded in Brazil. In 2019, in the first semester of the Bolsonaro government, homotransphobia was criminalized by the Supreme Court. This was supported by many activists who, up until then, had remained critical toward it and refused the false promise of protection and universal punishment, despite being dismissed as "unrealistic" (as they had the impossible as a horizon: penal abolitionism). This change in position was later justified by the feeling of being trapped between supporting the expansion of the penal code and the possibility of endorsing the conservative idea that queer lives were not worthy of protection. With fewer critics of criminalization remaining, support for the prison project widened among the Left.

The demands for penal cystem reform and the criminalization of LGBT phobia have both been ways of fighting anti-queer violence enacted by hegemonic (carceral) activisms. In this strategy, the decriminalization of queer people would be made possible precisely by the criminalization of LGBT phobia—penal agents engaging in anti-queer practices would be punished by the criminal cystem. Thus, this strategy relied on "the tools of the lord [which] will never bring down the big house" (Lorde 1984: 112).

LGBT phobia is a political, social, scientific, and religious issue. It is relevant to consider that it is not, ontologically, a crime. It was criminalized. Obviously, every crime has gone through a process of criminalization, but this is soon forgotten, as the solution to violence is outsourced to the law, and "crime" becomes a synonym for "problem." Narrowly defining LGBT phobia as "crime," which restricts possibilities for defining it along multiple other axes, thus obstructs the chances of understanding and overcoming it.

Indeed, most LGBT phobia is not directly punishable by the penal cystem, as shown by Jair Bolsonaro's politics. The president operates largely through a cis-heterosexism by denial, one that is no less violent than that punishable by law. Bolsonaro's politics operates largely through practices not directly punishable by the penal cystem, but no less violent, as cis-heterosexism by negation. During the 2018 presidential election campaign, multiple leftist social movements characterized Bolsonaro as an openly homophobic, transphobic, and racist politician. He had stated, for example, that his children would never marry a Black woman, nor would they be queer because, in his words, they would have been "well raised." Nonetheless, Bolsonaro claimed he was not racist or homophobic, arguing he had no prejudices and touting the open support of a group of white cis gay men and lesbians, as well as a group of Black and Native conservatives.

Since 2018 a public dispute has taken place between leftist LGBT activists and the president's gay and lesbian supporters, who deny not only Bolsonaro's violent politics but also LGBT phobia as a central feature of Brazilian society. Both sides converge, though, in that both bet on penal ways to bring justice and counter all forms of violence. One episode is exemplary of such similarity.

On December 15, 2019, in Rio de Janeiro, one of Bolsonaro's publicly lesbian supporters, Karol Eller, was publicly assaulted at a restaurant, an incident immediately reported by her as lesbophobia. Nonetheless, until then, she herself, along with other LGBT Bolsonaro supporters, had been accusing other gay, lesbians, and travestis of "playing the victim" when they exhibited homophobic attitudes. On December 17, Senator Eduardo Bolsonaro (2019), one of the president's sons, tweeted about the episode. He offered his solidarity to Eller's family and addressed the LGBT left by stating: "For the right-wing, the aggressor would have a harsh prison sentence. Do the leftists support such a measure?"

Senator Bolsonaro's statement disregarded that hegemonic leftist LGBT politics has been centered on carceral ways of responding to violence. It is exactly through a punitive logic that the hegemonic LGBT movement from 1999 to 2019 articulated a massive campaign to criminalize LGBT phobia. True to form, then, hegemonic LGBT activists replied to that tweet by stating that Eller should criminally prosecute those who attacked her. They also remembered that such an option was a possibility opened by the criminalization of homotransphobia, which was claimed as a (pyrrhic) victory of the leftist LGBT movement.

Despite their fundamental antagonism toward each other, Bolsonaro's supporters and a large part of his leftist opponents centered the same solution to that episode: rely on the penal cystem and its promises. This discursive game is played every time an episode of anti-queer violence becomes public, and presents itself as the only possible answer to violence. In such events, both in leftist carceral positions and conservative perspectives, it becomes impossible to show solidarity with the ones who were harmed without calling for severe punishment. As a result of carcerality's hegemony, contemporary queer solidarity has largely been reduced to requesting more jails and police, as if this were the only feasible and normal possibility.

The political rationale permeating hegemonic queer political struggles is based on the production of the criminal and victim as binary figures, a logic that claims the centrality of criminal law to call "us" the victims and that claims the right of the criminal law. These struggles over what the law says about queer people (Spade 2015) and the enforcement of criminal law over homophobic individuals fall short in several ways.

First, disputes over the criminalization of queers in the Brazilian legal cystem limit the scope of the overall debate on LGBT rights, as this criminalization occurs mostly outside formal law. Cis-heterosexism is allowed to operate in Brazilian society and in its cystems mainly through simple denial of its existence. Therefore, this violence cannot possibly be handled by the incarceration of a group of openly LGBT-phobic individuals.

Second, not only are these strategies ineffective at countering the foundational anti-queer, anti-Black, and anti-Native violence of this world, but by highlighting victimization, they have pinkwashed the colonial world. Brazil's murderous institutions, which have long been punishing and controlling Black, Native, and poor people, as well as queer dissidents, are now also desired by LGBT activists as a "solution" to violence.

Normative anti-queer violence is the foundation of this world, not its exception. In demanding the carceral as a remedy to this violence, these movements have limited themselves to an indisposition or inability to imagine and build paths of fighting LGBT phobia that would not reinforce racist and cis-heteronormative institutions.

Against the Carceral Ways: Toward an Anti-colonial Queer Abolitionism

The here and now is a prison house. We must strive, in the face of the
here and now's totalizing rendering of reality, to think and feel a *then
and there*. . . . We must dream and enact new and better pleasures,
other ways of being in the world, and ultimately new worlds.
—José Esteban Muñoz, *Cruising Utopia*

As we have shown, sexuality and gender have been a matter of prison and police in Brazilian history—both when queers have been persecuted by these institutions and when the LGBT movement has relied on them for "protection." Carceral activists, by supporting a violent anti-queer and anti-trans cystem to fight violence and counter LGBT phobia, have tied their desire for integration to the punitive terms defining what is normal in this world.

Abolitionist queer voices, most notably trans, travesti, and queer of color ones, have largely refused those paths and kept enunciating the end of prisons and police as a fundamental queer struggle; but so far, they have not been able to mobilize a large public debate among LGBT activists in Brazil. They have called for the abolition of both the penal cystem and gender and sexuality norms, and, above all, of the world in which these social relations are made possible. In this section, we seek to connect the voices of those who rejected carceral queer politics to theoretical reflections on the potentialities of intertwined queer, anti-colonial, and abolitionist struggles.

Dissident activists have publicly criticized the carceral paths chosen by the hegemonic LGBT movement in Brazil, which opted for the criminalization of homotransphobia as its main demand in the mid-2000s (Martins 2020). The politics of crime and criminalization was framed as a way of strengthening the carceral state. In their discourse, the target of the criminal cystem would continue being the same—Black youth from the poorest neighborhoods, including queer and trans people, who have been systematically punished and killed by a police force from which the hegemonic movement demands protection. By denying the neoliberal, carceral, and normalizing ways of hegemonic LGBT movements, these LGBT activists have kept alive the fire of queer anti-carceral and anti-policing struggles of the 1970s and 1980s.

From the global South, it is evident that anti-normalization struggles cannot be tied exclusively to sexual and gender issues, as they are linked at their core to all the dissidents of this world. In the face of ongoing colonial violence, a radical queer politics addresses all those whose practices and imaginaries have been persecuted as abnormal—like the cosmovisions and lives of Native and Black peoples. When we look at Latin American prisons, these "abnormals" are precisely the main targets of contemporary mass incarceration (Segato 2007). As the others of this world, certainly, the incarcerated masses must be read as queer, as suggested by Cathy J. Cohen (1997).

Although sexuality, gender, and raciality are inextricably imbricated in the (re)production of this world, these structures are not equivalent, nor can they be subsumed to one another—therefore, LGBT phobia is not a type of racism but a cystem imbricated in the racial reproduction of this world. Those structures have produced both the "normal" and the queer ones. Long before the global North brought institutional queer theory and queer politics to Ladin Amefrica, centuries of resistance against the colonial world and its racialized, gendered, and sexualized ways of living have taken place against the normal, even if the queers in the south of the world had other names, colors, and practices (Perra 2014).

Anti-colonial queer struggles refuse the promises of this world and do not aim to be included in the colonial, rational, and tolerant promises of the human—as inclusion in this world's (carceral) possibilities only reproduces deadly ways of living for most queers in these lands. They aim at a transformation beyond the limits of justice structured by raciality, coloniality, and its logic of obliteration (Silva 2007).

Prisons and police are structured by cisgender and heterosexual norms, capitalism, raciality, and coloniality (Spade 2015; Segato 2007). At the same time, as we have shown, they are at the center of the violent social reproduction of this world. For both reasons, anti-colonial queer struggles refuse the punitive logics of those institutions and are fundamentally abolitionist. They aim at abolishing not only punishment but also the racist, gendered, and sexual reproduction of this colonial world.

Just as Angela Davis (2011) has argued how these colonial cis-heteronormative constructs—race, gender, and sexuality—structure prisons, it is time to also point at sexuality, race, and gender as, in themselves, forms of policing, punishment, and, ultimately, as prisons. As gendered and sexualized subjects, we are continuously being policed around fantasies of coherence and continuity of our genders and sexualities; and multiple (im)possible gender and sexual practices, identities, and processes of subjectivation are controlled by punishment practices.

The punitive enforcement of gender and sexual norms goes along with the reification of sexual and gender identities. Both establish boundaries and reinforce desires of policing them. Queer abolitionist struggles, therefore, are at odds with not only carceral strategies but also the celebration and normalization of neoliberal sexual and gender identities.

If we take in a more literal sense José Estéban Muñoz's metaphor (2009: 1) that "the here and now is a prison house," we could take the colonial, racist, and cis-heteronormative present of this world as a prison in a double sense. On the one side, literal cages constrict the lives of Black, Native, and poor people, and on the other, gender, race, and sexuality as cages establish collective limits to life's possibilities. Abolishing all prisons and police that surround us and subject us implies, then, not only imploding actual cages but also destroying the metaphorical ones.

As "queerness is essentially about the rejection of a here and now and an insistence on the potentiality for another world" (Muñoz 2009: 1), queer abolition points to other potentialities beyond this colonial, carceral present. Therefore, going beyond our prison house implies radical transformation of the ways through which we think about collectivities, about ourselves, our present time, and our futurity. At its core, it requires, at least, (1) the construction of freedom for those who have been for centuries violated by the colonial criminal cystem; (2) the strengthening of solidarity and mutual aid networks for all the ones harmed by the production and reproduction of racial, gendered, and sexual norms; and,

(3) a queer refusal of desires of incarceration, punishment, and policing as far as they are the normalized effects of this world.

An anti-colonial, queer abolitionism aims at abolishing a society in which prisons are possible and at founding a new society (Moten 2018). Abolition is, mostly, a negation of the possibilities of this world, its promises, and its possibilities. A negation of humanity as the only way of life—a bet on monstrosity. It is a bet on queer world(s) in which all these prisons are not possible: cisnormativity, heteronormativity, raciality, capitalism, and coloniality.

Moreover, abolition is the refusal to reproduce the foundational violence that sustains this world in which queer subjects are not meant to be protected but to be persecuted and punished. Abolition is a negation enacted precisely by those who are obliterated in this world. It might well be an affirmation of the potentiality of queer lives and worlds beyond the ruins of this one.

Beyond the (Im)possibilities of the (Carceral) World: An Ethics of Incommensurability

The impossible world is the one that exists beyond the horizon of
our present thinking—it is neither the horizon of terrible war, nor
the ideal of a perfect peace. It is the open-ended struggle required
to preserve our bonds against all that in the world which bears the
potential to tear them apart.
—Judith Butler, *The Force of Nonviolence*

Queer abolitionisms are opposed to the political game of the "possibles" played by carceral LGBT politics. As a refusal of the ongoing pinkwashing of colonial institutions and their promises, anti-colonial queer abolitionisms are disruptive of the times and places of this world built on violence and punishment. In the game of the possibilities of this world, there is neither queer nor abolition futurity—there are only different ways of perpetuating coloniality, raciality, gender, and sexuality. Abolitionist practices point toward other political games and collective horizons, both as a promise of a liberatory queer future and as a process that takes the abolition of this world and all its foundational violence as an urgent task that cannot be postponed.

To refuse prisons and police, as well as punitive and carceral logics, requires that "we abandon the victim position—even though the state, the police, the white and the cisgender man have historically shown their inability to abandon the perpetrator position" (Mombaça 2021: 79). Leaving the victim and criminal positions is also abandoning the safety promises produced by the colonial world, available only to those who are completely human—not the queer, the Black, the Native, or the monsters of this world.

Our only possibilities may lie precisely at the practices and lives this world so fervently tries to make impossible—notably, trans and gender-nonconforming lives (Spade 2015). The impossibilities of this world demand the right to be neither a man nor a woman, but a monster. Argentinian travesti Susy Shock (2011) faces the normal, its possibilities and impossibilities, and declares monstrosity as a possible way of living. In her poems, being a monster emerges as a way of refusing to be seen as normal and as human by this world who built man in such a narrow, colonial form.

A queer monster abolitionism, thus, is much more than refusing criminal law to deal with violence for knowing it only brings more harm; it is the refusal of gender and sexuality as the world has known them and allowed them to be known. To be a monster may be read, then, as a refusal of gender and sexual integration possibilities. The condition of the monster, instead of the condition of man or woman, is "like a foot that moves towards nothingness, pointing the way to another world. . . . The monster is the one . . . whose face, body and practices cannot yet be considered true in a system of hegemonic power and knowledge" (Preciado 2020: 44). Monstrosity is, therefore, the key to other meanings of collectivities and (im)possible worlds.

The refusal of carceral and colonial "possibilities" and the betting on impossibilities are only a first step toward a politics of anti-colonial abolition. Beyond refusal, it is commonly asked how an abolitionist, anti-colonial world would look. Such a question implicitly tries to foreclose the construction of other worlds. At the core of decolonial and abolition struggles, there is a comprehension that "we will find out the answers as we get there" (Tuck and Yang 2012: 35). It is through the process of abolition that we will be able to create answers that the carceral and the settler colonialism make impossible to imagine. The formulation of new solutions by abolitionism, decolonization, and queer liberation is possible only through an "ethic of incommensurability" that refuses reconciliation with colonial normality, fundamentally an anti-normality ethics. As Eve Tuck and K. Wayne Yang write:

> *What will happen after abolition? What will be the consequences of decolonization for the settler?* Incommensurability acknowledges that these questions need not, and perhaps cannot, be answered in order for decolonization to exist as a framework. We want to say, first, that decolonization is not obliged to answer those questions—decolonization is not accountable to

> settlers, or settler futurity. . . . The Native futures, the lives to be lived once
> the settler nation is gone—these are the unwritten possibilities made pos-
> sible by an ethic of incommensurability. (35–36)

Anti-colonial Native futures, Black futures, and queer futures may come into being
only by the incommensurability of these futurities to this present prison house.
When queer abolitionists envision a world without prisons, racism, capitalism, cis-
heterosexism, "we are talking about a world that doesn't currently exist. But collectively dreaming up one means we can begin building it into existence" (Imarisha 2015).

　　Imagining other futures is central to the construction of possibilities
beyond this world. Other collective futures have long been imagined in the lives
and communities of both Native and Black peoples in this Ladin Amefrica, and
all the queer ones in the eyes of this world who continue to envisage other futures
beyond this *heteronación*.

　　Through a collective production of practices and imaginations that point at
other futures, it becomes possible to not only refuse and dream but also actively
build a collective process of redistribution of violence (Mombaça 2021). For this
process to take place, on one hand, it requires the naming of the world's norms, the
production of self-defense, and self-care (79–81). On the other hand, it demands
an ethic that conceives justice not as fixed and universal but "mutant, contextual
and provisional [and] that accepts that there is no safe answer to conflicts and
questions as paradoxical, complex, and improbable as the ones we deal with" (81).
Such a justice is the great impossibility of this world.

　　Essays like this and other collective practices are only a part of a long continuum of multiple sparks of those collective projects that since the imposition of
this world and its punishments in Abya Yala have been challenging and confronting its limits and (im)possibilities. These resistances and refusals of integration in
this world continue to point out how the colonial project and its fantasies of total
violence permanently fail to impose the possibilities of this world as the only ones
to exist.

　　In the anti-colonial and abolitionist battles to end this world, the paths
to be taken emerge precisely in the impossibilities of the (carceral) world. After
all, its possibilities have never protected us. Collective abolition practices have
long been barricades where we produce instruments for these ongoing battles and
where we may imagine a world in the ashes of this one.

　　The end of this world flashes in the horizons of anti-colonial, queer abolition struggles. By refusing the colonial, carceral possibilities, abolitionist practices

may be sparks of other worlds to come after this one is set on fire. Igniting abolitionist flames and multiplying them is an urgent task, for it may take us toward those worlds and those answers made impossible by this colonial present. In the South and the North of the world, our non-postponable collective responsibility is to keep these fires going—until this world, this prison house, burns, and from its ashes futurities of queer abolition may thrive.

Notes

1. Rather than Latin America, we use Ladin Amefrica/Améfrica Ladina as a way of proposing "a new and creative look to focus Brazilian historical-cultural formation" in which our ascendency, more amerindian and amefrican than latin, points at an "African America whose latinity, by its own inexistence, had its *t* changed by the *d*" (Gonzalez 1988: 69).

2. From vergueiro (2015: 15), we apply *cystem* as a reference to systems that produce "epistemic hierarchies in which . . . non cisgendered perspectives are excluded, minimized or silenced. The term 'cystem' . . . aims at emphasizing the structural and institutional character—'cystemic'—of cis+sexists perspectives, beyond the individualizing paradigm of the transphobia concept."

3. We understand colonialism not as a "political and economic domination that ended with the independence of the colonies, but a more broadened process, whose effect transcends the imposition of an administrative structure based on a colony-metropolis relation. The intention is to raise awareness to the fissure process caused by this relation of colonial dominance—the colonial wound" (Fernandes 2017). In this decolonial sense, the colonization of bodies, subjectivities, and political imaginations far exceed the colonial period—the current world as we know it is a colonial and racial one (Silva 2007).

4. In Brazil and other Ladin Amefrican countries, the feminine identity *travesti* went through many collective disputes regarding its meaning. They were treated as inherently criminal since the 1970s by the media and the criminal justice cystem; neglected by the public health cystem, while transexual women began having access to it for specific matters; denied the option to serve time in women's prisons by the Supreme Court, while transexual women first had such a concession; seen as sinners by conservative Christian sectors; and were targets for violent senses of humor. However, they appropriated this stigmatized identity, claimed the multiple meanings, and publicly pointed out what was the real basis of the motivation for rigorous distinction from transsexuality: racism and classist stratification. The meanings behind the difference became more diffuse as they conquered certain spaces, proving they were never ontological. See Berkins 2007; IACHR and OSRESCER 2020.

5. In the Brazilian LGBT movement there are multiple trends, strategies and political

practices, which may be analytically conceived of as two major trends. On one side is the more institutionalized, egalitarian sexual politics characterized as hegemonic; it focused mainly on legal rights and identity politics. On the other side, there is a minor trend of openly transgressive cultural politics, less institutionalized and overtly critical of the limits of identity politics and heteronormative horizons. Since the first years of the Brazilian gay movement, this difference has taken many forms, and in recent years the influence of queer theories and politics in the second, minor trend has become notable (Colling 2011). Nevertheless, both trends are self-referred and socially recognized as the "LGBT movement." To differentiate their strategies, we signal these trends as hegemonic and minor from this point on.

References

Aidoo, Lamonte. 2018. *Slavery Unseen: Sex, Power, and Violence in Brazilian History.* Durham, NC: Duke University Press.

Berkins, Lohana. 2007. "Travestis: Una identidad política." *E-misférica* 4, no. 2.

Bolsonaro, Eduardo (@BolsonaroSP). 2019. Tweet on solidarity to Karol Eller. Twitter, December 17, 2019, 11:54 a.m. https://twitter.com/BolsonaroSP/status /1206981031800320002.

Butler, Judith. 2021. *The Force of Nonviolence: An Ethico-Political Bind.* London: Verso.

Câmara, Cristina. 2002. *Cidadania e orientação sexual: A trajetória do grupo triângulo rosa.* Rio de Janeiro: Academia Avançada.

Cohen, Cathy J. 1997. "Punks, Bulldaggers, and Welfare Queens: The Real Radical Potential of Queer Politics?" *GLQ* 3, no. 4: 437–65.

Colling, Leandro. 2011. "Políticas para um Brasil além do Stonewall." In *Stonewall 40+ o que no Brasil?*, 7–21. Salvador: EDUFBA.

Curiel, Ochy. 2013. *La nación heterosexual: Análisis del discurso jurídico y el régimen heterosexual desde la antropología de la dominación.* Bogotá: Brecha Lésbica y en la Frontera.

Davis, Angela Y. 2011. *Are Prisons Obsolete?* New York: Seven Stories.

Fernandes, Estevão Rafael. 2016. "Quando o armário é na aldeia: Colonialidade e normalização das sexualidades indígenas no Brasil." In *Anais do X Simpósio Linguagens e Identidades da/na Amazônia Sul-ocidental*, 1–10. Rio Branco: Editora da UFAC.

Fernandes, Estevão Rafael. 2017. *Existe Índio gay?* Curitiba: Editora Prismas.

Glissant, Édouard. (1990) 2010. *Poetics of Relation*, translated by Betsy Wing. Ann Arbor: University of Michigan Press.

Gonzalez, Lélia. 1988. "A categoria político-cultural de amefricanidade." *Tempo Brasileiro* 92, no. 93: 69–82.

IACHR (Inter-American Commission on Human Rights) and OSRESCER (Office of the Special Rapporteur on Economic, Social, Cultural, and Economic Rights). 2020.

Report on Trans and Gender-Diverse Persons and Their Economic, Social, Cultural, and Environmental Rights. N.p.: IACHR. http://www.oas.org/en/iachr/reports/pdfs/TransDESCA-en.pdf.

Imarisha, Walidah. 2015. "Rewriting the Future: Using Science Fiction to Re-envision Justice." Blog, February 11. www.walidah.com/blog/2015/2/11/rewriting-the-future-using-science-fiction-to-re-envision-justice.

Latour, Bruno. 2013. *Chroniques d'un amateur de sciences.* Paris: Presses des Mines.

Lorde, Audre. 1984. *Sister Outsider: Essays and Speeches.* Trumansburg, NY: Crossing.

Lugones, Maria. 2008. "Coloniality and Gender." *Tabula Rasa*, no. 9: 73–102.

Martins, Alexandre Nogueira. 2020. "The Path to the Criminalization of LGBT-Phobia: Criminalizing Rationality, Neoliberalism, and Democratization." MA thesis, University of São Paulo, USP.

Mombaça, Jota. 2021. "Rumo a uma redistribuição desobediente de gênero e anticolonial da violência." In *Não Vão Nos Matar Agora*, 63–83. Rio de Janeiro: Cobogó.

Moten, Fred. 2018. "Gestural Critique of Judgment." In *Stolen Life*, 96–114. Durham, NC: Duke University Press.

Muñoz, José Estéban. 2009. *Cruising Utopia: The There and Then of Queer Theory.* New York: New York University Press.

Ocanha, Rafael Freitas. 2014. "Amor, Feijão, Abaixo Camburão: Imprensa, violência e trottoir em São Paulo (1979–1983)." MA thesis, Pontifical Catholic University of São Paulo.

Pereira, Pedro Paulo Gomes. 2019. "Reflecting on Decolonial Queer." *GLQ* 25, no. 3: 403–29.

Perra, Hija de. 2014. "Interpretaciones inmundas de cómo la teoría queer coloniza nuestro contexto sudaca, pobre, aspiracional y tercermundista, perturbando con nuevas construcciones genéricas a los humanos encantados con la heteronorma." *Revista punto género*, no. 4: 9–16.

Preciado, Paul. 2020. *Yo soy el monstruo que os habla.* Barcelona: Editorial Anagrama.

Rojas, Lucía Egaña. 2017. "Hago más traducciones que las malditas naciones unidas, de mierda." In *No existe sexo sin racialización*, edited by Leticia Rojas Miranda and Francisco Godoy Vega, 64–73. Madrid: Traficantes de Sueños.

Segato, Rita Laura. 2007. "El color de la cárcel en América Latina." *Revista nueva sociedad*, no. 208: 142–61.

Serra, Victor Siqueira. 2018. "Pessoa afeita ao crime: Criminalização de travestis e o discurso judicial criminal paulista." MA thesis, São Paulo State University, UNESP.

Shock, Susy. 2011. *Poemario trans pirado.* Buenos Aires: Nuevos Tiempos.

Silva, Denise Ferreira da. 2007. *Toward a Global Idea of Race.* Minneapolis: University of Minnesota Press.

Spade, Dean. 2015. *Normal Life: Administrative Violence, Critical Trans Politics, and the Limits of Law.* Durham, NC: Duke University Press.

Trevisan, João Silvério. (1986) 2000. *Devassos no paraíso.* Rev. 3rd ed. São Paulo: Editora Record.

Tuck, Eve, and K. Wayne Yang. 2012. "Decolonization Is Not a Metaphor." *Decolonization: Indigeneity, Education and Society* 1, no. 1: 1–40.

vergueiro, viviane. 2015. "Por inflexões decoloniais de corpos e identidades de gênero inconformes: Uma análise autoetnográfica da cisgeneridade como normatividade." MA thesis, Bahia Federal University, UFBA.

vergueiro, viviane. 2019. "Sou travestis: Estudando a cisgeneridade como uma possibilidade decolonial." Brazil: Padê Editorial.

Wynter, Sylvia. 2003. "Unsettling the Coloniality of Being/Power/Truth/Freedom: Towards the Human, after Man, Its Overrepresentation—An Argument." *CR: The New Centennial Review* 3, no. 3: 257–337.

"WE'RE HERE! WE'RE QUEER! FUCK THE BANKS!"

On the Affective Lives of Abolition

Alison Rose Reed

We are fun and creative, and we are trying to live abolition and
that is challenging, and that means challenging and questioning
and resisting as frequently as possible all the ways that we harm
each other and the ways that we are harmed and the ways that we
harm ourselves.
—kai lumumba barrow, "Perspectives on Critical Resistance,"
in *Abolition Now! Ten Years of Strategy and Struggle against
the Prison Industrial Complex*

Hope is a discipline. . . . we have to practice it every single day.
—Mariame Kaba, *We Do This 'til We Free Us: Abolitionist
Organizing and Transforming Justice*

Is love a synonym for abolition?
—Saidiya Hartman, "The End of White Supremacy, an
American Romance"

There's something strikingly queer, and queerly utopian, about abolition. Literalizing the metaphor of José Esteban Muñoz's (2009: 1) famous statement, "Queerness is not yet here. . . . The here and now is a prison house," this essay argues that the process of affectively reorienting space and minds toward abolition is a queer act. While surely, for 2.5 million people caged by the United States, the here and now is literally a prison house, abolition lives within its walls. An abolitionist analysis is queer in its strategic orientation toward futurity and its refusal

GLQ 28:2
DOI 10.1215/10642684-9608147
© 2022 by Duke University Press

to put faith into existing institutions, but as we will see, queerness is not always abolitionist. When paired, however, queer abolitionist affects can not only refuse the directives of racial capitalism and disrupt dominant discourses of surveillance, policing, and imprisonment but also imagine—in messy and imperfect ways, as kai lumumba barrow (Samuels and Stein 2008: 4) suggests above—a livable social world. As opposed to reformist logics of "broken" systems, queer abolitionist approaches to shrinking the carceral state recognize the constitutive violence of institutions and seek to reject normative frameworks of legibility. Abolition is here, and its affective lives are queer.

Like queerness, abolition—as both a "beautiful vision" and "practical organizing strategy"—refuses to limit horizons of possibility to the state's demand for simple solutions to complex problems (Shehk 2016). I use the term *queer* not in a strictly identitarian way (although I do not seek to erase queerness as lived experience), but in Cathy J. Cohen's (1997) canonical sense of a shared relationship to power that refuses to mobilize around its terms, as well as in Critical Resistance's (2004: 67) meaning as an organizing principle for transformative coalition building. Leaning into the unknown, dreaming new strategies to heal and reduce harm, and reimagining collectivity, abolition is at once intangible and concrete. This seeming paradox is the necessary precondition for refusing simplistic solutions to centuries-long problems, and moving beyond present impasses of carceral logics, which redouble harm in an effort to mitigate its effects. As Mariame Kaba (Haymarket Books 2021) affirms, in the radical Black feminist tradition of abolition, "'We will figure it out by working to get there' is praxis, not evasion. . . . Organizing is the how." Abolition thus exists in the here and now, from the reimagination of social life to networks of mutual aid to grassroots campaigns to demilitarize, defund, and dismantle the colonial-carceral state.

Queer affects, if not mobilized in service of carceral interests, can open portals to abolition. Such affects compel abolitionist practices if they are understood as orientations fostered over time rather than the outcome of a specific singular event. I here define *affect* capaciously to include intensities, sensations, feelings, and emotions, none of which are simply intrinsic to the body but are instead produced and situated relationally in dense networks of power.[1] Likewise, what Sara Ahmed (2006) describes as orientations trace directional movement toward or away from certain practices and bodies as a result of habitual training. As relationships provide the basic building block of organizing, queer affects can radically inform how to nurture those relationships in abolitionist ways. Therefore, abolition begins with affective and interpersonal relationships that strive toward delegitimizing carceral logics. But abolition does not end there.

Consider, for example, the tangible gains of Critical Resistance's coalitional work in 2019 to stop Urban Shield (a weapons expo and militarized police training) and the construction of two new jails in Los Angeles or, even more recently, the victories toward divesting in deadly institutions and investing in collective self-determination, such as with the Defund Oakland Police Department Coalition. Consider also the Black and Brown youth-led abolitionist campaign of #NoCopAcademy organizers, who fought to redirect $95 million to fund communities over and against the construction of a cop academy in westside Chicago. As both Kaba (2019) and Benji Hart (2019) write, even defeats can be wins for shifting the conversation around redefining "safety" and "community" to be centered on people and not property. Abolition also exists in the organized demands of prison strikes, in trans love behind and beyond bars, and in the sonic vibrations of Mumia Abu-Jamal's voice over Prison Radio.

In exploring the affective dimensions of queer abolition, this essay takes up the spatial and symbolic relationship between the Pride parade and the prison industrial complex (PIC), as the ideological and repressive management of complex social, economic, and political problems with a vicious racialized regime of criminalization, surveillance, policing, and caging.[2] In what follows I demonstrate the urgency of queer abolitionist constellations of affect.

First, I put Muñoz's critical utopianism in conversation with the work of carceral studies scholars and abolitionist organizers (distinct but overlapping categories). This section elaborates on how abolition, as a long-term organizing strategy often derided as utopian,[3] affectively and relationally aligns with the queer register of utopia. More specifically, I explore how both queerness as an analytic and abolitionist approaches can open portals to dream capaciously about intimate and coalitional relationships beyond the nuclear family model to more expansive visions of social life.

Next, I consider what happens when queerness is untethered from abolition via the example of No Justice No Pride actions protesting whitewashed Pride events as well as the LGBTQIA+ embrace of corporations and cops. No Justice No Pride's actions invoked Indigenous two-spirit ancestors, as well as trans and gender-nonconforming people of color as central to fighting state-sanctioned violence and building sustainable futures. The intersectional recuperation of these legacies of resistance to borders, binaries, pipelines, police, and prisons inspires this analysis of abolition's affective lives.

Then, I consider my work with Humanities Behind Bars (HBB), an abolitionist network of radical group-based study and mutual aid. While Pride's corporate capture is neither queer nor abolitionist, I explore how HBB's prison education program, in its vision and praxis, is ironically both queer and abolitionist in orientation—ironic because it takes place in a jail and exists within even as it pushes back against neoliberal instructional regimes with their pathologizing and patronizing attitudes toward incarcerated people. Humanities Behind Bars envisions its work as a way to build alliances and facilitate spaces for political education (of "teachers" and "students" alike) across prison walls. Surely, the program is not free from pitfalls, such as the risk of being shut down and its own complex dynamics as an organization. Humanities Behind Bars thus provides an opportunity to think about the tensions and contradictions of practicing abolition in a thoroughly carceral landscape to which it remains antagonistic. By bringing together an analysis of public protest and prison education, I posit that queer affects strengthen and sustain the relationships so vital to abolitionist world making.

Abolition (is) here; abolition (is) now!

Queer Feelings at the End of the World

Echoing Muñoz, queerness is not yet here, but its affective lives have a powerful existence in the present. Abolition requires this reorientation toward each other and away from racial capitalism as a "technology of antirelationality" (Melamed 2011: 78). Being careful not to fetishize the positionalities of queer people of color, Muñoz and Omise'eke Natasha Tinsley trace this orientation toward utopian futures, as the world is not yet ready for such expansive ways of loving, desiring, and relating to one another. As Tinsley (2018: 188) writes in homage to Muñoz, his "'forward-dawning futurity' is queer of color time, the warmly illuminated, unreal(ized) future where all our multiparented, unruly, well-loved black and brown children are free to desire creatively." This utopian vision does not preclude that creative desires thrive in the present; the beautiful imagination of other worlds exists alongside daily pockets of pleasure, as well as short- and long-term organizing strategies for a world where such relationships wouldn't be routinely severed by state violence.

The queer affects of abolition materialize utopian visions in daily practice. This "concrete possibility for another world" condenses my use of critical utopianism here (Muñoz 2009: 1), amplified by Black utopian thought (see Zamalin 2019). As Keno Evol (2020) writes of this latter tradition: "Utopia is the point of departure that ends in a non-arrival. Utopia is an infinite activity of relation." Queer utopianism strives to reclaim space in fugitive ways, dreaming of a world where resources and care are self-determined by communities in the name of the collective good. Yet I heed Eric Stanley's (2018: 491) positing of an "affective com-

mons" that comes together, but never arrives, to disrupt the settler-colonialist logics of such spatial reorganizations. Queer utopianism finds concrete expression in
the daily actions of creating a "decolonial future without borders or cages" that
abolition's affective lives are oriented toward (Walia 2020: 1).

As an affective mode, queer utopianism encapsulates what Muñoz
describes as a kind of desiring beyond the romanticization and particular pleasures of so-called negative emotions, which also do important work to give hope
dimension. Muñoz finds this hope, which the world seeks to annihilate, in the aesthetic realm as offering utopian blueprints of possibility. It is this "surplus of both
affect and meaning within the aesthetic" on which I focus here (Muñoz 2009: 3),
necessarily extending to the sphere of organized action. As Kaba (2021: 27) often
says, "Hope is a discipline. . . . we have to practice it every single day." This
study of affect remains attentive to differential relationships to carceral power and
how those relationships shape organizing spaces. A queer abolitionist analysis,
therefore, is informed by lived experiences of art and activism. Queer feelings can
exceed bodies in and through space; queer feelings aren't just felt by us queers.

Abolition and queerness overlap when they refuse to place faith in institutions to effect change, specifically through legal reforms that redouble the status
quo while shunning broader visions of liberation. In other words, abolition can
reorient space in a queer way by challenging normative paradigms of power and
its critique—thinking about relationship building capaciously, beyond the nuclear
family unit. This optic contests discourses of cultural pathology and personal
responsibility—popular in liberal dialogues about mass incarceration—that often
assert an insufficiently heteronormative family structure as the principal cause of
people's suffering, and redeemed fatherhood as the salve for structural racism. The
racialized rhetoric of personal responsibility here mutes a more complex, important engagement with how one lives with and among harm, including that of the
PIC. From the Moynihan Report to the mythic "superpredator," this discourse of
familial pathology came to shape national ideals in the wake of civil rights legislation in the 1960s, effectively blocking social welfare policy in the 1970s, and
continuing to attack civil rights gains in the 1980s and 1990s.[4] Moreover, the
discourse of cultural pathology taps into centuries-long myths of Black criminality
that bolstered massive post–World War II prison-building projects. Queer abolitionist frameworks, in contrast, understand love, family, and collectivity more
capaciously as social relations not of domination but of transformation.

Abolition requires an affective shift both against the genocidal project of
settler racial capitalism and toward forging alternative ecologies of repairing harm
and healing communities. These alternative ecologies address the root causes of

crime—itself a social construction. In the widely circulated web comic "Who's Left? Prison Abolition," illustrated by Flynn Nicholls, Kaba asserts: "I don't know what a world without prisons will look like, but it will fundamentally transform our relationship with other people" (Nicholls 2017). This important claim extends Dylan Rodríguez's (2010: 7; 2019: 1575) contributions about abolition as "in this moment, *primarily pedagogical*" and a "praxis of human being" to think about how relationships provide the foundation for abolitionist ways of knowing, doing, and feeling. Existing in the messy and always incomplete spaces between ideological purity or polarity, abolition's affective lives remain necessarily rooted in forming interpersonal relationships that reject the premise of the white supremacist construction of the "human" as such and its hierarchical, profoundly alienated social organization. Abolition necessitates replacing systems of coercion, criminalization, and control with deep forms of communal care. Of course, love as well as care work can become sites for the reproduction of carcerality; this analysis, however, charts possibilities embedded in movement toward its undoing. I seek neither to romanticize abolition as a pure category nor to cohere it as a static identity, but to trace its manifestations in practice.

Since abolition as a project exists now, it is temporally and ideologically enmeshed in both a less harmful world and the vast harms of this one. Abolition is not just a vital aspiration but a daily action that manifests queer affective orientations toward co-creating a reality that overturns structures of state power while existing antagonistically in relationship to them, understanding that an "outside" positionality is not always possible. To be clear, absolutely central to abolitionist organizing is the understanding that policing and prisons cannot be reformed from the inside and must be dismantled; yet the PIC is also imbricated in educational, political, and financial institutions, for example, from which total freedom presents contradictions and challenges. To secure the resources to survive, many folks negotiate some kind of strategic spatial situation within oppressive institutions, while battling against self-definition by and the sinister seductions of those very institutions; material survival must therefore be attended by soul work, to consider the consequences of one's attachments and labor. The queer affects of abolition imagine different social relations to move us from an unlivable social world to a livable one, but those affects exist in tension with the institutions on which people rely for material survival. This essay does not presume to proffer a solution but instead to recognize how in a constitutively violent society, unless one goes completely off the grid on previously uninhabited land (which already prefigures the colonial romance of Robinson Crusoe), material and spiritual survival will be at odds; the work is to imagine and enact ways of closing that gap collectively.

The queer utopian register of abolition insists—as a matter of spiritual survival—on possibility and pleasure amidst systemic pain, on alternative ways of organizing social life amidst economies of death. This reference to death economies does not seek to conflate grossly distinct experiences of violence but instead to acknowledge how the prison and military industrial complexes intentionally annihilate, both socially and materially, enemies and extras of the state's maintenance of racial capitalism. It also follows Dean Spade's (Stanley, Spade, and Queer (In)Justice 2012: 125) critique of how "rights strategies tend to affirm the law's role in creating and maintaining classes of undeserving outsiders marked for death." Precisely because abolition has often been pejoratively described as utopian—especially by liberal reformists who maintain a vested interest in the carceral state, and whose strategies do not question the notion of "legitimate" state violence—the utopian can be strategically reclaimed to emphasize how abolition delineates an epistemological and practical position beyond just being anti-police and anti-prison, to one firmly grounded in agitating for another world.

To reference a specific idiom from Saidiya Hartman (2020) and others on how anti-blackness fundamentally shapes modern institutions, which in turn cannot be reformed but must be razed, abolition signifies "the end of the world." Abolition dwells—affectively and relationally—in the space between the end of this world and the beginning of another. This imaginative capacity to envision new social relations is rooted in the ineffability and necessity of love, notwithstanding its fragile beauty and betrayals. As Hartman (2020) asks, "Is love a synonym for abolition?" Of course, the context for this question grapples with love's "temporary reprieve" or temporal respite from the violence of whiteness. Yet amid impossibility, the demolition of this world is exercised in the present through collective practices of care that combat constitutive anti-blackness.

The end of the world recognizes that the tragic is part of the fabric of daily living, channeling James Baldwin's ([1963] 1993: 91–92) statement in *The Fire Next Time* about feeling "responsible to life," precisely because life is tragic: "It seems to me that one ought to rejoice in the *fact* of death—ought to decide, indeed, to *earn* one's death by confronting with passion the conundrum of life." This responsibility refuses to organize death-in-life "totems, taboos, crosses, blood sacrifices, steeples, mosques, races, armies, flags, nations," and other myths of civilization premised on hierarchy, exclusion, subordination, and violence. In other words, Baldwin's vision makes clear the need to abolish violent containers of meaning (e.g., the false binaries of free/unfree, innocent/guilty, legal/illegal, man/woman and the edifices that consolidate them, such as cages). As an entry point to leaning into the impossible, an abolitionist analysis embraces life, how to love capaciously and heal harm, and the space of imagination, where one might feel portals opening to another world. As Ruth Wilson Gilmore (Kushner 2019) says of abolitionist alternatives to the constitutive violence of the military and prison industrial complexes, "where life is precious, life is precious."

No Justice, No Pride

On June 13, 2013, I spent a boozy afternoon at a Pride celebration in Santa Barbara, California, bumping into old flames, flirting with a future girlfriend, and dancing merrily to drag queens performing onstage. When I returned home, nothing was more sobering than learning of George Zimmerman's acquittal for the murder of Trayvon Martin, as another tragic example of how the state sanctions Black death. My beach day of romance and glitter suddenly felt perverse, complicit even. The violent simultaneity of corporatized Pride events held unwittingly against the backdrop of stolen Black lives has stuck with me ever since.

The example of Pride's coinciding with Zimmerman's acquittal parallels Chandan Reddy's (2011: 39) theorization of freedom with violence, or how "socially and institutionally produced forms of emancipation remain regulatively and constitutively tied to the nation-state form." For example, Reddy (17) literalizes the metaphor of amendments (e.g., how the Matthew Shepard and James Byrd, Jr. Hate Crimes Bill Prevention Act amends the 2010 National Defense Authorization Act, which allocated the largest budget for the Department of Defense in history, and the 1969 Civil Rights Act) to reveal in part how rights-based and legal forms of social emancipation remain linked to global violence and racial capitalism, with race as the "political unconscious" of sexuality. It comes as no surprise, then, given Reddy's analysis of how sexuality amends race, that the partial overturning of the Defense of Marriage Act went hand in hand in 2013 with the dismantling of the Voting Rights Act of 1965.

But that, of course, is not the end of the story. Zimmerman's acquittal and subsequent mass mobilizations around Justice for Trayvon reverberated locally and across the country, as students of color at the University of California, Santa Barbara (where I was a PhD candidate at the time) took the lead organizing the Santa Barbara Coalition for Justice. This collective of students, faculty and staff, seasoned activists, and community members organized to hold a series of actions, from a silent vigil to teach-ins to a march through downtown, disrupting onlooking shoppers funneling in and out of bourgeois boutiques. The wealthy white areas of Santa Barbara—downtown State Street being a prime example—are aggressively policed, as rich retirees and vacationing celebrities funnel funds into police departments protecting their multimillion-dollar beachfront properties. The march's route intentionally proceeded down State Street for maximum disturbance to business as usual. Protestors sang and shouted rallying cries, while holding signs with messages such as "#NoMoreEmmettTills." We had thrown a poster-making party in the days leading up to the march, so many of the signs themselves were confrontational art statements in fluorescent colors. As a legal observer at the crowd's periphery, I witnessed the stark boundary of powerful resistance and the eyes of outsiders, looking on in curiosity or contempt. That is to say, the affective energy of the marchers, expressing righteous rage and loving solidarity, an emotional pulse that vibrated through my body, was met with the opposite facial expressions of confusion, guilt, or disdain by shoppers sipping brunch cocktails on outdoor patios lining the street.

Affect is itself a performance of boundary. Affect can demarcate both belonging and unbelonging in a given space. Affective responses to art and activism can create a border of feeling with and for state power or protestors against it. While protest itself can be contained and incorporated by the state, its affective afterlives, in their intangibility, cannot so easily be erased from space. As I observed at the march and during its aftermath, participating in protest can cohere queer feelings, radicalizing people.

Meanwhile, some faces continue to twist and warp at a hashtag, or say #BlackLivesMatter in the same breath as calling for community dialogues with cops, or redirect what "defund the police" means to soothe the feelings of liberals, whose fantasies of safety smooth over the carceral state's constitutive violences. Such responses produce support for reforms that bolster the state by pouring more money into its brutal machinations. Abolition, however, as a way of knowing and doing, posits that justice does not look like a multicultural or legal Band-aid but is a broader call for systemic transformation, as well as a way of organizing social relations in the present that recognizes the limited authority of the dominant. Inclusion never equals transformation when its terms are a morally bankrupt ascension to racial-colonial carceral violence.

As is evident by the marriage equality movement, lesbian and gay people have entered the mainstream and appealed to corporate markets; however, trans radicals of color, Indigenous two-spirit folks, abolitionist queers, rebel dykes, and otherwise antiassimilationist LGBTQIA+ people continue to refuse the narrow terms of mainstream Pride campaigns, organized around overwhelmingly white, middle-class, corporate, pro-military, and pro-cop interests. For example, "We're Here! We're Queer! Fuck the Banks!," an anticapitalist Pride chant heard in Oakland, California, in June 2017, rails against the corporate co-optation of Pride month from its roots in the 1969 Stonewall uprising, which was not an isolated event in history but preceded and followed by protests and organizing against the criminalization and brutalization of queer and trans people (such as the Compton's Cafeteria Riot of 1966). This historical militant queer victory was not just about fighting back against the police but also about mobilizing for queer liberation for all those vulnerable to state violence, including people of color, poor queens, trans folks, sex workers, and unhoused youth.[5] After all, queerness as an analytic should not be divorced from self-identified queer people, but must remain tied to its attendant radical organizing praxis that refuses the myopia of single-issue identity politics. As Stanley writes (Stanley, Spade, and Queer (In)Justice 2012: 116), "Many trans/queer people have found ways to exist beside, build community in spite of, and struggle against the police state. From alternative methods of accountability and organizing direct actions, to collective self-defense, including these forms of resistance helps build a more expansive definition of abolition." The Pride chant referenced above, therefore, expresses abolition's affective charge, which reclaims space ("We're Here!") with a queer energy that remains hostile to racial capitalist institutions ("We're Queer! Fuck the Banks!"). Likewise, a queer abolitionist analysis moves beyond the profit-motive myth of incarceration (see Kushner 2019) to the more complex relationship between finance capital and the PIC, as an overwhelmingly public (i.e., government) institution.[6]

To combat intensified voices of ever-present hate in the fascistic era of Donald Trump (before the election of Joe Biden provided false comfort to liberals), community organizers amplified the abolitionist critique of assimilationist politics and the recuperation of queer and trans of color legacies of resistance. During the summer of 2017, Pride events were scheduled in the aftermath of Officer Jeronimo Yanez's acquittal for the devastating video-recorded murder of Philando Castille—as well as the brutal murders of Charleena Lyles and Nabra Hassanen on the heels of each other, as just three examples of anti-Black, racist, sexist, and Islamophobic forms of structural hate. No Justice No Pride actions sprang up at Pride parades from Washington, DC, to New York City to Seattle—protesting the long-standing collusion of Pride events with corporate interests and cops. As No Justice No Pride's (2017) Facebook event page announced, "We are the dreams of our indigenous two spirit ancestors who existed pre-colonization. We must remember that our liberation has been led by trans and gender-nonconforming people of color who had nothing to lose. PRIDE WAS BORN FROM RESISTANCE TO STATE SANCTIONED VIOLENCE!" Of course, activists often necessarily inhabit contradictions; their anticapitalist statement is here made on a corporate platform. Even so, as these demonstrations against corporatized Pride affirm, struggles against state power cannot always exist outside it, but organizers aspire toward the idea that liberation cannot be rooted in someone else's oppression. While such aspirations may seem like theoretical sentimentalism, a queer abolitionist analysis traces the affective and relational labor people perform in their daily lives. This labor is complicated, sometimes chaotic, and always incomplete. As barrow (Samuels and Stein 2008: 4) explains: "It's important for us to communicate with folks that we don't have answers; we are like everybody else, trying to figure out how to change the world."

No Justice No Pride protestors, in coalition with decolonial abolitionist groups such as Hoods4Justice, were harassed and arrested by police across the country.[7] Yet liberals continue to fantasize about, and remain affectively invested in, cops. For example, in an article titled "Straight New York City Cop Shares Pride Message You Won't Soon Forget," Greg Hernandez (2017) writes about one New York Police Department officer who shared a message of "solidarity" with Pride-goers that went viral: "He identifies himself only as 'Huge Fat Loser' and posts a photo of himself wearing a T-shirt that reads: 'I may be straight but I don't hate.' He then shares a list of reasons why he worked last weekend's Pride event. It's a thorough and thoughtful list that any LGBTI person can identify with." The direct second-person address in the title, combined with the absence of *Q* in its catalog of queer identities, implies a normative reader who seeks fellowship with the police. The officer's Facebook post explains that he plans to work PrideFest with the shirt under his uniform, as if sartorial layering could create a peaceful palimpsest of state violence and love-driven politics. His dedication includes cops and gay 9/11 victims, while positioning the police as protectors of queer people: "For every call I went to where someone got kicked out of their house or who's [*sic*] family just didn't understand. For anyone who's had to hide who they are. I've got your back. Love is Love." He ends his emotional appeal with hashtags #LoveIs-Love, #Pride, #PrideParade, #NYPD, #IGotYou, and #FreeHugs. People flocked to his Facebook post to embrace this cop's promise and celebrate his supposedly progressive celebration of law-abiding Pride attendees. This co-opted version of Pride, in bed with cops and the system of criminalization and caging they actively maintain, is a dystopian rather than utopian horizon. When love means not only accepting but also openly embracing the agents of state violence, a queer abolitionist analysis posits the urgency of reclaiming love not as love but in struggle, as a form of communal care and spiritual sustenance.

When we, following Grace Lee Boggs, Robin D. G. Kelley, and other visionaries,[8] offer up a transformative politics of relationality, then, we must be specific about what we mean by love. That is to say, we must continue to disrupt the active investment in celebrating cops under the banner "Love Is Love." Against the sanitized multicultural celebration of empathy, compassion, and love for others as a solution to social ills in and of itself, the Black radical tradition (and other revolutionary epistemologies) reclaims love's transformative power when used toward dismantling carceral power and building toward another world. Love, anger, and other affects that can compel action remain vital to the ongoing work. Grand narratives of social histories can deemphasize the micro-movements people make in their everyday psychic and social lives, punctuated by grief and joy. Pointing to the coexistence of such affects scales the study of social movements down to the subtle transformations of daily relational praxis. As adrienne maree brown (2020: 2–3) writes, "We must work hard at getting abolitionist practice functional at a small scale so that large-scale abolition and transformative justice are more visible, rootable, possible."[9] While always imperfect, our approach to relationships must strive to acknowledge power dynamics and honor the best in each other and ourselves, collectively cultivating radical visions of love as an everyday practice and organized commitment to healing harm without resorting to carcerality.

Abolitionist Prison Education?

Before COVID-19 moved classrooms online, or in the case of some prison education programs, postponed courses altogether, every week I would pack my mesh tote with photocopied reading materials separated by hot-pink sticky notes, dry-erase markers, writing utensils, extra ballpoint pens, and a yellow pad of discussion prompts or impromptu lecture ideas, before making the eight-minute drive from my apartment to the local jail, tucked so squarely behind the downtown courthouse so as to be visible only from the freeway. After collecting my ticket and driving through the pay lot partition to park, I would leave my cell phone, wallet, and other personal belongings in my glove compartment aside from the driver's license required for entrance. Walking from the parking structure to the jail entrance, I would often nod to folks coming from the courthouse or jail, while avoiding the gaze of cops leaving a shift and the catcalls of construction workers nearby. In front of the never-ending construction zone, thrown into relief by neon-orange makeshift mesh fencing, I would pass a sign before being buzzed through a heavy security door after saying the magic words to gain admittance: Humanities Behind Bars (HBB). The aluminum reflective sign does more than indicate to visitors that a byzantine parking structure surrounded by other city administrative buildings, all brutalist in architectural design, is in fact connected to the jail; it reads "Jail/Public Safety." This conflation of a space that cages humans awaiting trial or transfer with "public safety" provides an unwelcome reminder of the violent logics of carceral society.

Once past the main entrance, you walk a little way longer through an additional parking lot to another heavy blue door that leads to the receiving dock and security checkpoint. Once, a cop startled me by emerging through that door with gun pointing eye level, as if whoever just so happened to be there could serve as a practice target. I'll never know why I was greeted that way (he offered no explanation), but these kinds of arbitrary flashes of state violence become routine, making it necessary to decompress after leaving such an intentionally traumatic space—a privilege not afforded to those caged by the state and whose experience of that trauma and violence is, it goes without saying, far more severe. Once through security (the see-through bag must go through the metal detector, the body must be inspected with a handheld scanner), the programs director or someone else summoned in the office would meet me at security and escort me to the classroom. Its location changed over time, ranging from a table bolted to the floor between two occupied cellblocks, where attorneys would consult with their clients, to an actual classroom with a whiteboard on the newfangled programming block. When that classroom was being renovated, I remember once meeting in a recently emptied cellblock. Behind the bars where the jail staff left us, you could still smell the sweat and waste of bodies. We retooled the space to make it our own, covering over an exposed urinal with the thick plastic of a shower curtain. This was our last class, and the relationships we had formed over the course of a semester were meaningful to us. The jail library was no longer accepting donations, and students criticized how they never had proper access to books anyway, with guards arbitrarily confiscating their class materials on the regular. Due to and despite these facts, I had brought in some books I picked out for each student, tailored to their interests, from the HBB library of donations for future book drives. That day, in our unusually quiet corner of the jail, we read each other poetry we had written that was inspired by the course, "The Poetics and Politics of US History." Studying, plotting, and planning with jailed students can teach valuable lessons about abolitionist organizing and the imperative to listen carefully not just to famous political prisoners, whose revolutionary thought can easily be romanticized, but also to everyday people whose analyses of the state and of interpersonal harm dwell in the messy, troubling zones where important work takes place.

In 2016 Meghan G. McDowell and I cofounded Humanities Behind Bars, which began as a prison education program and later added a pen-pal project, radical inside–outside study group, mutual aid network, and local bail fund. We started as a strategic partnership between the city jail and the university we both taught at, but the only source of funding from the university was a research assistantship sponsored by the graduate school. This assistantship was one of the first things to go with budget cuts made under the auspices of COVID-19 austerity measures. The university nonetheless continues to selectively honor and claim HBB as its own, despite the fact that we are a grassroots community-based organization with no official relationship to the university and no paid staff. All the money we raise goes toward supporting currently and formerly incarcerated people, directly through the mutual aid and bail funds, and indirectly through our minimal general operation costs for the prison education and pen-pal programs (e.g., books and supplies for classes, stamps and envelopes for letter-writing sessions). Well aware of the necessary critique of the nonprofit industrial complex (see INCITE! 2007), HBB decided over time to become a registered 501(c)(3) because otherwise we could not legally fundraise in the state of Virginia, a litigious issue that concerned enough of HBB's members to take action. We collectively decided, after many meetings with the core team and consultation with longtime organizers and movement lawyers, that despite the problems of such incorporation, we wanted to ensure our long-term sustainability; this proved strategic, as in 2020 HBB raised over $100,000 for the Tidewater Solidarity Bail Fund (modeled after and in relationship with the Richmond Community Bail Fund). We take seriously the work of organizing mutual aid and political education by building solidarity with people across prison walls. Networks of mutual aid "work to meet survival needs and build shared understanding about why people do not have what they need" (Spade 2020: 9). Mutual aid is political education in action.

We often reflect on the seeming incommensurability of abolition as well as mutual aid with "prison education," as such programming often relies on neoliberal modes of instruction and charity models of benevolent saviorism under state-captured notions of social justice and public engagement. Indeed, HBB cofounders have elsewhere written not only on the seeming incompatibility and generative im/possibility of prison education and abolition, but also on how affective shifts in classroom spaces and the formation of prohibited forms of conviviality disrupt the neoliberal carceral presumptions of such programming (McDowell and Reed 2018). Because of our abolitionist orientation, which we don't flaunt to guards or administrators but is evident in the content and comportment of our courses, our program is always at risk of being shut down and has come close on a number of occasions; for example, class has been interrupted for questioning by panels of cops, and educators have been disciplined for breaking the rules (of appropriate attire, for instance).

By content and comportment, I refer to what and how we teach, even though the state often explicitly prohibits the formation of bonds over texts in the Black radical tradition. As a mundane example, HBB educators have been instructed by some jail staff to never make eye contact with "inmates," state language that consolidates supposed criminality into an identity formation. After the mandatory jail training, HBB includes its own orientation in which we unpack the problems with such belittling actions and language, and discuss our efforts to study *beside* and not teach *to* those who elect to participate. Humanities Behind Bars has to maintain this strained and strategic relationship to the state in order to study and organize with jailed artists and activists.

Although we use the classroom space to make collective organizing decisions and mobilize around student demands, HBB members have often discussed the uncomfortable knowledge that our program, as one of many at the jail, feeds state narratives of humane and rehabilitative jailing by providing educational services free of charge. While not all HBB educators are affiliated with nearby universities, the fact that its cofounders are college professors lends the program additional legitimacy. Adding to the tensions and contradictions of HBB is student participation. Because we are not a degree-granting program, students choose to be there not for credentialing purposes but for a myriad of other reasons, certainly including but not limited to the desire to study or, more practically, work toward a GED (such courses are offered at the jail) or other degree (upon release). Either way, programmatic participation reflects well on incarcerated people when they go to court. The jail, however, only allows "non-violent offenders" to take courses, which further reinforces the worthy/unworthy divide that structures the neoliberal university and prison education alike.

Despite these constraints, courses remain spaces to organize as well as to study, and students have expressed gratitude for the way HBB extends those spaces—and the contributions made therein—into the community. Abolitionist organizing, after all, takes its lead from currently and formerly incarcerated people who bring vital analyses to the table, while not romanticizing those analyses as beyond critique. Some students, for complex reasons, rehearse harmful state logics in constructing their own redemption narrative by appealing to the category of "worthy" that disappears the allegedly unworthy. Organizing with currently and formerly incarcerated students also presents difficulties in finding ways to collectively secure people's material needs to survive without reproducing the moral citizenship/charity model of the nonprofit sector and the regulatory function of "reentry" programs. In sum, being in tactical relation to institutions at times operates from a place of constrained need. Abolitionist analyses must continue to critically address the ethics of this interpersonal and institutional messiness, refuting false binaries of working within oppressive institutions or existing outside them.

Teaching in a jail or prison is marked by violent affective incommensurability: the cruelty of cages and those invested in them, against the fugitive laughter and other affects brought on by the togetherness formed through a positioning against the carceral state via conspiratorial study of its mechanisms, and toward how the radical imagination dreams otherwise amidst it. For example, once, while staging Black feminist Marita Bonner's one-act play *The Purple Flower* at the jail, a usually shy student belted out a dramatic line with such gusto that the class burst out in uproarious laughter with him. This moment reminds me of the significance of shared laughter, movement, and joy when studying serious topics, while remaining attentive to people's lived experiences. To be sure, whether at a jail or on campus, I am not suggesting we treat traumatic histories—and people's embodied relationship to them—lightly. For example, when discussing the play's setting, students theorize Bonner's spatialization of racial power in relationship to their condition of incarceration. Yet all the more so in a space where trauma is everywhere felt, this seriousness must be balanced with the social possibilities of riotous laughter and other fugitive affects.

Of course, the relational possibilities embedded in such affective shifts, and the comradeships formed between jailed "students" and HBB "educators," exist amidst a deep well of pain that can never be resolved—the existence of cages. Abolitionist affects of love and rage, then, insist on possibility not out of some romantic sense of messianic rupture detached from the weight of experience, but precisely because to not insist with urgency on another world leads quite literally to spiritual and material death. These containers of human cages are intentionally traumatic. Moreover, one cannot simply go on living as before while knowing a loved one is incarcerated. It is a heaviness, the freedom of movement weighted by close proximity to profound unfreedom. Therefore, queer utopianism is not a refuge but an insistence that social relationships and collective creativity remain vital to survival. Relationships, with all their messiness and loss, joy and pleasure, rowdiness and rebelliousness, breakdowns and breakups, grief and tragedy, impasses and irreconcilabilities, teach vital lessons and make social movements possible. As HBB activist-poet and former student Dom Roscoe (2020) writes, in a dreamy, elliptical mode that breathes on the page, reclaiming space: "I'm not an incarcerated mind, but a MIND'S EYE OF INCARCERATION spinning . . . . . [Freely] . . . . . What does it cost to pay attention?—Nothing; So listen, are you free?—." Replacing the liberal discourse of dehumanization with an insistence on his privileged optic on power—whereby he focuses attention on the inhumanity of its active and complicit agents—Roscoe redefines freedom within a new economy of value, the exhortation to pay attention to the ongoing Black liberation struggle. He asks his reader, "are you free?," demanding a reconsideration of the very terms of freedom of mind and body. Roscoe's poem serves as a powerful indictment of carceral logics and a reminder that as long as millions remain in cages, none are free.

Against Incorporation

Abolition exists in the everyday work being done in people's intimate relationships and on the ground to create a world without the structuring logics and edifices of cops, cages, and borders. This work uses a variety of tactics and strategies to get closer to that world, existing in antagonistic relationship to institutions. Its mode of queer utopian feeling is already here as process, in concerted actions to break down the prison industrial complex while nurturing collectives of care and exercising commitments to being an enemy of the carceral state.

Like queer and trans social identities and organizing work, abolition has seen heightened mainstream attention in the twenty-first century. Increased visibility can paradoxically obscure as it reveals, incorporating bodies and ideas absent commitments to struggle.[10] The proliferation of conversations about "mass incarceration" (as if simply less incarceration encapsulates the solution) has seen the obfuscation of what abolition means in the present day. Myopic understandings of history will lead to misguided propositions for change; an abolitionist analysis of the carceral state seeks to make real gains toward its dismantling, because of and not in spite of its refusal to cooperate with cops and corporations.

While a more thorough analysis of these recent developments is beyond the scope of this essay, I want to note them in closing to emphasize that a co-opted version of abolition that reconciles itself to cop-friendly or corporate viewpoints is another form of carceral antiracist incorporation that, as Joy James (2020) writes, has become popularized in academia. This righteous warning against the untethering of abolition from the revolutionary demands of Black freedom struggle makes clear the tensions and contradictions of fighting for another world while working within this one. Transformative social change lies not with politicians or within university walls but with the people, within community organizing spaces as well as "the cultivation of the Black radical imagination." As Charlene A. Carruthers (2018: 33) writes, "It is within the spaces of imagination, the dream spaces, that liberatory practices are born and grow, leading to the space to act and to transform."

At this historical conjuncture, in the wake of sustained uprisings dur-

ing the COVID-19 summer of 2020, emergent possibilities are being materialized in daily life, and the radicalization of liberal publics is happening seemingly
overnight. It's a moment indicative of the power of ongoing social movements. Of
course, this people power will meet backlash, incorporation, and new challenges,
but the point is the people do have power. We are now seeing long legacies of abolitionist organizing led by Black feminists, queer and trans people, and incarcerated
activists play out in the streets, on social media, and in quarantined classrooms.
Without minimizing the very real presence of state-sanctioned carceral terror and
the deep grief born out of it, abolitionist affects (from love to rage) provide an alternative to the soul-crushing status quo. As abolitionist organizers like to joke, we
always throw the best parties. And we say this not because we value fancy things
or kitschy drinks but because we value each other, our shared laughter, and inde-
fatigable passion for building another world. Abstract analyses of power speak only
shallowly to material realities. The poetry of life, from protests to parties, engages
both in critique and celebration.[11] Again, understanding the "party" as a metaphor
for the strength of relationships in building movements and dismantling the prison
industrial complex, abolitionists have been saying, of late, welcome to the party!
Glad you have arrived.

Notes

I want to extend gratitude to the anonymous reviewers and special issue editors for
their generative and generous feedback, which greatly improved the piece. I am also
deeply appreciative of Shannon Brennan, Jessica Lopez Lyman, and Kristie Soares,
who provided incisive commentary on earlier drafts, as well as Felipe De Jesús
Hernández, who provided brilliant insights as the work neared completion. This essay
is dedicated to the fierce and loving memory of E. T.

1. See, for example, Ahmed 2013.
2. This definition is adapted from Critical Resistance's widely circulated version, avail-
    able on their website (criticalresistance.org).
3. For a hotly contested example of dismissing abolition as simply "pie-in-the-sky imag-
    inings," see Lancaster 2017.
4. For more on the Moynihan Report, see Ferguson (2004: 119–23).
5. For instance, in 1970 Sylvia Rivera and Marsha P. Johnson founded STAR (Street
    Transvestite Action Revolutionaries), which countered liberal, exclusionary agendas.
6. For more on this relationship, see Gilmore 2007.
7. See Grinberg 2017 and Ring 2017.
8. See, for example, Kelley 2015.

9.   For more on the scalar dimensions of social movement(s), see brown 2017.

10. See Tourmaline, Stanley, and Burton 2017.

11. This formulation of critique and celebration is indebted to Fred Moten. See Moten 2016.

References

Ahmed, Sara. 2006. *Queer Phenomenology: Orientations, Objects, Others*. Durham, NC: Duke University Press.

Ahmed, Sara. 2013. *The Cultural Politics of Emotion*. Abingdon, UK: Routledge.

Baldwin, James. (1963) 1993. *The Fire Next Time*. New York: Vintage.

brown, adrienne maree. 2017. *Emergent Strategy: Shaping Change, Changing Worlds*. Chico, CA: AK.

brown, adrienne maree. 2020. *We Will Not Cancel Us: And Other Dreams of Transformative Justice*. Chico, CA: AK.

Carruthers, Charlene A. 2018. *Unapologetic: A Black, Queer, and Feminist Mandate for Radical Movements*. Boston: Beacon.

Cohen, Cathy J. 1997. "Punks, Bulldaggers, and Welfare Queens: The Radical Potential of Queer Politics?" *GLQ* 3, no. 4: 437–65.

Critical Resistance Abolitionist Toolkit Workgroup. 2004. *The Abolitionist Toolkit*. criticalresistance.org/resources/the-abolitionist-toolkit/.

Evol, Keno. 2020. "George Floyd and What Black Utopian Thinking Can Offer Us." Mn Artists, May 29. mnartists.walkerart.org/george-floyd-what-black-utopian -thinking-can-offer-us.

Ferguson, Roderick A. 2004. *Aberrations in Black: Toward a Queer of Color Critique*. Minneapolis: University of Minnesota Press.

Gilmore, Ruth Wilson. 2007. *Golden Gulag: Prisons, Surplus, Crisis, and Opposition in Globalizing California*. Berkeley: University of California Press.

Grinberg, Emanuella. 2017. "At Pride Celebrations, Protesters Chant 'No Justice, No Pride.'" *CNN*, June 25. www.cnn.com/2017/06/25/us/no-justice-no-pride-protests /index.html.

Hart, Benji. 2019. "How #NoCopAcademy Shook the Machine." *Chicago Reader*, April 26. chicagoreader.com/columns-opinion/how-nocopacademy-shook-the-machine/.

Hartman, Saidiya. 2020. "The End of White Supremacy, an American Romance." *BOMB*, June 25. bombmagazine.org/articles/the-end-of-white-supremacy-an -american-romance.

Haymarket Books. 2021. "We Do This 'til We Free Us: Abolitionist Organizing and Transforming Justice." Webinar, February 23. YouTube video, 1:26:19. youtu.be /xWL9a1f9uW0.

Hernandez, Greg. 2017. "Straight New York City Cop Shares Pride Message You Won't Soon Forget." *Gay Star News*, June 28. www.gaystarnews.com/article/straight-new -york-city-cop-shares-pride-message-wont-soon-forget/.

INCITE! 2007. *The Revolution Will Not Be Funded: Beyond the Non-profit Industrial Complex*. Cambridge, MA: South End.

James, Joy. 2020. "Airbrushing Revolution for the Sake of Abolition." *Black Perspectives* (blog), July 20. African American Intellectual History Society. www.aaihs.org /airbrushing-revolution-for-the-sake-of-abolition/.

Kaba, Mariame. 2019. "A Love Letter to the #NoCopAcademy Organizers from Those of Us on the Freedom Side." *Prison Culture* (blog), March 13. www.usprisonculture .com/blog/2019/03/13/a-love-letter-to-the-nocopacademy-organizers-from-those-of -us-on-the-freedom-side/.

Kaba, Mariame. 2021. *We Do This 'til We Free Us: Abolitionist Organizing and Trans- forming Justice*. Chicago: Haymarket Books.

Kelley, Robin D. G. 2015. "Thinking Dialectically: What Grace Lee Boggs Taught Me." Praxis Center, Kalamazoo College, October 13. www.kzoo.edu/praxis/thinking -dialectically.

Kushner, Rachel. 2019. "Is Prison Necessary? Ruth Wilson Gilmore Might Change Your Mind." *New York Times*, April 17. www.nytimes.com/2019/04/17/magazine /prison-abolition-ruth-wilson-gilmore.html.

Lancaster, Roger. 2017. "How to End Mass Incarceration." *Jacobin*, August 18. www .jacobinmag.com/2017/08/mass-incarceration-prison-abolition-policing.

McDowell, Meghan G., and Alison Reed. 2018. "Humanities Behind Bars: Toward an Abolitionist Praxis in Prison Education Programs." *Abolitionist: A Publication of Critical Resistance*, no. 30: 9–11.

Melamed, Jodi. 2011. *Represent and Destroy: Rationalizing Violence in the New Racial Capitalism*. Minneapolis: University of Minnesota Press.

Moten, Fred. 2016. Panel commentary presented at "Profiles of Abolition: Abolition and the Radical Imagination," hosted by Critical Resistance and Los Angeles Poverty Department, Los Angeles, February 20.

Muñoz, José Esteban. 2009. *Cruising Utopia: The Then and There of Queer Futurity*. New York: New York University Press.

Nicholls, Flynn. 2017. "Who's Left? Prison Abolition." Illustrated by Flynn Nicholls with text by Mariame Kaba. Medium.com, December 24. https://medium.com/@icelevel /whos-left-mariame-26ed2237ada6.

No Justice No Pride. 2017. "No Justice No Pride—DC Day of Action." Facebook event, June 10. www.facebook.com/events/mcpherson-sq-nw-washington-dc-20005-united -states/no-justice-no-pride-dc-day-of-action/1848794345393661/.

Reddy, Chandan. 2011. *Freedom with Violence: Race, Sexuality, and the US State*. Dur- ham, NC: Duke University Press.

Ring, Trudy. 2017. "Anti-corporate Protesters Plan Action for NYC March." *Advocate*, June 19. www.advocate.com/pride/2017/6/19/group-interrupted-dc-pride-plans -action-nyc-march.

Rodríguez, Dylan. 2010. "The Disorientation of the Teaching Act: Abolition as Pedagogical Position." *Radical Teacher* 88: 7–19.

Rodríguez, Dylan. 2019. "Abolition as Praxis of Human Being: A Foreword." *Harvard Law Review* 132: 1575–1612.

Roscoe, Dom. 2020. "Mind's Eye of Incarceration." *HumanitiesBehindBars.org*, "Student Writings." Accessed September 30. https://humanitiesbehindbars.org/student -writings/.

Samuels, Liz, and David Stein, eds. 2008. "Perspectives on Critical Resistance." In *Abolition Now! Ten Years of Strategy and Struggle against the Prison Industrial Complex*, edited by CR10 Publications Collective, 1–14. Oakland, CA: AK.

Shehk, Mohamed. 2016. Emcee commentary presented at "Profiles of Abolition: Abolition and the Radical Imagination," hosted by Critical Resistance and Los Angeles Poverty Department, Los Angeles, February 20.

Spade, Dean. 2020. *Mutual Aid: Building Solidarity during This Crisis (and the Next)*. London: Verso.

Stanley, Eric. 2018. "The Affective Commons: Gay Shame, Queer Hate, and Other Collective Feelings." *GLQ* 24, no. 4: 489–508.

Stanley, Eric A., Dean Spade, and Queer (In)Justice. 2012. "Queering Prison Abolition, Now?" *American Quarterly* 64, no. 1: 115–27.

Tinsley, Omise'eke Natasha. 2018. *Ezili's Mirrors: Imagining Black Queer Genders*. Durham, NC: Duke University Press.

Tourmaline, Eric A. Stanley, and Johanna Burton, eds. 2017. *Trap Door: Trans Cultural Production and the Politics of Visibility*. Cambridge, MA: MIT Press.

Walia, Harsha. 2020. "A Decolonial Future without Borders or Cages." *Abolitionist: A Publication of Critical Resistance*, no. 32: 1, 7.

Zamalin, Alex. 2019. *Black Utopia: The History of an Idea from Black Nationalism to Afrofuturism*. New York: Columbia University Press.

REPRESENTATIONAL REFUSAL AND THE EMBODIMENT OF GENDER ABOLITION

Lorenzo Triburgo and Sarah Van Dyck

The crisis of mass incarceration has made its way into US mainstream politics in the last five years due in large part to the transgender activists of color who have been at the forefront of prison abolitionist movements for the last five decades. While mainstream media displays a seemingly insatiable visual appetite for trans and queer bodies, transgender women and trans-queer people—particularly those of color—continue to experience violence and criminalization at increasingly high rates (Grant et al. 2011; James et al. 2016). If we are to understand the prison industrial complex (PIC) as an infrastructure of oppression upheld in part by the dominant narrative that people of color, poor people, and queer people are dangerous to what bell hooks (2015) describes as the white supremacist capitalist patriarchy, it is critical to examine the visual language of criminalization while remaining wary of the traps of visibility.[1] My projects *Policing Gender* and *Shimmer Shimmer* seek to explore these traps and possibilities.

The PIC cultivates and maintains its power in a multitude of ways, including by, as Critical Resistance (n.d.) states, "creating mass media images that keep alive stereotypes of people of color, poor people, queer people, immigrants, youth, and other oppressed communities as criminal, delinquent, or deviant." Criminalization through representation and the visual as a mode/method of dehumanization has been well established and disseminated through a range of media including Ava DuVernay's film *13th* (2016), art installations such as *Mirror/Echo/Tilt* at the New Museum in New York (Crean, Leonardo, and Smith 2019), and the writing of scholars across disciplines who form the foundation of Visual Studies (hooks 2015; Mercer 1994). Through pedagogies established by carceral and managerial

GLQ 28:2
DOI 10.1215/10642684-9608161
© 2022 by Duke University Press

regimes including advertising, film, and crime reporting, the field of the visual has also been weaponized. Therefore, as a transqueer artist invested in the potential of lens-based images to propel liberation, the process of creating a project about mass incarceration from a queer perspective necessarily required consideration of the connotations I would be creating. Once a photograph is made and shared digitally, it can be difficult to control where it ends up and impossible to know what meanings others will derive from it. I created *Policing Gender* out of a determination to create prison abolitionist photographs that subverted connections between queerness, deviance, and criminality.

Recognizing incarcerated individuals as a protected group, the assurance of informed consent and the importance of anonymity were also at the forefront of my mind. Although I had gained permission to photograph within a number of jails and prisons during the research phase of this project, I did not believe that these substantial ethical concerns could be resolved with depictions that included any visual signifiers of criminality—even cinder blocks, for example. I also addressed the concerning fact that photographers and other artists need not undergo any kind of peer review before working with human subjects. In lieu of a review board, I connected with activists, educators, journalists, and scholars such as Dr. Susan Sered who was generous enough to share time with me in discussing how best to approach my project (telephone conversation, September 19, 2014). I joined the national grassroots prison abolition organization Black & Pink (B&P), and my local chapter of Critical Resistance. Through B&P I became pen pals with over thirty LGBTQ incarcerated individuals with whom I ended up writing on a monthly basis for over two years.

We discussed our upbringings, relationships with religion, books, plays, music, cars, and art—things you talk about when you are getting to know someone and becoming friends—and importantly here, I asked for input on my ideas for the project and what they thought would be most helpful in support of LGBTQ incarcerated individuals. The response was overwhelmingly a desire to educate people on the outside about the reality of their lives as incarcerated individuals and the corruption of the prison system. As one of my pen pals states in the audio that accompanies the photographs in *Policing Gender,* "At least out there you have cell phones to record this stuff. In here it's complete secrecy." While invisibilizing incarcerated individuals is a dehumanizing tactic employed by the US prison system that also works to uphold neoliberal normalization of systemic violence against specific communities for the benefit of others, I was concerned about creating direct representations of queer-identified incarcerated individuals, owing to the risk of reinforcing a conceptualization of incarcerated people as a racialized, gendered, and sexualized threat (Dillon 2018) to white supremacist capitalist patriarchy (hooks 2015).

I resolved my ethical, conceptual, and aesthetic concerns through the figureless "portraits," aerial images, and audio that compose the project. The photographs of draped fabrics recall the use of textile as a symbol of wealth, power, and beauty by Renaissance portraitists such as Hans Holbein, who influenced Catherine Opie's (1994) use of fabric backdrops in her well-known portraits of the 1990s including *Self-Portrait/Pervert*. The fabrics are styled and lit as though for a portrait but with no figure present; absence becomes the subject. This absence is both a reference to the millions of incarcerated individuals absented from our communities, and an act of refusal.

The aerial photographs in *Policing Gender* serve as metaphors for the surveillance that is integral to the functioning of the PIC. In contrast to the lush, color photographs of draped fabrics made in the studio, the aerial images in the series are black-and-white and were photographed in the field. These are modes associated with so-called straight photography on which the myth of photographic truth is sustained. I made these photographs from a hot-air balloon, knowing that the first aerial reconnaissance photographs were made during the American Civil War using a hot-air balloon. The aerial vantage point necessarily places the viewer in the position of power, looking down on the field of vision I provided. The location of these photographs is nondescript and not important. There is no truth to be found in them. Again, I am intentionally depriving my viewer of their expectation of access but, more importantly, calling attention to the presence of mass surveillance.

The audio that accompanies the photographs consists of a mix of my pen pals' voices describing their experiences of being queer on the inside (recorded with their permission) and edited with field recordings from within prisons and jails. I added one constructed sound to the mix at the end that ramps up on volume and persistence as a way to bring even the tiniest sliver of the experience of living in constant, aggressive noise to the installation of the project. Together, these components ask my audience to contemplate and reflect more than consume and judge, as is so often the default.

I name "voyeuristic entitlement" as the expectation of visual access to the likenesses, experiences, and spaces of those who have been othered. Photographic images are increasingly consumed with such ease and thoughtlessness that the act of looking—of being a see-er (a position not possible for incarcerated individuals)—is an unchecked privilege. Acknowledging the voyeuristic entitlement of my potential viewers, I refused to create representations of my pen pals. In addition to a

Figure 1. Lorenzo Triburgo, "For Rye," 2015. Archival pigment print, 40 × 30 in., from the series *Policing Gender*.

power differential between subject and viewer that could never be redistributed, I use absence in *Policing Gender* to challenge the privileged expectation of visual access (see figs. 1–2). In our current moment wherein neoliberal machinations of dominant cultural production simultaneously commodify and criminalize trans and queer bodies, I argue that this "representational refusal" is a viable tactic in

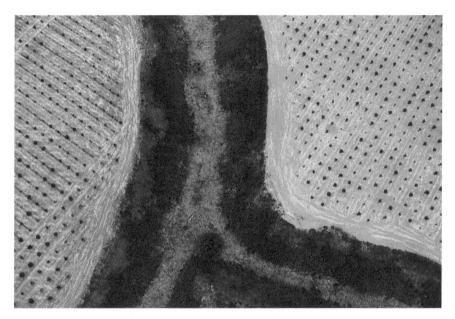

Figure 2. Lorenzo Triburgo, "Hot Air Aerial 03," 2015. Archival pigment print, 16 × 22 in., from the series *Policing Gender*.

claiming power for marginalized identities in visual media. Incarcerated individuals do not have the option to create publicly shared self-representations, and my use of representational refusal leaves the power of representation in their hands, even if they are restricted by the prison system from expressing it.

Harnessing and subverting the expectations of representation and access that are always already embedded in photographs is one way to undermine the medium as a tool of oppression. When the Trump administration released a memo in 2018 outlining an initiative to legally define gender at the federal level as unchangeable and determined by one's genitals, another mode of visual communication was called for. Following the news of this Department of Health and Human Services memo, trans activists quickly organized "We Will Not Be Erased" rallies, and the hashtag #WontBeErased was amplified on social media. By this time, I had also been frustrated for years by "passing" as "male" or being read as a "man." I am transqueer, and passing all the time felt like being involuntarily closeted, being rendered invisible. I recognized the need to utilize the privilege of self-expression that I harbored in order to stand in solidarity, not be erased, and shed the gendered confines I found myself within. I was awarded an artist residency in 2019 and used my time to explore ways of imaging my yearning to embody a new subjective space. I decided to stop taking testosterone after ten years of "hormone therapy" to see if I could physically and metaphorically represent gender abolition, which I understand as a state in which we move beyond a mentality of legal reform and into an expanded field of self-determination—creating space for what we have yet to imagine (Bassichis, Lee, and Spade 2015). I am in a partnership, and our respective gender presentations inform how one or the other of us is read. My queer-femme partner Sarah Van Dyck has also been made invisible as queer by heteronormative assumptions about our genders. It became clear that the project of gender abolition was necessarily a collaboration.

Van Dyck and I created *Shimmer Shimmer*, a series of photographs featuring my nude, glitter-adorned, transqueer body in familiar, gendered, art historical gestures, but with subtle shifts in gaze and posture that play alongside the physical ambiguity of my body to defamiliarize the viewer (see figs. 3–4). We made all the photographs in the winter and early spring of 2020 at the queer section of New York City's People's Beach at Jacob Riis Park (Riis Beach), our queer sanctuary. The title *Shimmer Shimmer* intimates the aesthetic of the images but also speaks to the use of glitter as a metaphor for shifting, changing, or liminal spaces.[2] Alongside the figurative images, we created photographs of glitter in the studio that, at first glance, might be mistaken for images of constellations. In this way, we are suggesting that, while a visual reference to "Venus" might be familiar to the viewer as "female" or "Mars" as a "male" god, in fact we are referring to planets and the queering of astrology that is important to how we and our community make meaning. The shimmering glitter, idyllic skies, and warm glow achieved by the mix of ambient and artificial lighting also lend a campiness to the photographs that is accentuated by the ambiguous gender of my transqueer figure.

The embrace of visual representation in *Shimmer Shimmer* is a response to the shift in the political climate in which we were living. The decision to stop taking testosterone and to become more visually genderqueer, on and off camera, was also informed by a desire to claim my body as a political tool in service of gender abolition. In 2018 the creation of representations of transqueerness felt urgent, not only to proclaim our existence but also to counter the assimilationist narratives that have been produced by dominant media over the previous ten years. To disrupt the binaries that have attempted to trap us and render us invisible, a queer-femme gaze and agency formed the foundation of the project and informed the resulting images. It is Sarah behind the lens of the camera in *Shimmer Shimmer*. Her direction dictated my body's movements, and her gaze is what viewers are experiencing. Whereas the ethical and political considerations in creating *Policing Gender* resulted in representational refusal, the new political state calls for a proclamation of presence that works toward gender abolition. If we continue

Figure 3. Lorenzo Triburgo and Sarah Van Dyck, "Venus," 2020. Archival pigment print, 48 × 32 in., from the series *Shimmer Shimmer*.

Figure 4. Lorenzo Triburgo and Sarah Van Dyck, "Luna," 2020. Archival pigment print, 36 × 24 in., from the series *Shimmer Shimmer*.

to critically engage with the visualization of queerness, dismantle aesthetics of oppression, while claiming agency over our bodies and representations, then photographic images can propel gender abolition.

Notes

1. For in-depth analyses and nuanced discussion on the complex and inverse relationships between the lived experiences of transgender people and increased media representations, as well as the complexity of "opportunities" for transgender artists, see Tourmaline, Stanley, and Burton 2017.

2. The title "Shimmer Shimmer" is in reference to Roland Barthes's (2005: 51) notion of the shimmer—"This integrally and almost exhaustively nuanced space is the shimmer . . . : the Neutral is the shimmer: that whose aspect, perhaps whose meaning, is subtly modified according to the angle of the subject's gaze"—and trans media scholar Eliza Steinbock's (2019) use of this to describe visualizing transness.

References

Barthes, Roland. 2005. *The Neutral*, translated by Rosalind E. Krauss and Denis Hollier. New York: Columbia University Press.

Bassichis, Morgan, Alexander Lee, and Dean Spade. 2015. "Building an Abolitionist Trans and Queer Movement with Everything We've Got." In *Captive Genders: Trans Embodiment and the Prison Industrial Complex*, expanded 2nd ed., edited by Eric A. Stanley and Nat Smith, 21–46. Edinburgh: AK.

Crean, Melanie, Shaun Leonardo, and Sable Elyse Smith. 2019. *Mirror/Echo/Tilt*. Exhibition, New Museum, New York, June 18–October 6.

Critical Resistance. n.d. "What Is the PIC? What Is Abolition?" Accessed September 30, 2021. criticalresistance.org/about/not-so-common-language/.

Dillon, Stephen. 2018. *Fugitive Life: The Queer Politics of the Prison State*. Durham, NC: Duke University Press.

DuVernay, Ava, dir. 2016. *13th*. Sherman Oaks, CA: Kandoo Films. Netflix.

Grant, Jaime M., Lisa A. Mottet, Justin Tanis, Jack Harrison, Jody L. Herman, and Mara Keisling. 2011. *Injustice at Every Turn: A Report of the National Transgender Discrimination Survey*. Washington, DC: National Center for Transgender Equality and National Gay and Lesbian Task Force.

hooks, bell. 2015. *Black Looks: Race and Representation*. New York: Routledge.

James, Sandy E., Jody L. Herman, Susan Rankin, Mara Keisling, Lisa Mottet, and Ma'ayan Anafi. 2016. *The Report of the 2015 U.S. Transgender Survey*. Washington, DC: National Center for Transgender Equality. www.ustranssurvey.org/reports.

Mercer, Kobena. 1994. *Welcome to the Jungle: New Positions in Black Cultural Studies*. New York: Routledge.

Opie, Catherine. 1994. *Self-portrait/Pervert*. Chromogenic print, 101.6 × 76.2 cm. (40 × 30 in.), Guggenheim Museum, New York.

Steinbock, Eliza. 2019. *Shimmering Images: Trans Cinema, Embodiment, and the Aesthetics of Change*. Durham, NC: Duke University Press.

Tourmaline, Eric A. Stanley, and Johanna Burton. 2017. *Trap Door: Trans Cultural Production and the Politics of Visibility*. Cambridge, MA: MIT Press.

(TRANS)GENDERING ABOLITION

Black Trans Geographies, Art, and the Problem of Visibility

Jaden Janak

*A*rt represents an understudied yet full archive of Black trans resistance. Though political speeches, organizational documents, and other ephemera hold visions of Black trans futures, visual media contain important insights into how Black trans people envision worlds of safety, care, and community beyond the carceral system. This essay focuses on literature, film, and music because these art forms remain undertheorized as vehicles for abolitionist world building. In contrast to hate crime legislation and other anti-violence ventures that paint Black transness as primarily rooted in victimhood (Snorton and Haritaworn 2013: 67), this work seeks to complicate those portrayals by analyzing visual media for traces of Black trans abolitionist freedom dreams that embrace the complexity of Black trans life and our theories of social change.[1]

"(Trans)gendering Abolition" engages the paradox of Black trans visibility: visual media make Black transness legible, and yet visibility-based activism is a road that leads to flattened understandings of Black trans life. Visibility, at least in the traditional sense, is a fraught project for trans people, whose moment of coming into visibility is often the moment of violence. As abolitionist Miss Major Griffin-Gracy (2019) asserts, "I don't really understand why we need a day of visibility, when for most of us, especially us Black girls, we are as visible as we need to be. Our visibility is getting us killed." Griffin-Gracy's statement on Trans Day of Visibility contradicts moves being made to diversify popular culture and media through the inclusion of transgender people and our stories. With the 2014 *Time Magazine* article "The Transgender Tipping Point" (Steinmetz 2014) as well as shows like *Orange Is the New Black* and *Pose*, Black and Brown trans people are as visible as they have ever been in popular media.[2] But as Griffin-Gracy elucidates, this visibility often comes at a cost for Black trans women, whose proximity to the criminal (in)justice system places them in the crosshairs of the state's crimi-

GLQ 28:2
DOI 10.1215/10642684-9608175
© 2022 by Duke University Press

nalizing apparatus. The visibility of trans people as victims in media, whether that be in news coverage or in film or music, can contribute to our simultaneous hyperinvisibility and hypervisibility, only further obscuring personhood. Black trans scholar Cypress Amber Reign Johnson and Black feminist hip-hop scholar Robin Boylorn note the paradoxical notion that hypervisibility can bring about erasure, so much so that certain populations are never seen in the public imaginary beyond stereotypes or statistics (Johnson and Boylorn 2015: 6). The often-blurry line between visibility and invisibility energizes this project.

Artists analyzed in this project construct Black trans geographies that embody abolitionist world(s) and Black trans futures. Building on the Black geographies analytical framework presented by Katherine McKittrick and Clyde Woods (2007: 1), as well as Ruth Wilson Gilmore's (2017) notion of "abolition geographies," Black trans geographies refuse simplistic categorization, build new ways of being, and create community in the midst of statal notions of individualization. In the midst of "locations of captivity" that have oppressed Black trans people, new modes of theorizing space, place, and freedom have emerged in these spaces and places of un-freedom (McKittrick 2006: xvi–xvii). Black trans creativity prompts new ways of imagining the world and moves toward a pluriversal concept—one that recognizes our ability to bend time and space and to shape new universes with our creative works (Escobar 2018: 6). It is important to note that Black trans geographies are not inherently radical by virtue of one's racial and/or gender identity markers. Rather, Black trans geographies rely on a deeply engaged political analysis and praxis that question the prison-industrial complex and ultimately imagine a world beyond it. The *Black* in Black trans geographies "stems from its escapeful somethin' else-ness" and is a queer and feminist fugitive stance (Bey 2019: 96). That is, Blackness (like abolition) is creative in its manipulation of the possible and refuses to be collapsed into prescriptive ideas of normativity; this marks Blackness as both queer and feminist in nature. Black trans geographies, then, are a refusal to be categorized and an acceptance of coalitional politics that recognize the interconnected nature of political struggle. Black trans gazes that challenge the legitimacy of carceral binaries—like *violent* and *nonviolent* or *good* and *bad*—are "oppositional gazes"[3] that both reveal the violence of carceral systems and constitute a force that is counter-hegemonic to that violence.[4] Through a study of literature, film, and music, I argue that Black trans possibility making can be revealed through an artistic approach that emphasizes Black trans abolitionist geographies.

Though the intellectual roots of abolitionism date back to struggles of slavery abolition and marronage, the concept of prison-industrial complex (PIC) abolition has only recently entered the lexicon of the broader public. With features included in popular publications such as the *New York Times*, the project of abolition is perhaps more known in the United States than it ever has been. And yet, what prison abolition actually entails can be lost in the popularization of the term. Prison abolition is a liberatory, visionary project that places its sights of revolution at the site of the prison (and beyond).[5] According to Eric Stanley (2011: 6), the criminal (in)justice system as we know it is arranged in what is called the prison-industrial complex—the pervasive network of surveillance and captivity that infects carceral institutions like jails and prisons; practices such as community policing, stop and frisk, and background checks; and organizing structures such as liberal democracy, capitalism, and the nation-state. Abolition, then, acknowledges that the criminal (in)justice system cannot be reformed because reform efforts attempt to resolve the system's inadequacies through legislative and material changes that leave the system's core structure intact. Rather, with the material needs of incarcerated people front and center, abolitionists balance the need to "change everything" (Gilmore 2021) and the imperative to support those currently living under state captivity.

The trans futurist dreams of a post-prison world are best expressed through art because art is a medium in which the impossible can become realized. As Robin D. G. Kelley (2002: 11) writes, "When movements have been unable to clear the clouds, it has been the poets—no matter the medium—who have succeeded in imagining the color of the sky, in rendering the kinds of dreams and futures social movements are capable of producing." Often labeled by cynics as a far-off vision, abolition becomes more readily seen through artistic depictions of its principles. Literature, film, and music relay the complexities and nuances of Black trans abolitionist futures in ways perhaps speeches at rallies cannot. Moreover, art is a readily accessible mode through which many more communities can participate, which opens opportunities for the visions of oppressed communities to be seen and heard. A study of abolitionist art, then, is necessary to understand Black trans geographies, which may not appear through a traditional organizational history of abolition. My cultural studies approach establishes a more robust intellectual archive of prison abolition and generates new possibilities for encountering Black trans theories of social change. The examples that follow are just some of the many ways artists use abolitionist principles to deconstruct, reconstruct, and dismantle the color of the sky.

Telling Our Stories: *Redefining Realness*

In 2014 Janet Mock, now producer and director of *Pose*, released her first book, *Redefining Realness: My Path to Womanhood, Identity, Love, and So Much More*. Mock's memoir delves into her childhood, transition, abuse she's faced, and her engagement in sex work at a young age to fund her transition. Imbued with an abolitionist resistance to binaristic flattening, *Redefining Realness* works against carceral feminist logics that view Black trans women and their bodies within a liberated-versus-victimized dichotomy (Stallings 2015: 207). *Redefining Realness* presents an abolitionist argument for embodied freedom that embraces the nuances of sex work for minors and the importance of community building outside state apparatuses.

In Mock's (2014b) book, she demonstrates the importance of community building in the deconstruction of carceral regimes that target Black trans people, especially women. While living with her mother who was using drugs and unable to fulfill her promise of funding Mock's transition, Mock turned to sex work so that she could fund her own transition process (167). One of many trans girls and women who looked for work on Merchant Street in Honolulu, Hawai'i, Mock cultivated communal structures of mutual accountability with the women she worked alongside. Described as "an underground railroad" of Black trans mutual aid, the workers of Merchant Street pushed past capitalistic notions of individualism to create a world of safety when the state and their own families refused to do so themselves (Mock 2014a). For example, the women and girls of Merchant Street looked after one another by devising covert ways for announcing which clients were undercover cops, giving surgeon recommendations, and making sure everyone got tested for sexually transmitted infections and human immunodeficiency virus (178). In a world where medical gatekeeping, poverty, and racism limit Black trans access to necessary health care, the community of Merchant Street "used the resources [they] had—[their] bodies—to navigate this failed state" and be a source of protection for each other (187). Merchant Street, a place of transaction and exchange, is transformed by the trans women and girls whose community allows them to persevere, survive, and use their bodies to create their own futures and destinies. This Black trans abolitionist geography redefines what family is and reiterates that communities can provide better for each other than an antagonistic state can.

Though sex work provided Mock agency to litigate her own body and life, survival sex work made her Black trans body even more precarious. Poignantly asserting her own agency in making the decision to enter sex work while also critiquing the systems that forced her decision to be made, Mock claims, "My experience with sex work is not that of the trafficked young girl or the fierce sex-positive woman who proudly chooses sex work as her occupation. My experience mirrors that of the vulnerable girl with few resources" (177). The sex trade gave Mock, and the many Black transgender women, men, and gender-nonconforming people who also engage in it, the ability to have more options, even as these choices are still limited. Indeed, Mock's experience cannot be couched within the simplistic narrative that sex work was Mock's way of expressing her much desired freedom, nor can her experience be described as solely brutal. Though Mock's employment included working at clothing stores, fast-food restaurants, and more, sex work provided her with the ability to make enough money to purchase her own hormones and eventually save up for her desired gender-confirmation surgeries (Mock 2014a). Mock maintains that sex work gave her the confidence to "not feel shameful about my body and sexuality"; however, this "was under the guise of doing a job that was full of stigma" (207). Mock's systemic analysis complicates dominant narratives within feminist discourse that paint sex workers as either human trafficking victims or entirely agential figures. That is, as a mode of Black trans abolition, Mock's account refuses yet another carceral binary logic.

Speaking back to these binary views of sex work, *Redefining Realness* critiques carceral solutions aimed at the sex work industry. Feminist advocates in anti-violence sectors have long embraced carceral responses to the sex work industry. As Sarah Lamble (2011: 236) points out, "Some feminist, queer, and trans activists have also been too quick to equate justice with imprisonment" as a means to "protect" sex workers from the violence that exists within their occupation. Anti-violence and feminist advocates who equate justice for women with incarceration of sex work clients are often referred to as carceral feminists.[6] Carceral feminists often assume that sexual violence (many include sex work under this umbrella) is an individual problem to be remedied by the punishment of individual perpetrators. To carceral feminists, Mock's experience as a Black, trans, sixteen-year-old sex worker may mark her as a victim of sex trafficking. But that is not the story Mock tells. She proclaims, "No one *person* forced me or my friends into the sex trade; we were groomed by an entire system that failed us and a society that refused to see us" (213). Though Mock called the police after a particularly violent encounter with a client, she soon realized the police and carceral system would not protect her, nor would she ever receive justice from such a system. Indeed, this system is the very "cruel and unusual punishment" it seeks to rectify. Mock's brave and illuminating look into her experience as a sex worker challenges carceral feminist notions of sex workers as in need of saving. Instead, Mock rightly understands that sex workers have autonomy and use community safety to stay well at work. The police do not protect or serve sex workers (or anyone else for that matter). Communities protect themselves from the "service" of the government.

By demonstrating the mutual aid community of Merchant Street sex workers and by engaging in abolitionist refusal to be defined solely as victimized or agential, *Redefining Realness* charts an abolitionist vision for community building and safety that does not rely on state formations of carcerality.

Moving away from notions of "rescue feminism" (Maynard 2012: 33) that deem Black trans women in need of protection via the carceral "justice" system, Mock's writing understands that Black trans women sex workers are indeed exposed to violence and risk of disease and that Black trans women create structures of accountability to keep themselves safe. Mock's work reminds us that Black trans abolitionist geographies refuse strict categorization by living in liminality—Black trans sex workers, like Mock, are exposed to undue harm via their occupation, and they create survival mechanisms to make their communities safer. The ties of solidarity and community that bind the workers of Merchant Street together illustrate what an abolitionist world is—not absent of harm but full of communal strength and safety.

The Merchant Street group acts as a pod, or a small-scale illustration of what these worlds look like. Pod communities are those we can rely on in emergency situations and that also hold us accountable for our actions and inactions (Mingus 2016). For Mock, the Merchant Street community of street workers represented this kind of pod community. Police and other state-functioning mechanisms failed Merchant Street and often added to the precarity involved in their work. So, they turned to one another for advice on accessing hormones outside the medical industrial complex, on fighting food insecurity, on self-defense techniques, and the implementation of boundaries within underground economic work. As they helped one another, they formed kinship networks that fought to provide material support as well as camaraderie in the face of organized abandonment. This community is one in a long line of experiments that imagine in real time what abolition can look like by creating Black trans abolitionist geographies. *Redefining Realness* shows how abolition is built (and rebuilt) one pod experiment at a time.

Cinema Views: Gender Transgression in *Stranger Inside* and *Free CeCe!*

Separated by fifteen years, *Stranger Inside* and *Free CeCe!* are two films that explore the experiences of incarcerated trans and gender-nonconforming people. *Stranger Inside* (Dunye 2001) follows a young Black person, Treasure Lee, as she attempts to locate her incarcerated mother by purposefully getting incarcerated herself. In

Treasure's quest to find her mother, she creates familial relationships with other prisoners to survive. Director and cowriter Cheryl Dunye worked with incarcerated women and gender-nonconforming people to craft her compelling fictional portrayal of their lives. Working with them for months, Dunye employed a methodology of abolitionist care that ameliorated (but did not eradicate) the power differentials between the prisoners and herself (Outfest 2020). In contrast, *Free CeCe!* (Gares 2016) is a documentary about the real lived experience of formerly incarcerated prison abolitionist activist CeCe McDonald. Featuring interviews of McDonald conducted by activist and actress Laverne Cox, *Free CeCe!* uplifts McDonald's harrowing story while also highlighting the experiences of Black trans women, like McDonald, who are often incarcerated in male facilities and placed in solitary confinement. *Free CeCe!* explores how McDonald embodies abolitionist practices while still incarcerated. These two films offer robust critiques of the carceral system and depict the many ways trans and gender-transgressive people, especially those who are incarcerated, make systems and structures that enable our survival.

In the making of *Stranger Inside*, Dunye employed a practice of care that poured into the incarcerated communities about which she wrote. Dunye participated in the 1998 Critical Resistance conference hosted in Berkeley, California, to do research for the film (St. John and Dunye 2004: 327). This three-day conference of over thirty-five hundred participants brought together prison abolitionists, formerly incarcerated people, as well as scholars and artists (all overlapping rather than distinct categories) for the expressed purpose of creating an international movement for the abolition of the prison-industrial complex (CR10 Publications Collective 2000: 6). Confronting the difficult reality that "the prison industry is both perpetuated by and perpetuates isolation and disconnection," Dunye reduced the gap between the prison walls and the so-called free world by forming connections with incarcerated people to better portray their experiences through the characters in *Stranger Inside* (336). In workshopping sessions over the course of two months, Dunye met with incarcerated individuals at the Shakopee Correctional Facility for Women in Minnesota for an exchange of information: the women would share what their lives were like, and Dunye shared screenwriting skills (329–30). Abolitionist scholars and organizers have termed this kind of power redistribution in service of a collective "mutual aid" (Spade 2020: 25). Dunye intentionally attempted to mediate power relations between the incarcerated women and herself as a filmmaker by hosting readings at the prison both by the incarcerated women and by world-renowned actors Laurie Carlos and Sonja Parks. By co-creating work with the prisoners at Shakopee, Dunye engages in an abolitionist praxis of community building that centers incarcerated people in its formation of solidarity.

Dunye's *Stranger Inside* (2001) utilizes score and production choices to establish the haunting history of incarceration and forced labor through a construction of rival prisoner geographies. At a gathering of the cast and crew as part of Outfest, Dunye discussed her need to ensure that *Stranger Inside* reflected the lived realities of Black gender-nonconforming, queer, and trans people. Dunye intentionally incorporated sonic allusions to the Alan and John Lomax recordings from Parchman Farm, the Sunflower County, Mississippi, prison and former plantation within *Stranger Inside* (Outfest 2020; Lomax 2014). In *Stranger Inside*, the camera moves closely to Brownie as she insists that the past no longer matters, and Treasure needs to protect her because they are blood relatives. The next scene shows the women of the prison marching down the yard in cadence to a work song that goes, "How many months do I love my mama / Every month of the year." This disturbing juxtaposition of the Black guard escorting the mostly Black gender-nonconforming prisoners across the yard with the work song about loving families exposes the haunting of incarceration. Though their kinship bonds sustain them, the prisoners are still separated from their families outside the prison walls. Mimicking the functionality of chattel slavery, prisons, like the one in *Stranger Inside*, tear apart families, disappearing family members from their loved ones in some cases for the remainder of their lives. Much like the hold of the slave ship, the prison segregates, separates, and splices familial connections that result in a yearning for these bonds (Sharpe 2016: 76). By recovering this history through song, Dunye uplifts the narratives of those ensconced in early twentieth-century convict leasing and recovers the memories of those lost to histories of violence and death. Dunye's filmic choices, rooted in historiography, demonstrate a clear commitment to imagining how incarcerated people construct their own geographies that contradict the ones established for them.

Especially interested in the ways gender-nonconforming people create networks of survival in prison, Dunye's *Stranger Inside* illustrates the complicated methods that prisoners utilize to create familial structures. As Dunye became a mother herself, she became fascinated with parent/child relationships and how captured people "balance . . . being an inmate, being a mother, being a member of a family or a clan, or a group that got them in—one that they support or have to support" (St. John and Dunye 2004: 329). Characters Brownie and Treasure, then, showcase how their imagined relationship as parent and child coexists and clashes within the nonbiological familial universes they created to survive imprisonment (Dunye 2001). Brownie is the head of household for a family within the prison that Treasure eventually infiltrates, marking her as both a biological daughter (this is dispelled later) and a member of Brownie's kinship network called Enlisted. To continue the "family" business of selling drugs, Treasure becomes wrapped in a cycle of violence to protect the family's earnings and Brownie's reputation through any means necessary. This unstable and violent family dynamic reflects the brutality of the carceral system, which deems them property.[7] The muddled nature of this fictionalized relationship reveals the complicated nature of community building within carceral systems for real people—survival networks in prison, much like that of Mock in Hawai'i, are complex creations that are not immune from harm. Taking care of one another in the face of organized abandonment can look like replicating some of the harmful aspects of the state (Gilmore 2007: 178). Through continuing to experiment and cultivate deeply flawed mechanisms for meeting one another's needs, communities like Brownie and Treasure's represent an abolitionist perseverance and ingenuity.

Approaching the relationality between prisoners and the "free" world somewhat differently, *Free CeCe!* is a true story about CeCe McDonald, who fostered bonds of mutuality with fellow incarcerated folks and those advocating for her release on the outside. McDonald, who was sentenced to forty-one months in prison but served thirty-two months (including parole), used the time as an opportunity to engage with her fellow prisoners in geographies of struggle through discussion groups about topics ranging from toxic masculinity to prison abolition and activism.[8] With the help of support campaigns led by the CeCe Support Committee, McDonald was able to connect with activists on the outside such as Angela Y. Davis, whom McDonald credits with giving her the tools and language to begin identifying as an abolitionist. Davis (2003) shared her pivotal prison abolitionist text *Are Prisons Obsolete?* with McDonald and also conversed with her about Davis's own experience of incarceration. As part of *Free CeCe*, filmmaker Jacqueline Gares arranged for McDonald to interview with Laverne Cox, who played Sophia, an incarcerated Black trans woman, on Netflix's *Orange Is the New Black* (Anderson 2016). The conversations between McDonald and Cox highlight how McDonald's case, though harrowing, is in no way singular (NCTE 2018). Using these conversations as a platform, McDonald shared with her fellow incarcerated peers the plight facing Black trans women, and *Free CeCe!* exists to inform the general public about these same concerns.

Though McDonald benefitted in many ways from the increased awareness of her case by way of the documentary and other support efforts, McDonald herself is critical of visibility as it comes to trans people. She shares in an interview with abolitionist Joshua Allen that "[her] case brought attention to trans visibility, especially the violence against trans women of color, specifically [B]lack trans women," but this came with a downside (Fischer et al. 2018: 185). McDonald still struggles to survive in the world as someone convicted of a felony and at times cannot afford to pay her bills. For McDonald (Gares 2016), "visibility" for trans people in the media is meaningful only when systems and structures of oppression are challenged. Understanding that she has a robust platform as a result of the popularity of *Free CeCe!* and the support she amassed over the years, McDonald seeks to use that attention to push the public to fight against liberal reforms like gender responsive prisons—which are prisons that are allegedly safer for trans people because they are built with us in mind (Braz 2006: 87). Departing from liberal notions of visibility as equality or liberation, McDonald's abolitionist vision makes visible the value of a world without a prison-industrial complex.

Both *Stranger Inside* and *Free CeCe!* allow the viewer to approximate seeing the interior lives of incarcerated people, though one film does so through fiction and one through the mediated form of the documentary genre. In addition to showcasing how incarcerated people construct relational lives, both films depict the violence of the carceral system that is often hidden from the general public. In *Stranger Inside*, Dunye depicts the horrors of solitary confinement through the jailed segregation of Kit and Treasure from the general population of the prison. Though this phenomenon is dramatized in *Stranger Inside*, many Black trans people find themselves in solitary confinement in real life. For most of the twenty-eight months she served in prison, McDonald was kept in solitary confinement allegedly to protect her from the "violence" of her peers, though by McDonald's (2017: 243) own admission she faced more abuse from guards and officials than she did her fellow incarcerated persons. Indeed, McDonald was sexually assaulted while incarcerated and faced difficulties receiving her hormones. *Free CeCe!* does not shy away from these tougher moments in McDonald's experience; rather, the documentary confronts these moments with full force to illustrate how common McDonald's experience with incarceration is for Black trans women. *Stranger Inside* and *Free CeCe!* allow viewers to begin to see the interiority of Black trans incarcerated people's geographic lives for what they are—beautiful, horrific, and complex. These stories reveal the necessity of collaboration, building, recreating, and building again an abolitionist society.

We, Too, Sing of Freedom: The Soundtrack of Trans Resistance

Soundscapes from protest chants to freedom songs have always been integral to the vitality of social movements and the futures they imagine (Brooks 2016; Kernodle 2008; Stewart 2005). During the civil rights and Black power movements especially, sonics uplifted the messages of organizations such as the Student Nonviolent Coordinating Committee and the Black Panther Party (Freeland 2009: 272). Indeed, drumbeats of Black social movements have long attempted two tasks: the need to protest injustice and the need to imagine otherwise. Kelley (2002: 11) makes this dual responsibility clear when he writes, "The most radical art is not [just] protest art but works that take us to another place, envision a different way of seeing, perhaps a different way of feeling." This section explores the role of music in the work of abolition. In a world where Black trans people often become visible only in the midst of trauma, this short meditation uplifts the work of Saint Louis Black trans artist and prison abolitionist organizer Jay-Marie Hill (stage name: Jay-MarieisHoly), whose songs "Past Time (In Conversation with Lamia Beard)" (2016) and "Here, Queer, and Staying" (2018) lament trans lives lost while also propelling us toward a future.[9]

Hill's song "Past Time" (2016), part of a Movement for Black Lives–inspired album with Rev. Osagyefo Sekou titled *The Revolution Has Come*, mourns the murder of Black trans woman Lamia Beard. Hill opens the lamentation song as their deep tenor sings the words "Trans sis I'm here to hold you / Shot down in cold blood." Beard was found shot to death a year before the song's release (Kellaway 2015). Conveying the sadness of the song, Hill incorporates blues-inspired elements, including light piano and the deep sound of the bass guitar, Hill's primary instrument. Hill continues, "Sister, sister / I know I'm late / My hands are bloody and that's on me." For Hill, the fault for Beard's death lies with more than just the person directly responsible for killing her; rather, a culture of ramped trans-misogynoir and hyperinvisbility for Black trans women claimed Beard's life—a culture in which Hill acknowledges they also participate. The song refuses to allow Beard's death and other Black trans women's deaths to seem inevitable. Hill sings beautifully, "You were always meant to live," a message to Beard and her fallen sisters that their murders were not divinely ordered; instead, they occurred because of a culture, a society, and a world that kills us (Snorton and Haritaworn 2013: 68). The heaviness of the song and the seriousness of the matter at hand are unmistakable. Hill's instrumentation, their words, and the feeling behind both eulogize Beard and the lifelessness of a world that allowed Beard's murder.

The second half of "Past Time" is a self-reflexive meditation on the precarity of love for Black trans people, who, when murdered, often die by our own hands or those of lovers (Kaur 2019; Lee 2014). Hill references past relationships that left them feeling dismissed as a trans person: "Lover, lover you love my body / Love my body, but not my soul." Here, Hill acknowledges how their personal experience with cisgender partners, who wanted them for their body but not for who they are as a trans nonbinary person, connects with Beard's murder. Here, a body/

soul binary is useful for the purposes of disaggregating sex, gender, and the understanding of one's inner essence. For the song's narrator, their essence as a person cannot be contained within biological or identitarian fixtures; rather, their soul is more than their sexual output or their bodily features. Hill goes on to sing, "I dream of you / Loving me, not killing me." In this way, Hill relates the rejection from intimate partners with a sort of emotional death but, more than that, underscores how these intimate rejections can lead to actual physical death. Hill continues the above distinction between the body and soul when they state that loving them means accepting them for their soul, not just their body. When they are accepted for only their body, this facilitates a spiritual death that can manifest into a physical one through extralegal violence and self-harm. Continuing, the voice of the song shifts to implore cisgender people and all other comrades to view the struggle for Black trans women's lives as a fight for our own. Making a rhetorical move against the separation of struggle between Hill as a Black nonbinary person and Beard as a Black trans woman, Hill sings, "Stranger / It's past time to love me / cause my time has come too early." Hill's work, then, understands that their liberation is intimately tied with Beard's, though their struggles are not the same. Paradoxically, love for Black trans people and others of marginalized genders can result in our deaths, and yet it is in loving that we find our freedom.

Released two years later, Hill's debut single, "Here, Queer, and Staying" (2018), envisions Black trans joy amid terror. Hill opens the song with the familiar steady beat of their bass guitar and the solemn words, "Round the cycle we still go / Mourning what we hate to know / New dead new dead." Hill's discussion of the terror facing trans people continues as they sing, "Wishing I ain't have to see / So much death in front of me . . . This pain is a job that's never done." Given the terrain of violence affecting trans people, Hill's song could have focused exclusively on the terror we face. Instead, they meditate on how trans people practice joy by proclaiming, we are "here, queer, and staying / we're here / and we ain't goin nowhere." In the music video accompanying Hill's work, they feature pictures of murdered Black trans individuals alongside smiling faces of Black trans people from Saint Louis and around the country (Jay-Marie is Holy 2018). As Hill gallivants through the streets of Saint Louis, they stop and smile at attractions, proving that our lives are still worth living even as we face violence. Hill refuses to succumb to fear as they move through their city and invites listeners to "redefine living" by creating abolitionist geographies of joy within the cityscapes of carceral terror. Hill's work forces us to see Black trans women and trans people for more than our murder statistics. "Here, Queer, and Staying" is a Black trans rallying cry to live fully and joyfully.

"Past Time" and "Here, Queer, and Staying" represent a small subsection of trans freedom songs inspired by abolitionist movements like the Movement for Black Lives, and these songs exemplify how to mourn the loss of trans life while still visualizing the fullness of trans personhood. Hill, who has served as the Transgender Education and Advocacy Program coordinator for the American Civil Liberties Union of Missouri, uses their music to animate the organizing work they do. Their musical repertoire, in addition to their organizing around decriminalizing sex work, demonstrate Hill's personal commitment to the principles of prison abolition. Moreover, their sonic creations bring to life their organizing work by making seen the possibilities that abolitionist organizing bears. When considered alongside organizing work, music can be a receptacle for unveiling Black trans geographies that dream of ways to cultivate community amidst state forces of isolationism. Examples like Hills's work, and the work of organizing musical anthologies such as *The Black Joy Experience* by Black, queer, feminist organization Black Youth Project 100, showcase the need to expand where scholars trace the archive of abolitionist theorization. These movement-based artistic creations contain imaginations of the sky that lament state violence while at the same time creating trans-futuristic conceptions of freedom.

When They See Us: Conclusion

Abolitionist practitioners and scholars ought to look toward art that fundamentally (re)imagines a world beyond—a world in which trans people thrive. In the foreword to *Captive Genders: Trans Embodiment and the Prison Industrial Complex*, CeCe McDonald (2015: 3) writes "It's fucked up to hear about the murders of trans women every day, but I don't think prison is the answer. . . . For me in a post-prison world . . . it will be a trans-topia." This trans-topia would be a world where the dreams that trans media render are a reflection of complex lived experiences. To achieve this trans-topic world, we need a revolution, one that can be seen in art that works to dismantle the prison-industrial complex and makes these trans-topic dreams a reality.

Black trans abolitionist art generates unique aspects of abolitionist world making by envisioning the specifics of what worlds without carceral logics and geographies look like in practice. Through years of activism alongside incarcerated women, prison abolitionist writer Victoria Law (2009) has shown the necessity of art in the form of zines to envision life beyond the walls of the prison.[10] My project builds on this work by exposing how forms like literature, film, and music can do similar geographic work in scaffolding abolitionist terrains. *Redefining Realness*,

Stranger Inside, Free CeCe!, and the music of Jay-MarieisHoly create geographies that paint the freedom dreams of abolition. The study of these artistic renderings presents more full depictions of Black trans subjects beyond the valence of victimhood. By studying these depictions, scholars, political organizers, and community members gain the opportunity to encounter more expansive visions of abolition and Black trans people themselves.

There once was a time without prisons, and that time will one day come again.

Notes

1. Carceral studies texts have long focused on the role of the media in proliferating carceral discourse and realities. From *13th*, the Netflix documentary about mass incarceration and in part media's depiction of the war on drugs (DuVernay 2016), to Stuart Hall's *Policing the Crisis: Mugging, the State, and Law and Order* (Hall et al. 1978), visual media forms are analyzed for their propensity to define who and what are criminal. In contrast, my work turns to mediated forms to understand how these forms can become vehicles for abolitionist dreaming.

2. For more information, see Katy Steinmetz's (2014) *Time Magazine* article, "The Transgender Tipping Point," which lays out the contemporary struggles of transgender people as well as the history of transgender people in popular memory through interviews and a speech given by Laverne Cox.

3. Here, I am invoking bell hooks's term *oppositional gaze* from her foundational text, "The Oppositional Gaze: Black Female Spectators" (1992). In her work, she discusses at length how white feminists have talked about Black women in media, and how those discussions further the invisibility of Black women. She offers that Black women filmmakers and cultural producers invent new possibilities within their work— possibilities that create more livable lives for Black women. For the purposes of this article, I want to push hooks's formation further by inviting us to consider how Black trans people are viewed and view themselves in media. How might that differ from hooks's ideas about Black female spectatorship?

4. Building on the work of Pavithra Vasudevan and Sara Smith (2020: 3), I use their theoretical formation of "domestic geopolitics" to understand how colonial powers work in intimate ways, and how that intimacy always forges a counter-hegemonic resistance within domestic spaces and places.

5. It is equally important here to highlight what prison abolition is not. Hailed by reformists, liberals, and conservatives alike as idealistic and impractical, PIC abolition has been lampooned as a white political project, a project including only people accused of certain offenses, and, perhaps most perniciously, abolition has been said to put survivors of intimate assaults at further risk of harm. None of these accusations are true.

Abolition is a multiracial, coalitional effort that prioritizes harm reduction including sexual and gender-based violence. For more information about the connections between survivor-affirming groups and abolition efforts, see Miriam Perez-Putnam (2020) and INCITE! and Critical Resistance (2001).

6. Carceral feminism is a theoretical concept describing how mainstream feminism's efforts to address gender-based violence such as sexual assault, human trafficking, and the like became deeply entrenched in the prison-industrial complex. Purveyors of carceral feminism may conflate the need for accountability with the need for punishment of sexual and gender-based violence perpetrators. Ultimately, carceral feminism is rooted in a logic of Western saviorism that views women and people of other oppressed genders as objects to be saved rather than people with complex personhoods navigating systems of domination. Carceral feminism, though seeking to end violence against people of oppressed genders, merely spreads this violence through the proliferation of the prison-industrial complex. For more on anti-carceral feminism, see Richie 2012, Thuma 2019, and Davis et al. 2021.

7. Incarcerated people are legally considered to be property of the state. Because of this provision, if an incarcerated person finds themselves injured and receives medical attention within their facility, they can be given a disciplinary charge of "Damage (or Destruction) of Government Property" (18 U.S.C. § 1361).

8. Jaden Janak, personal correspondence with McDonald, Saint Louis, Missouri, March 21, 2018.

9. The song credit for "Past Time" can be found under Rev. Sekou and the Holy Ghost. Despite Hill having written the vast majority of the album, Hill is never mentioned by name in the artist credits.

10. See *Resistance behind Bars: The Struggles of Incarcerated Women* (Law 2009) and *Tenacious: Art and Writings by Women in Prison* (Law 2003–).

References

Anderson, Tre'vell. 2016. "LAFF: Why Laverne Cox Is Lending Her Voice to the 'Free CeCe' Documentary." *Los Angeles Times*, June 3. www.latimes.com/entertainment /movies/la-et-mn-laff-free-cece-documentary-20160525-snap-story.html.

Bey, Marquis. 2019. *Them Goon Rules: Fugitive Essays on Radical Black Feminism*. Tucson: University of Arizona Press.

Braz, Rose. 2006. "Kindler, Gentler, Gender Responsive Cages: Prison Expansion Is Not Prison Reform." *Women, Girls, and Criminal Justice*, October/November: 87–91.

Brooks, Daphne. 2016. "How #BlackLivesMatter Started a Musical Revolution." *Guardian*, March 13. www.theguardian.com/us-news/2016/mar/13/black-lives -matter-beyonce-kendrick-lamar-protest.

CR10 Publications Collective. 2000. "The History of Critical Resistance." *Social Justice* 27, no. 3: 6–10.

Davis, Angela Y. 2003. *Are Prisons Obsolete?* New York: Seven Stories.

Davis, Angela Y., Gina Dent, Erica Meiners, and Beth Richie. 2021. *Abolition. Feminism. Now.* Chicago: Haymarket Books.

Dunye, Cheryl, dir. 2001. *Stranger Inside.* New York City: Home Box Office.

DuVernay, Ava, dir. 2016. *13th.* Sherman Oaks, CA: Kandoo Films. Netflix.

Escobar, Arturo. 2018. *Designs for the Pluriverse: Radical Interdependence, Autonomy, and the Making of Worlds.* Durham, NC: Duke University Press.

Fischer, Mia, Sarah Slater, CeCe McDonald, and Joshua Allen. 2018. "Transgender Visibility, Abolitionism, and Resistive Organizing in the Age of Trump: A Conversation with CeCe McDonald and Joshua Allen." *QED* 5, no. 3: 181–203.

Freeland, Gregory K. 2009. "'We're a Winner': Popular Music and the Black Power Movement." *Social Movement Studies* 8, no. 3: 261–88.

Gares, Jacqueline, dir. 2016. *Free CeCe!* New York City: Jac Gares Media, Inc. Amazon Video on Demand.

Gilmore, Ruth Wilson. 2007. *Golden Gulag: Prisons, Surplus, Crisis, and Opposition in Globalizing California.* Berkeley: University of California Press.

Gilmore, Ruth Wilson. 2017. "Abolition Geography and the Problem of Innocence." In *Futures of Black Radicalism*, edited by Gaye Theresa Johnson and Alex Lubin, 57-77. New York: Verso Books.

Gilmore, Ruth Wilson. 2021. *Change Everything: Racial Capitalism and the Case for Abolition.* Chicago: Haymarket Books.

Griffin-Gracy, Miss Major. 2019. "Miss Major on Trans Day of Visibility 2019." March 27. YouTube video, 2:06. youtu.be/3zGZ5a9a0Lo.

Hall, Stuart, C. Critcher, Tony Jefferson, John Clarke, and Brian Roberts. 1978. *Policing the Crisis: Mugging, the State, and Law and Order.* London: Macmillan.

Hill, Jay-Marie. 2016. "Past Time (in Conversation with Lamia Beard)." Track #6 *The Revolution Has Come*, FarFetched LLC, Spotify.com. open.spotify.com/track /4KruPMoLw9cLNHDnVRdLQ5.

Hill, Jay-Marie. 2018. "Here, Queer, and Staying." Self-released, May 30. Bandcamp. jay-marieisholy.bandcamp.com/track/here-queer-staying-debut-single.

hooks, bell. 1992. "The Oppositional Gaze: Black Female Spectators." In *Black Looks: Race and Representation*, 115–32. Boston: South End.

INCITE!, and Critical Resistance. 2001. "Statement on Gender Violence and the Prison Industrial Complex." incite-national.org/incite-critical-resistance-statement/.

Jay-Marie is Holy. 2018. "Here, Queer, and Staying x Jay-Marie is Holy." *YouTube* video, 4:33, October 26. www.youtube.com/watch?v=cgBovQbgQFg.

Johnson, Cypress Amber Reign, and Robin Boylorn. 2015. "Digital Media and the Politics of Intersectional Queer Hyper/In/Visibility in *Between Women*." *Liminalities: A Journal of Performance Studies* 11, no. 1: 1–26.

Kaur, Hermeet. 2019. "At Least Twenty-Two Transgender People Have Been Killed This

Year. But Numbers Don't Tell the Full Story." *CNN*, November 18. www.cnn.com
/2019/11/18/us/transgender-killings-hrc-report-trnd/index.html.

Kellaway, Mitch. 2015. "Trans Woman Killed in Virginia; Media Again Misgenders Her."
Advocate, January 23. www.advocate.com/politics/transgender/2015/01/23/trans
-woman-killed-virginia-media-again-misgenders-her.

Kelley, Robin D. G. 2002. *Freedom Dreams: The Black Radical Imagination*. Boston:
Beacon.

Kernodle, Tammy. 2008. "'I Wish I Knew How It Would Feel to Be Free:' Nina Simone
and the Redefining of the Freedom Song of the 1960s." *Journal of the Society for
American Music* 2, no. 3: 295–317.

Lamble, S. 2011. "Transforming Carceral Logics: Ten Reasons to Dismantle the Prison
Industrial Complex through Queer/Trans Analysis and Action." In *Captive Genders:
Trans Embodiment and the Prison Industrial Complex*, edited by Eric A. Stanley and
Nat Smith, 235–65. Oakland, CA: AK.

Law, Victoria. 2003–. *Tenacious: Art and Writings by Women in Prison*. New York: Published by the author.

Law, Victoria. 2009. *Resistance behind Bars: The Struggles of Incarcerated Women*. Oakland, CA: PM.

Lee, Cynthia. 2014. "The Trans Panic Defense: Masculinity, Heteronormativity, and the
Murder of Trans Women." *Hastings Law Journal* 66: 77–132.

Lomax, Alan, Anna Lomax Wood, Bruce Jackson, and Heuston Earms. 2014. *Parchman
Farm: Photographs and Field Recordings, 1947–1959*. Atlanta, GA: Dust-to-Digital.

Maynard, Robyn. 2012. "Carceral Feminism—The Failure of Sex Work Prohibition."
Fuse Magazine 35, no. 3: 28–33.

McDonald, CeCe. 2015. Foreword to *Captive Genders: Trans Embodiment and the Prison
Industrial Complex*, edited by Eric A. Stanley and Nat Smith, 2–5. Oakland, CA: AK.

McDonald, CeCe. 2017. "'Go beyond Our Natural Selves': Prison Letters of CeCe McDonald." *TSQ* 4, no. 2: 243–65.

McKittrick, Katherine. 2006. *Demonic Grounds: Black Women and the Cartographies of
Struggle*. Minneapolis: University of Minnesota Press.

McKittrick, Katherine, and Clyde Woods. 2007. "No One Knows the Mysteries at the Bottom of the Ocean." In *Black Geographies and the Politics of Place*, edited by Katherine McKittrick and Clyde Woods, 1–13. Cambridge, MA: South End.

Mingus, Mia. 2016. "Pods and Pod Mapping Worksheet." Bay Area Transformative
Justice Collective, June. https://batjc.wordpress.com/resources/pods-and-pod
-mapping-worksheet/.

Mock, Janet. 2014a. "On Sex Work and Redefining Realness." YouTube video, 1:52.
www.youtube.com/watch?v=Xd55yq4LMC8.

Mock, Janet. 2014b. *Redefining Realness: My Path to Womanhood, Identity, Love, and So
Much More*. New York: Atria.

NCTE (National Center for Transgender Equality). 2018. *LGBTQ People behind Bars: A Guide to Understanding the Issues Facing Transgender Prisoners and Their Legal Rights*. Washington, DC: National Center for Transgender Equality. transequality.org /sites/default/files/docs/resources/TransgenderPeopleBehindBars.pdf (accessed November 25, 2019).

Outfest. 2020. "*Stranger Inside* Live Q&A with Cheryl Dunye, Effie Brown, and Cast and Crew." YouTube video, 39:28, August 21. www.youtube.com/watch?v=or C20p1gUVE.

Perez-Putnam, Miriam. 2020. "Surviving Rape as a Prison Abolitionist." *Wear Your Voice*, January 10. www.wearyourvoicemag.com/surviving-rape-prison-abolitionist/.

Richie, Beth. 2012. *Arrested Justice: Black Women, Violence, and America's Prison Nation*. New York: New York University Press.

Sharpe, Christina. 2016. *In the Wake: On Blackness and Being*. Durham. NC: Duke University Press.

Snorton, C. Riley, and Jin Haritaworn. 2013. "Trans Necropolitics: A Transnational Reflection on Violence, Death, and the Trans of Color Afterlife." In *Transgender Studies Reader 2*, edited by Susan Stryker and Aren Z. Aizura, 66–76. New York: Routledge.

Spade, Dean. 2020. *Mutual Aid: Building Solidarity during This Crisis (and the Next)*. New York: Verso.

Stallings, L. H. 2015. *Funk the Erotic: Transaesthetics and Black Sexual Cultures*. Champaign: University of Illinois Press.

Stanley, Eric A. 2011. "Fugitive Flesh: Gender Self-Determination, Queer Abolition, and Trans Resistance." In *Captive Genders: Trans Embodiment and the Prison Industrial Complex*, edited by Eric A. Stanley and Nat Smith, 1–11. Oakland, CA: AK.

Steinmetz, Katy. 2014. "The Transgender Tipping Point." *Time*, May 29.

Stewart, James. 2005. "Message in the Music: Political Commentary in Black Popular Music from Rhythm and Blues to Early Hip Hop." *Journal of African American History* 90, no. 3: 196–225.

St. John, Maria, and Cheryl Dunye. 2004. "Making Home/Making 'Stranger': An Interview with Cheryl Dunye." *Feminist Studies* 30, no. 2: 325–38.

Thuma, Emily. 2019. *All Our Trials: Prisons, Policing, and the Feminist Fight to End Violence*. Champaign: University of Illinois Press.

Vasudevan, Pavithra, and Sara Smith. 2020. "The Domestic Geopolitics of Racial Capitalism." *Environment and Planning C: Politics and Space* 38, nos. 7–8: 1160–79.

A TRANS WAY OF SEEING

Nadja Eisenberg-Guyot and Kitty Rotolo

Something miraculous happened the last time we saw each other, at the end of October 2020 in the painted concrete, half-full visiting room of the Eastern New York Correctional Facility, surrounded by the soft chatter of masked imprisoned people and their visitors, seated at tables playing checkers, or eating vending-machine food, as the corrections officers surveilled us, arms crossed: you laughed. Not the self-contained, almost-whisper giggle demurely hidden behind your hand as you glance around the room to make sure no one is watching—the gentle, sad laugh cloaked in self-consciousness borne from decades of confinement, no. Not that. This laugh was full-bodied, riotous, righteous—don't care who hears and don't give a damn who is watching—infectious, joyous. Laughter not despite being imprisoned, but laughter momentarily expanding the boundaries of your con-finement, like an exhalation of breath pushing those concrete walls back, back, back—a laughter that crinkled out from the edges of your face and sent static electricity reverberating, a laughter that could explode the room. Kitty Jayne, I had never heard you laugh like that before. In the years of visiting you at the Rose M. Singer Center on Rikers Island and now in the prison where you're doing state time, four-to-ten. Two years in on your bid is the first time I heard that laugh. Kitty Jayne, that laugh just might bring the prison down. Kitty Jayne, in that laugh, freedom reverberates.

I've learned to value my freedom. No human being should be locked up in cage all day and night.

The first time I met you, I was sitting at the front desk of the Sylvia Rivera Law Project in Chelsea, probably answering the phone. I'm sure your head didn't actually graze the top of the elevator doorway opening directly into the office, but it could have. Your presence

GLQ 28:2
DOI 10.1215/10642684-9608189
© 2022 by Duke University Press

immediately filled the space. I didn't know anyone could emerge from
a narrow, rickety elevator like they were stepping onto a catwalk until
I saw you do it.
—Nadja, to Kitty Jayne, Eastern New York Correctional Facility,
Napanoch, New York

*I would describe you, Nadja, as the cutest political trans activist that I
know! I remember the first time we met and I thought to myself, what
a cute young man! And the first time you came to visit me [in the
Transgender Housing Unit at the Rose M. Singer Center] proved to me
what kind of individual you really are, to take time out of your busy
schedule to come to Rikers Island to spend time with me.*
—Kitty Jayne, to Nadja, Clinton Hill, Brooklyn, New York

In February 2020 we bought Kitty Jayne a clear plastic typewriter for
$225 from a mail-order catalog that specializes in prison-approved[1] commodities
and began to write this piece together, two white trans people born twenty years
apart, Kitty Jayne in New York, Nadja in California, who first encountered each
other at the Sylvia Rivera Law Project in 2018.[2] Our cowriting is stretched by
distance—the space and time between us, ten days on average between when a
letter is dropped in the mail and when it is received—and mediated by the threat
of censorship and the ever-lurking, if invisible, fact of surveillance. (How many
hands have fingered our letters? How many prying eyes have tried to read through
the lines of our trans storytelling searching for clues of prison break and conspir-
acy? Are the smudges at the edges of the envelope yours, or a trace of the audience
to our friendship we cannot avoid?) Reflecting on our friendship and the possibilities for mutual recognition that queer kinship has afforded us, these letters reveal
transness as a practice of seeing—ourselves and each other—through lines of
sight athwart transphobia.[3] For us, a "trans way of seeing" isn't about trans visibility; instead, it's a doing, a mode of embrace, the labor required to sustain the lines
of sight that allow us to see each other while preserving forms of opacity (Stanley
2017) that enable trans survival in a transphobic world.

The structure of this text is unconventional and unwieldy. This was our first
time writing together, and the strictures imposed on us by the prison stretched our
creativity and methods to the limit. As much as possible, we wanted to avoid the
conventional ethnographic mode in which Kitty Jayne's story is presented as "raw
material" and Nadja's work is to "interpret" what Kitty Jayne says. We're still figuring out how to interweave our voices while preserving our distinct positionalities.

Throughout this cowritten article, lines directly from Kitty Jayne are represented in italics. Where *we* is used, it refers to Kitty Jayne and Nadja. Where *I* and *you* appear in non-italic text, the *I* is Nadja (writing letters to Kitty Jayne), and the *you* is Kitty Jayne.[4]

Trans liberation to me means to be a free agent, to flaunt pure beauty. To me, transwomanhood means to be a beautiful person. Together, we explore how Kitty Jayne has negotiated incarceration in men's prisons, and how, through the transphobic violence of prison, she has articulated and lived transness—as individual identity, as resistance, as affinity, as collectivity, and as practice—inside.

I've seen one or two girls hang up their garter belts during incarceration. In claiming a trans way of seeing, Kitty Jayne's womanhood keeps what incarceration denies: that garter belts can be picked up off the penitentiary floor. In holding her sisters' garters, she refuses the severing state violence requires. *It might have a little something to do with the social unacceptance that we are subject to.* While forever holding on to the knowledge that *you have to have a thick layer of skin in order to survive on those runways and in these prisons,* we describe some of the modes of identification and self-elaboration that are possible while you are being disposed of.[5] We ponder how living with carceral dispossession and expulsion may make radical modes of trans becoming possible, or how Ms. Kitty Jayne remains *very proud to be (one of the) the original trans girls in the penitentiary. It comes easily enough for me.*

The prospect of reflecting on my life is very exciting because it's almost like reliving my life. And it will bring to mind so many loved ones who are no longer with us. So it is very appealing to me, my friend. The most important part of telling my story will be of reliving being a transwoman back in the day. We didn't have all of the politically correct terms that we have now. We were just drag queens. I would describe myself as a very tall eccentric devious cunning baffling beautiful woman. Someone who has been around the block a few times with both wisdom and personal knowledge of everything LGBTQI.

Marsha P. Johnson and I were great friends. She one day pulled my hair back and told me what a pretty girl I could be. When I looked at what she had done in the mirror I KNEW THAT I WAS MEANT TO BE A GIRL. I was very excited by this new discovery. Marsha was like my gay mother, and she always made me feel more comfortable. And understand myself.

Even before I started getting locked up, the police and jails were a big part of my life. Because all of my lovers and friends were always getting locked up. Marsha had been arrested for prostitution 100 times. Back then, you only got three days, time served for prostitution. I used to date the guy that they made the movie Dog Day Afternoon *about.*[6] *He was on federal parole, and always in trouble!*

    Back in the day, there was A LOT of corruption with the 6th precinct. They were always beating the queers up. And forcing them to have sex in order to not get arrested. Scandalous. On more than one occasion, while arrested for prostitution, I was offered to be released in exchange for a blowjob. Going through the system in the 80s was a real pain in the ass. Because when I got arrested in broad daylight, I'd have my working clothes on, fishnet stockings and a garter belt, a pair of heels and a corset. But I never took them up on their offers. Other times, I was asked to rat out the drug dealers, or other people who had committed a crime. Of course I never did that either.

    For the past forty years, I have been boosting expensive artwork and antiques. I do it for the money. I also used to boost high-end fashion mink coats. Kitty Jayne does it for the money, but she also does it for her sisters. *Yes, of course I know Lady S. That's my bitch! Fat Black queen with a bald head, right? Please send her my love. And yes, I do remember showing the boys on Rikers Island my titties. I've been known to do that every now and again (lol). I have a total of about five years on Rikers, six months one time, 9 months, a year, etc., etc. I can remember how shady it always was. Back in the 80s, all the way up to about 1997, they had gay housing. The homo guards. It was quite fabulous. 31 cells, 16 for boys, 15 for us girls. EVERYONE was married. And it was quite the fuck fest. We used to have Balls with cookies and cakes from the commissary as the grand prizes.*

    The week after Kitty Jayne pleaded guilty to the charges that led to her current term of incarceration, we sat in the Rose M. Singer Center visiting room discussing the case.

    Getting into the visiting room at Rosie's is itself an ordeal. The first thing I prepare for is the waiting—punctuated at intervals by drug-sniffing dogs, metal detectors, ion drug scanners—it's been two hours or more, and I probably haven't seen you yet. The walls at Rosie's are cinderblock, painted my favorite color, lilac, and I wonder who could believe that lilac could soften cinderblock. From the floor to the walls, everything in the Rosie's visitors' center was made by incarcerated people upstate: the linoleum, the lockers, the chairs, the wooden booth where the guards sit, the toilet paper holders in the bathroom, the plastic purple armchairs that appear in the waiting room one week and then disappear the next (to be jumbled in the back of the visiting room, unused, in front of the "mother and child" play area). A stencil on the visitor's exit door reads, "Women are like angels. Even when you clip our wings, we still can fly." I'm obsessed by this quote. I tune out the waiting room TV blaring the Rachael Ray morning show and the corrections officers glaring at visitors and stare at the grotesque phrase, written in gold cursive, curling across the bullet-proof Plexiglass of the door. Jail is just a bump on the road to women's uplift, I guess.[7]

My transmasculinity confuses the guards when it comes time to be searched before finally entering the visiting room. Sometimes they call me "young man," and yet I'm also asked to shake and snap the bottom of my bra (I don't wear one), and when I can't produce the characteristic snap of an elastic band, I'm admonished that next time it will be "no contact"—as though without the snap of a bra band they can't confirm that I haven't smuggled drugs or weapons.[8] So we sit, holding hands over the foot-high Plexiglass barrier jutting out of the wooden table between us, feet planted firmly on the floor ("Don't cross your legs!," snapped the guard, every damn time), you coming from a strip search, me carrying a trace of the guard's gender bemusement, both of us being told we must wear bras on the visiting floor or risk losing visits, as though the visibility of our transness converges for the jail at the fleshy point of our nipples,[9] and we talk about boosting. *I stole $40,000 of luxury handbags*, you say. *Not just for me, but for the girls. You know I never show up anywhere without a gift, even when I'm as broke as a drag queen's limp wrist.* I tell you I think no one deserves luxury purses more than the girls; I tell you "fuck rich people"; I say you're a queen of wealth redistribution; I tell you I made people call me Robin Hood when I was five after I saw the Disney cartoon; I tell you I think it's revolution or bust, baby. Your eyes widen as you lean back slowly and say *boy, you're a real radical, huh. Okay, Robin Hood.*

In 1981, my husband Mark and I followed a man into his building on St. Mark's. Mark had a BB gun on him. Although you'd never have known it as it looked so real. We announced a robbery and took off in Mark's car with the guy's wallet. We didn't get three blocks away when a sanitation truck parked in front of us so we couldn't pass. The police came quickly behind us. For that we got 5 years' probation. I was like a kid, Nadja, 16 years old. I was scared to death. No, it didn't feel exciting at all to break the law.

Driving back from our most recent visit, I find a trailhead and pull over, walking for an hour into the snowy dense forest. Eastern New York Correctional is nestled in state parks: Vernooy Kill, Minnewaska, Witch's Hole, Shawangunk Ridge, Awosting. Alone in the forest, I ask myself a question I can't answer: what would I risk for your freedom? If in your lawbreaking and storytelling I conjure spaces of trans freedom—liberated luxury purses for all the girls and *freedom feels like being able to fuck when you want to* and *the ballroom scene full of feathers, plumes, bugle-beads, and thick cigarette smoke*—I think about the price you've paid for snatching freedom where you could get it, how the relentless criminalization of trans life and community means even when "in the free world," you've lived in the penumbra of the penitentiary. *Being locked up is a mess. It really takes a mental toll on all of us. If I could change anything about myself it would be to erase all of my criminal activity.* Even as I cast you as the heroine of my outlaw romances—conjure your fabulous flights of fancy as trans freedom and play necessarily against the law—you remind me that there's nothing heroic in being *criminalized*, however audaciously you have had to live. At the prison you said, *I wish you could bust me out of here. Snatch that guard's gun and we'd just run.*[10] What would I risk for your freedom? It's not that I can't answer this question. It's that I'm afraid that my answer is not enough to get you free.

When I was at this particular prison ten years ago, we had a pretty large community of LGBT people, plus all of our fans. Yet, we had no place to call our own. No court, no classroom to study our history, while every other group had their own space to do their thing. So I wrote a proposal complete with bylaws . . . and got signatures from all the people who ran the six other organizations supporting us. But instead of giving us a classroom with gay history tapes, they sent me to the Time Allowance Committee and they gave me a release date to go home, thus silencing and putting to rest my proposed project. Made to choose between transness as freedom and freedom from incarceration, transness as collectivity and transness as individual identity, the state predicated your freedom on severing relations from your sisters inside. Yes, the prison thought you were too much of a nuisance and yes, you always deserved to be free, but I think the prison also saw that *your* sisterhood was dangerous.

It's possible to find a sisterhood with other girls [in here]. If memory serves me, it was much easier to make friends with the girls back in the 90s. They were mostly no-nonsense, thoroughbred battlecats, like myself. . . . There was this one boy whom I met in 1994, in Elmira CF, his name was DJ. He was white, and very banjee. He used to buy me hormones, bras, and panties. He was a closet queen. I couldn't get him to come out for anything. It made me very sad, Nadja, to see him living a lie. He had a lot of time to do. I tried to hook him up legally with medical so he could get hormones. He wasn't having it. But very recently, I received a message from him. He's close by, in Woodbourne CF, that he finally got himself out of the closet. And that he's a woman now. I've met a lot of butchqueens who've discovered that they were really trans. They all thanked me for bringing it out of them. So yes. I've brought several people out to the light.

It's not just the incarcerated queens that you've brought out into the light, Kitty Jayne. Your ways of seeing me resound deeply within experiences that I never thought I could articulate enough to share with another, like how, for as long as I can remember, I've always felt fastened in kinship to animals, from Robin Hood the fox to Gus, Cinderella's mouse friend wonderstruck by the proximity to her princess-hood, to the dinosaur books in the bedroom and the Prospect Park raccoon that no one else cares I saw (no matter how much I try to testify to the beauty of her emergence in the winter twilight), but whose seeing me is a feeling that lingers five years on. *And yes! Of course you are at peace with the animals because you are trans. THEY KNOW.* I laugh with delight when I receive this letter; it's just so perfectly true. It's a whole world in a sentence.[11] *I think you should both face, as well as challenge, your fears, and get that shot of testosterone. I recommend the injections because it's been clinically proven to give you the maximum effect. BUT ONLY DO SO IF YOU WANT A BEARD. I personally think you should do it if it's a BIG step in living your life as you want to be.* You make me feel brave. Paradoxically perhaps, given all that you have endured at the hands of this transphobic world, you make me feel like liberation is possible.

I want to be remembered as a trailblazing mentor and fierce advocate for trans people. Sometimes when we're sitting in the visiting room talking, we tell stories of prison breaks and Robin Hoods and jostlers and till toppers and the old ball scene like they're folk tales, but you remind me that they're legendary—that you're legendary—not mythological. The dramatic, extravagant narrative form through which you bring forth Chelsea, The Village, The Piers—

> *the ballroom scene back in the late 70s–80s was like a magical kingdom. Full of feathers, plumes, bugle-beads, and thick cigarette smoke. It was a festival of shade. The competition was FIERCE! It was only my pleasure to walk the Balls for the Legendary House of Patricia Field. The spectators were the shadiest characters of all. And if you snatched a trophy for your category, you were the It Girl. If you snatched two trophies, you were LEGENDARY*

—itself reverberates with the materiality of trans ways of living: luxurious, riotous, joyous. I understand what you mean when you write *the prospect of reflecting on my life is very exciting because it's almost like reliving my life*: because the way you write is the way you have lived, "creat[ing] your own future as a practice of survival" (Campt 2017: 114). I tear open a letter from you and magical words tumble forth (words that to me conjure elusive dreamworlds[12] but to you conjure the materiality of memory); I picture you at your typewriter finishing a paragraph about the House of Field and flipping your hair; I hear the drawl in your voice and the swish in your walk (even in those prison-issued pants) and know that the way you write isn't mere rhetorical flourish: embellishment is a way of being, of elaborating, fashioning, a self in a world that has always criminalized your womanhood.

Prison abolition is the space to be myself, move freely, without fear or confinement. [A world without prisons] would be full of animals. And human beings interacting as one, helping each other out, holding each other down. I also picture a world where children have a say in the everyday decisions that adults make and adults respect what children have to say. Freedom means everything to me. Yes, I can be truly free in this world. Because after this bid is done, I'll have 35 years locked up. And truly without my freedom.

If I were on the outside, I would feel most like myself and comfortable if I were on stage performing. But in here, I would have to say it's right after the last count, when the lights are off. Just laying in bed waiting to go to sleep. When my mind and body are relaxed.

Kitty Jayne, why is romance the genre through which we communicate? What do love stories give us? As we write about freedom, I try to write in ways that love you, and you write in ways that make me believe that love is possible *I was fucking a family of four brothers and each one swore me to secrecy. It was quite amusing.* And so I honor the things you cannot or will not say, as a way to be together on the terms that you choose (impossible to think that you choose, and yet, you do): our narrative is a romance. A romance of how you describe freedom to me, Kitty Jayne. Not just determined by what has been denied you—not just the absence of confinement—freedom is tangible, a way of being in the world in the here and now, a form of self-fashioning not at all outside the enclosures and violence you've endured, but an "alternative future [created] by living both the future we want to see, while inhabiting its potential foreclosures at the same time" (Campt 2017: 107). *One never heals correctly once sexual violence has come into play. Accountability in the penitentiary is nil. Only one part of the parties concerning people incarcerated are accountable. The victims, because the administration, who are most certainly guilty, are never ever held accountable.* Kitty Jayne, I've stopped probing the silences you erect around violence and confinement, the resolute way in which domination is the frame of your letters but not the protagonist, not because the violence doesn't matter but because there is nothing to be done with its brute facticity, no way to narrate it that is not capitulation to its overdetermining power (cf. Snorton and Haritaworn 2013). I guess I'm saying we tell love stories because the romance figures a somewhere we can be together. I guess I'm saying that there's no resolution to this tension, in this world anyway, but you keep on figuring a freedom that will blow the walls of the prison back.

So, I try to resist my romance with your resistance at that same time as I try to give back to you what you love, a trashy, forbidden romance, the narrative that holds you together—*the Latin King was chased to hell and back for loving me; I had my name tattooed on his ass*—as I think about you, and as this paper takes form and shape through letters exchanged and sentences written and written again, visits still prohibited now a year into the COVID-19 pandemic, the ache of not seeing you for months—*Can you believe they cancelled PRIDE, Nadja? What are all the screaming Mimis and Bulldaggers going to do without PRIDE, Nadja?. . . All of the staff and half of the prisoner population are walking around with masks on, it looks like a robbery in progress*—but how to express the romance of you, Kitty Jayne, a romance that leaps off the page, that *wakes up shakes your ass and exercises your freedoms whatever they may be*. How to express that I fall in love with you more and more as I read and re-read the creased letters, typewriter ink already fading, but like your laugh, shimmering around the edges with the promise of freedom? This is a love letter.

Notes

1. New York State Department of Corrections and Community Supervision (DOCCS) Directive 4911 "establishes the policy of the Department concerning packages and articles sent or brought to facilities and received through facility Package Rooms." See NYS DOCCS 2020 for the full list of rules and restrictions.

2. *I stay connected to community by keeping in contact with people like yourself Nadja. I used to write to ALL of the outside organizations. But not so much anymore.*

3. Drawing on José Esteban Muñoz's *Disidentifications* (1999), we describe transness as a way of seeing in order to highlight the intersubjective, dialogic, and collective nature of trans identifications. Alongside Muñoz's analysis pointing toward disidentification as a mode of queer political performance, "descriptive of the survival strategies the minority subject practices in order to negotiate a phobic majoritarian public sphere that continuously elides or punishes the existence of subjects who do not conform to the phantasm of normative citizenship" (4), a "trans way of seeing" emphasizes how we see each other through, between, and beyond transphobia and points toward seeing itself as a site and strategy of trans politics. As Kitty Jayne narrates her own entry into trans womanhood—*Marsha P. Johnson one day pulled my hair back and told me what a pretty girl I could be. When I looked at what she had done in the mirror I KNEW THAT I WAS MEANT TO BE A GIRL. I was very excited by this new discovery*—as Kitty Jayne's gender is refracted through Marsha's and Kitty Jayne's seeing, her womanhood becomes visible: called forth through trans sight. As with disidentification, we propose that this trans way of seeing "envision[s] and activate[s] new social relations" (5); indeed, it can only be realized and sustained intersubjectively. Thus, while a trans

way of seeing is perhaps part of "revisionary identification," or "different strategies of viewing, reading, and locating 'self' within representational systems and disparate life worlds that aim to displace or occlude a minority subject" (26), our emphasis here is not on locating the "self" but seeing the other or, more precisely, *offering to the other a way of seeing themself. I've met a lot of butchqueens who've discovered that they were really trans. They all thanked me for bringing it out of them. So yes. I've brought several people out to the light.* Our use of *seeing* here is also responsive to recent work by Black trans scholars documenting the "traps" of visibility for trans people, especially Black trans women, often only in their deaths (cf. Tourmaline, Stanley, and Burton 2017). Rather than approaching transness as axiomatically visible, or the problem of trans representation in a heteropatriarchal society being "invisibility," we instead offer ways of seeing to signal toward the communal and ethical practices through which trans people receive each other, and we suggest that cultivating these ways of seeing is part of prefiguring trans liberation while still unfree.

4.   We are grateful to Orisanmi Burton, who suggested letter writing as a way to collaborate on this project, and whose ongoing work with imprisoned Black radicals inspires us.

5.   We are indebted in our thinking to the tradition of radical, especially Black, trans and queer organizing and critique, which grounds our rejection of the politics of respectability and the false promises of liberal inclusion (cf. Cohen 2004; Ferguson 2004; Snorton 2017). What we recognize—from our different social locations and histories— is that there is no liberation to be found through inclusion in a white, bourgeois, gender-normative, capitalist order, and that our liberation as white trans people necessitates the destruction of racial capitalism and its logics of heteropatriarchy and institutions of policing and incarceration. We understand transphobia to be profoundly and inextricably anti-Black in its logic and operation. We recognize that the prison industrial complex intentionally and systematically targets Black people in the United States. *Do you see that building over there? It's the Corrections Officers' Mess Hall. Prisoners serve the COs wearing special all-white uniforms. It looks like slavery.* As a white imprisoned trans woman, Kitty Jayne is collateral of the state's genocidal war on Black people (or, as a mother in the abolitionist organizing collective Mothers Reclaiming Our Children explains in Ruth Wilson Gilmore's *Golden Gulag* (2007: 227), "You have to be white to be prosecuted under white law, but you do not have to be Black to be prosecuted under Black law." Yet simultaneously, since rigid gender differentiation has long been constructed as the apotheosis of "civilized" whiteness (Schuller 2018), criminalizing and punishing the gender nonconformity of trans and gender-nonconforming people (especially trans women) is part of white supremacy's project to "purify" whiteness of gender deviance. Although there are forms of respectable trans womanhood that may be recuperable within white gender-normative strictures of womanhood (homemaking, passing, veteran of imperialist wars, bourgeois, invested in cisness), inclusion would require that Kitty Jayne abandon her embod-

ied desires and practices of community and kinship (boosting, fucking in the streets, walking the balls with her sisters and picking their garters off the penitentiary floor, living fast, doing drugs, preferring men's prisons to women's). If Kitty Jayne's disreputable trans womanhood is thus construed as a threat to whiteness from within whiteness, since the prison functions as a zone of containment to protect whiteness and white innocence, then Kitty Jayne's incarceration is an effect of the white supremacist logic of the prison.

6. John Wojtowicz, who in 1972 attempted to rob a bank in Brooklyn to pay for his wife Elizabeth Eden's gender-affirmation surgery.

7. As Estelle Freedman (1984) argues, women's prisons have long been constructed as sites of women's uplift and domestic training, part of the project through which bourgeois women tended to the "souls" of their "fallen sisters." Women's prisons would, according to this perspective, teach persons imprisoned there "first of all[,] to be good women" (55).

8. Beauchamp's (2019: 6) *Going Stealth: Transgender Politics and U.S. Surveillance Practices* asks the question, "How are transgender and gender nonconforming populations caught up in ongoing state surveillance practices that almost never explicitly name transgender as a category of concern?" The surveillance practices at Rosie's are a tangled web of misogyny and transphobia. This interaction reveals both that bodies with breasts and bras are presumed to characteristically conceal and smuggle (bras must be snapped but not the waistbands of boxers), and that trans and gender-nonconforming bodies are presumptively deceptive, concealing the "truths" of our bodies and contraband (drugs) in equal measure.

9. I am fascinated by this policy, unable to ascertain if the bra requirement applied to people presumed to have breasts or people presumed to be women, which are obviously overlapping but not coextensive categories. I can't reckon the structure of the joint readings of our trans bodies that results in both of us needing to wear bras at all times, all while the correction officer's (mis)recognition of our genders (*Sir* and *Ma'am* thrown every which way, at both of us in equal measure) is volatile and constantly shifting. Even for Kitty Jayne, for whom the order to wear a bra could perhaps be seen as acknowledgment of her womanhood, it overrides and subdues her own embodied experience of her breasts. *I never wear a bra. Why would I, with my itty bitty titties?* Of course, even if proffered as a sort of procedural recognition of her womanhood, the bra mandate actually serves to discipline Kitty Jayne toward gender normativity and proceeds with indifference toward the actual material experientiality of her body.

10. I omitted these lines about prison break from the versions of the article that I sent to Kitty Jayne, to avoid subjecting her to punishment.

11. I feel the sentiment that animals know that we are trans to be a refutation of the white supremacist project of anthropomorphizing animals as heterosexual to naturalize "sex" difference and of reifying the boundary between human and animal—a constructed boundary that, as Mel Y. Chen 2012 and Zakiyyah Iman Jackson 2020

have shown, has always been anti-Black. Kitty Jayne's animals offer knowledge about ourselves to trans people: they are subjects, not objects, of knowledge.

12. You help me, in Muñoz's (1999: 34) words, "imagine an expansive queer *life*-world . . . one in which the mysteries of our sexuality are not reined in by sanitized understandings of lesbian and gay identity, and finally, one in which we are all allowed to be drama queens and smoke as much as our hearts desire."

References

Beauchamp, Toby. 2019. *Going Stealth: Transgender Politics and U.S. Surveillance Practices*. Durham, NC: Duke University Press.

Campt, Tina. 2017. *Listening to Images*. Durham, NC: Duke University Press.

Chen, Mel Y. 2012. *Animacies: Biopolitics, Racial Mattering, and Queer Affect*. Durham, NC: Duke University Press.

Cohen, Cathy J. 2004. "Deviance as Resistance: A New Research Agenda for the Study of Black Politics." *Du Bois Review* 1, no. 1: 27–45.

Ferguson, Roderick A. 2004. *Aberrations in Black: Toward a Queer of Color Critique*. Minneapolis: University of Minnesota Press.

Freedman, Estelle. 1984. *Their Sisters' Keeper: Women's Prison Reform in America, 1830–1930*. Ann Arbor: University of Michigan Press.

Gilmore, Ruth Wilson. 2007. *Golden Gulag: Prisons, Surplus, Crisis, and Opposition in Globalizing California*. Berkeley: University of California Press.

Jackson, Zakiyyah Iman. 2020. *Becoming Human: Matter and Meaning in an Antiblack World*. New York: New York University Press.

Muñoz, José Esteban. 1999. *Disidentifications: Queers of Color and the Performance of Politics*. Minneapolis: University of Minnesota Press.

NYS DOCCS (New York State Department of Corrections and Community Supervision). 2020. Directive 4911. doccs.ny.gov/system/files/documents/2020/11/4911.pdf.

Schuller, Kyla. 2018. *The Biopolitics of Feeling: Race, Sex, and Science in the Nineteenth Century*. Durham, NC: Duke University Press.

Snorton, C. Riley. 2017. *Black on Both Sides: A Racial History of Trans Identity*. Minneapolis: University of Minnesota Press.

Snorton, C. Riley, and Jin Haritaworn. 2013. "Trans Necropolitics: A Transnational Reflection on Violence, Death, and the Trans of Color Afterlife." In *The Transgender Studies Reader 2*, edited by Susan Stryker and Aren Z. Aizura, 66–76. New York: Routledge.

Stanley, Eric A. 2017. "Anti-trans Optics: Recognition, Opacity, and the Image of Force." *South Atlantic Quarterly* 116, no. 3: 612–20.

Tourmaline, Eric A. Stanley, and Johanna Burton, eds. 2017. *Trap Door: Trans Cultural Production and the Politics of Visibility*. Cambridge, MA: MIT Press.

RACE, SEX, AND GOD

Travis M. Foster

Queer Faith: Reading Promiscuity and Race in the Secular Love Tradition
Melissa E. Sanchez
New York: New York University Press, 2019. x + 337 pp.

*Make Yourselves Gods: Mormons and the Unfinished Business of
American Secularism*
Peter Coviello
Chicago: University of Chicago Press, 2019. 304 pp.

*Beside You in Time: Sense Methods and Queer Sociabilities in the
American Nineteenth Century*
Elizabeth Freeman
Durham, NC: Duke University Press, 2019. xii + 228 pp.

Readers of queer American literature require no introduction to the conceptual rewards that arise when writers intermingle sex and God, queer experience and theology, freedom and religion. Think of Alice Walker's *Color Purple* and Shug Avery's elaboration of the nonbinary theology presenting God as "It," a project taking prayer, faith, and divinity as vital components of Avery's womanist and queer thought. As Michael Cobb (2006: 170) notes of the theology in Walker's novel, "So much of what should not be said can be said by a religious language of 'It,' which inaugurates the important project of making the stories open to revision, reflection, play, and impression." Picking up on the broader insights undergirding Shug Avery's sacred rhetoric—that religious potentials need not compete adversarially with queer potentials, that they might instead collaborate in shared flourishing—queer studies has seen a resurgence in the religious, including, most

GLQ 28:2
DOI 10.1215/10642684-9608203
© 2022 by Duke University Press

recently, a special issue titled "Queer Political Theologies" (January 2021) in this very journal. Reading through this work, we come to understand what so many of us already knew: that, perhaps more often than not, religious and queer practices seek in similar ways to explore, expand, and embrace the porous nonautonomy of the self, the meeting of matter and spirit, the malleability of seemingly entrenched social systems, the call to action produced and then reproduced within spaces of ritual, pleasure, care, and being together. As Mark Jordan (2007: 565) writes in an earlier *GLQ* review essay, queer theory stands to benefit only when it acknowledges theology as "its rival, its beloved, its heir."

The three books under consideration here explore these potentialities in the past, from the mid-first-century theology of Paul the Apostle to the 1930s modernist fiction of Djuna Barnes. Such a vast spread might indicate that the three hardly belong side by side in a single review. Yet, fundamentally, these monographs take up the same crucial question: what forms of queer life has religion made possible? For readers, the stakes determining just how crucial it is to ask this question here and now make themselves clear in the refreshingly jarring unexpectedness of the books' answers. In *Queer Faith: Reading Promiscuity and Race in the Secular Love Tradition*, Melissa E. Sanchez pursues the queer affordances of religion within those theological and poetic traditions—from Paul and Augustine to Petrarch, Martin Luther, and Shakespeare—that might otherwise be taken to cement the heterosexual, monogamous couple as the ideal option for sexual life. In *Make Yourself Gods: Mormons and the Unfinished Business of American Secularism*, Peter Coviello pursues queer religious histories in the social inventions, theology, and polygamy of the early Mormon Church. And in *Beside You in Time: Sense Methods and Queer Sociabilities in the American Nineteenth Century*, Elizabeth Freeman finds queer worlds emerging out of a variety of practices, some of them religious, including the ecstatic enthusiasms of the Shakers and Djuna Barnes's repurposing of Catholic sacraments, especially baptism and the Eucharist. As a group, the three monographs reveal how religion facilitates queer collective, social, and conceptual alternatives to those made available by the antisocial thesis.

In the process, all three provide expanded genealogies of race as the historically enabling and constitutive influence on modern sexual categorization and queer sexual politics, and all three historicize the whiteness—which is to say, the white supremacy—of contemporary homonationalism. In so doing, they resist the distinctions and divisions of modern thought generally and, with it, a good deal of queer studies scholarship, specifically. If, as Ashon Crawley (2017: 30) argues, racialization produces categorical distinction as a "strategy of containment" and "epistemological constraint," creating the "serrations of racialization" that enable continuation of white supremacist hierarchy, then the foremost ambition of these three projects lies in their insistence on entangling histories of sex, religion, and race. By centering race, moreover, all three for the most part avoid (or, perhaps better, are prevented from succumbing to) what Kadji Amin (2017: 4, 8) identifies as "the idealizing engine of queer studies," in which the "romance of the alternative" leads to series of triumphalist narratives marking all nonnormativity as resistant, often heroically so. Or, rather, Sanchez, Coviello, and Freeman multiply the significances they wish readers to find in their volumes. All three are interested in the queer practices and possibilities of the past both as the kinds of idealizing resources Amin critiques as too monopolistic within queer studies and as cautionary tales primarily about how white supremacy, with its capacious drive toward the incorporation of intraracial white difference, is all too eager to make use of nondominant alternatives. So, for example, in her introduction Melissa Sanchez cites Freeman's previous book, *Time Binds: Queer Temporalities, Queer Histories*, to describe one piece of her project ("I . . . practice what Elizabeth Freeman describes as 'close readings of the past for the odd detail, the unintelligible or resistant moment' in order to 'treat these texts and their formal work as theories of their own, interventions upon both critical theory and historiography'"), even as she describes as parallel the project of historicizing how "distinctions between transgression and normativity, emancipation and repression . . . have shaped queer as well as normative associations of erotic choice with modernity, secularization, and whiteness" (18, 15; citing Freeman 2010: xvi–xvii). Through such a parallel focus, these three volumes contain an implicit critique of previous work within white queer studies: namely, that the field's "romance of the alternative" was purchased through the white supremacist luxury of ignoring race.

The central ambition of *Queer Faith*—one at which it is fantastically successful—is to convince readers that Christian theology provides an indispensable resource for queer theory, helping it to think more deeply about the inevitable failure of our commitments to one another, to account for and even find value in our unavoidable infidelities, and to historicize how white queer aspirations toward freedom and resistance are so frequently premised on racial and colonial exclusions. It makes this case through two trajectories, one tracking the influence of the apostle Paul's theological notion of the divided self through Christian intellectual history, particularly the writings of Augustine, Luther, and John Calvin, and another tracking how the same concept inserts a rigorous advocacy of promiscuity, infidelity, and divorce into the Petrarchan poetic love traditions otherwise known for the celebration of monogamy. As Sanchez carefully details, Pauline theology centers on a core truth: we cannot attain absolute control over our selves and are instead "continually coopted by foreign forces within and without" (200). Hence our necessary *promiscuity*, a term Sanchez uses to signal not only romantic and sexual openness but also sacred, social, and, as she elaborates in the book's coda, scholarly and professional attachments. Faith, self-knowledge, confession, and fidelity to God and to each other can exist only as aspirational qualities. And hence, she argues, "theology is useful to think with because, like psychoanalysis, it denies the liberation that it promises" (203).

The value of these claims is at once critical and ethical. The critical contribution exists insofar as queer studies scholars expand our archives and conceptual resources for challenging the anti-queer foundations—such as the privatizing of love within institutional frameworks—of heteronormativity, racial capitalism, and neoliberalism and for tracking "the exclusions upon which freedom may be premised" (159). Sanchez's ethical contribution emerges as she tracks within her archive an epistemology that precludes both innocence and the morality of victimhood. Foregrounding the limits of autonomy and commitment, an ethics of promiscuity "is neither a systematic nor deliberate ethics for living." Instead, promiscuity "is an intimate relation—always itself improvised and irregular—with the humbling, even shaming, compromises that shape our existence as impure creatures in an unjust world" (244). The book pursues these aims with great care, through five chapters on Augustine's elaboration of Pauline theology; the racial hierarchies of Shakespeare's sonnets; Luther's, Calvin's, and Edmund Spencer's elaboration on the indignity of even conjugal sex; the ethics of adultery and divorce as key features in John Milton's divorce pamphlets as well as Philip Sidney and Lady Mary Wroth's adulterous sonnet sequences; and the lyrics of John Donne written from the point of view of the unfaithful lover. Moreover, it does so with a robustly promiscuous citational style, engaging in conversation with not only a great number of scholars but also with scholars from a great number of different fields. The result is a lively, exuberantly peopled book that exposes just how mistaken can be the advice to bury citations all too frequently passed along by scholarly mentors.

In chapter 4, "The Optimism of Infidelity: Divorce and Adultery," for example, Sanchez places readings of Sidney, Wroth, and Milton alongside a myriad of twentieth-century and contemporary critics, including Laura Kipnis, Theodor Adorno, Lauren Berlant, Dale Martin, Janet R. Jakobsen, John D'Emilio, Elizabeth Freeman, Adam Phillips, Deborah H. Rhode, Jack Halberstam, Lee Edelman, and others. Out of this conversation emerge key claims about the ethics and politics of love, from the early modern era to our own. In Milton's divorce tracts, we find a theological argument "that ethical love need not be sanctioned by, and actually may be opposed to, the institution of marriage" (174). In Sidney's

Astrophil and Stella, addressed to a married woman, and Wroth's *Pamphilia to Amphilanthus*, modeled after Wroth's adulterous affair with William Herbert, we find the dissolution of any opposition between fidelity and infidelity, "for fidelity to the true love requires infidelity to the legal spouse and vice versa" (182). Such a project allows the chapter to "consult documents of the more distant past that critique the psychic violence inherent in the legal enforcement of lifelong fidelity, even as the racial exclusions and aggressions they enact in the name of freedom must give us pause about any liberatory project, then or now" (166–67). To make this second point, Sanchez carefully analyzes the appearance of racial divisions in Milton, Sidney, and Wroth, which limit freedom to those exhibiting what for them is a racialized mode of moral capacity and depth of self solely available to whites. This racialization of interior life serves to quarantine the freedom of free love, linking it to the selfhood of the white Christian whose very existence they define through opposition to religious and racial others seen as manifesting diminished affective capacity. The writings of Milton, Sidney, and Wroth, as Sanchez puts it, thus remind "us of the exclusions inherent in ideals of autonomous desire, even as they expand its parameters" (199).

In *Queer Faith* Pauline theology and the Petrarchan tradition provide today's queers with affirmative and negative models from the usable past. In *Make Yourself Gods*, these models come from the nineteenth-century history and theology of the Latter-day Saints. A glowing *BYU Studies Quarterly* review of Coviello's monograph cautions its readers that the "average Latter-day Saint reader will . . . be at odds with its use of queer critique," and it's quite possible that many queer and feminist readers might find ourselves at odds over its energetic celebration of Mormonism's vigorously heterosexual mode of polygyny (which Coviello refers to as plural patriarchal marriage) as a vital component of nineteenth-century US queer history (MacKay 2020: 186). Yet the book makes two mostly persuasive cases for just that. The first is that modern-day queers can find in nineteenth-century Mormon history a trajectory of loss that parallels our own. Queers might see our downward spiral from radical and perverse outsiders to celebrated aisle walkers in the historical shift from Mormon polygyny—with its "queer devotionality," "perversity of gender, of sex, and of proper belief," "radical vision of embodied life," "carnal theology," "counterdiscipline," "*deviant carnality*," and "intimate form built explicitly to recognize, rather than rebuke, the pleasures of carnality"—to Mormon monogyny, with its much more sedate, secular, and liberal institution of respectable sex (55, 83, 85, 217, 88; emphasis in original). The second is that this transition occurs in no small part through the force of secularization, a biopolitical force that mirrors hetero- and homonormativity in its capacity to constrain the possibilities for human existence and flourishing. Moreover, as Coviello carefully tracks, both of these histories occur alongside, through, and in the service of American white supremacy.

To reveal to his readers the queer perversity phase of Mormon history, Coviello turns to Mormon theology. His book's title, *Make Yourselves Gods*, comes from Joseph Smith's "King Follett Discourse," an 1844 sermon encouraging followers to amplify their very beings in a process toward becoming divine, gods on earth. For Smith, this transition occurs through polygyny, a way of imitating Old Testament saints like Abraham and of, through carnal pleasure, mapping "out an exaltation of the human not *beyond* the flesh but toward a divinity *already present* in the mortal world (67; emphasis in original). As a radical alternative to marital monogamy that reshapes all aspects of familial and social existence, polygyny touches even the most quotidian of practices with the divine. Building on the work of Nancy Bentley, Saba Mahmood, and others, Coviello resists secularism's narratives about the subjection of religious women and instead tracks his argument to the lives of Mormon women by charting how polygyny not only led to profound loneliness and longing but also carved out "an extraordinary breadth of authority": "I want to suggest," he writes, "that in the lives and writings of early polygamous women we find an especially vivid testament to an understystematized theology of the flesh working itself out negotiation by negotiation, and doing so not least through the bodies of women" (93). While we might wonder at the phrase "polygamous women"—to what degree is a person polygamous if she is limited by plural patriarchal marriage to just one sex partner—more convincing is the claim that polygyny altered social norms in ways that enabled new embodied experience and thought.

Such counternormative experimentation led non-Mormon whites to portray the Latter-day Saints as racially suspect, anti-American, and sexually perverse. And, as Coviello tracks it, as the turn of the century approached, the church responded through a settler-colonial project of whitening and liberal reform. "To put it compactly: the Saints are a people disciplined out of their devotionally charged carnality, into monogamy, and eventually into the secular American whiteness for which that disciplined sexual comportment was, all along, a neat metonymy" (175). Ultimately recasting themselves through a kind of hypernormativity, the Mormons, "in their efforts to destigmatize their own religio-erotic errancy through the fervent performance of a countervailing normativity" and their embrace of the white imperial state, foreshadow precisely the kind of recent histories that have, for many, so depleted queer life. (Coviello describes this as "proto-homonationalism" [229]).

Yet, the book argues, it's not enough to describe these histories as the biopolitics of racism or as the force of state imperialism, and he instead identifies throughout the book the impact of a third historical force: not just settler colonialism and "exterminatory racism" but also "the disciplinary sociality of secularism into a generalized politics of life" (234). Indeed, secularism occupies the project's central focus. This shows up not only in its subtitle, "Mormons and the Unfinished Business of American Secularism," but also in its introduction, which aims to do for the study of secularism what Eve Kosofsky Sedgwick, in her introduction to *Epistemology of the Closet*, did for queer theory: lay out a set of guiding axioms. These run from what for many students of secularism and postsecularism will be familiar claims (such as axiom 2 claiming that the negative of secularism isn't religion but bad belief and axiom 3 that secularism is a disciplinary project) to those that may be novel or at least less familiar (such as axiom 4 on secularism's embodiment and axiom 5 on secularism as a biopolitics). The result is a work that falls within the rubric of queer studies (along with that of many other fields), while also expanding our field's purview and encouraging further study into the alignment of errant religious, gender, and sexual practices and identifications.

Queer Faith and *Make Yourselves Gods* locate in their respective histories of religion both queer world making and cautionary tales about the readiness with which such world making can morph into the liberal belonging and racial hierarchy of white supremacy. *Beside You in Time* does these things as well, but it stands apart by focusing less explicitly on religious practices than on what Freeman terms "sense methods." Her case studies of these sense methods include religious practices of the nineteenth-century United States, including Shaker dance, the ecstatic worship represented in Gertrude Stein's "Melanctha," and the reconfiguring of sacraments in Djuna Barnes's *Nightwood*. But they also include other practices, including playing dead in African American literature and performance and libidinal historicism in Mark Twain's *Connecticut Yankee in King Arthur's Court* and Pauline Hopkins's *Of One Blood*. Arguing that "subjugated knowledge is often lodged in the flesh itself, and lives as timed bodiliness and as styles of temporally inflected sociability," the book describes sense methods as the kind of temporal encounters we experience that foreground "time itself as a visceral, haptic, proprioceptive mode of apprehension—a way of feeling and organizing the world through and with the individual body, often in concert with other bodies" (8). Doing so, *Beside You in Time* builds on Freeman's previous book, *Time Binds*, treating time as a practice within historical and contemporary queer world making. If our experience of time is instrumental for how we occupy our overlapping social worlds, then our sense methods, our temporal encounters, have the capacity not only to align us with dominant social structures but also to align us with others occupying subordinated social space.

These temporal encounters constitute a queer method of embodied togetherness. They are, Freeman argues, always relational, emerging through interactions between bodies; they thus provide "a queer theory of relationality" irreducible to genital sexuality. (The book instead incorporates Audre Lorde's more expansive notion of the erotic as a mutual rhythm, a way of placing bodies into concert.) And they sit apart from both the antisocial or antirelational model of gay white male queer theory and the optimization of life Michel Foucault theorizes as biopolitics. Queerness in this book aligns less with the death drive and the shattering of the ego than with "a drive toward connectivity, conjugation, and coalescence . . . which cannot be equated with the biopolitical understanding of life as that which must be optimized at the expense of those deemed unworthy of life" (13). Such a queer hypersociability, for Freeman, manifests "along axes and wavelengths beyond the discursive and the visual" (14). Nor is queer hypersociability limited to interactions between bodies in the here and now; instead, in ways that build on work by scholars such as Christopher Nealon, Carolyn Dinshaw, and J. Samaine Lockwood, it has the potential to link present and historical bodies. Given this conceptualization of hypersociability, it comes as no surprise when Freeman describes "ecstatic religion" as possibly "the most extreme example" of "the long nineteenth century's extralinguistic, sensory modes of belonging and becoming," for such a wayward practice links worshippers to behaviors, collectivities, and senses of time decidedly apart from the liberal subjectivity of modern secularism. As Freeman puts it, when taken together, such acts constitute "small-scale temporal coincidences between bodies, achieved through corporeal praxes opening out from face-to-face community toward the larger population and toward other moments on the historical timeline" (190).

Hence in chapter 1, "Shake It Off: The Physiopolitics of Shaker Dance, 1774–1856," Freeman traces how the Shakers' celibacy along with their countervailing rhythms and movements facilitated collective experimentation with ways of living outside patriarchal gender hierarchies, compulsory heterosexuality, and, indeed, compulsive sexuality itself: "Shaker rhythms were, precisely, both queer and sacred, for they lifted the Shakers out of various earthly tempos and united them with one another in a spiritual form of belonging that might be thought of as not only akin to queer world making but also truly, radically Christian, if we remember that Jesus instructed his followers to abandon their biological families" (50). Just as aberrant religious and sexual habits racialized Mormons, so too were the Shakers racialized through association with Native (when considered "wild") and Black (when considered oversimilar and monotonous) rhythms and ways of being. By "shaking off" their sexual desires through dance, affirming asexuality as a practice of queer sociality, Shaker dancing exemplifies Freeman's analysis of how being out of step together can place bodies, people, and communities apart from the dominant temporality of heterosexuality and white supremacy. At the same time—while this point is frequently less explicit in *Beside You in Time* than it is in either *Queer Faith* or *Make Yourselves Gods*—the book treats nondominance and anti-normativity as categories that, by themselves, cannot simply be taken as radical or resistant. As a group, all three thus remind us of the robust synergies between religious and queer studies, while suggesting how we might better understand the field's long-standing emphasis on nonnormativity within rather than against histories of racist and colonial exclusions.

References

Amin, Kadji. 2017. *Disturbing Attachments: Genet, Modern Pederasty, and Queer History.* Durham, NC: Duke University Press.

Cobb, Michael. 2006. *God Hates Fags: The Rhetorics of Religious Violence.* New York: New York University Press.

Crawley, Ashon. 2017. *Blackpentecostal Breath: The Aesthetics of Possibility.* New York: Fordham University Press.

Freeman, Elizabeth. 2010. *Time Binds: Queer Temporalities, Queer Histories.* Durham, NC: Duke University Press.

Jordan, Mark D. 2007. "Religion Trouble." Review of *Que(e)rying Religion: A Critical Anthology*, edited by Gary David Comstock and Susan E. Henking; *Gay Religion*, edited by Scott Thumma and Edward R. Gray; and *The Sexual Theologian: Essays on Sex, God, and Politics*, edited by Marcella Althaus-Reid and Lisa Isherwood. *GLQ* 13, no. 4: 563–75.

MacKay, Michael Hubbard. 2020. Review of *Make Yourselves Gods: Mormons and the Unfinished Business of American Secularism. BYU Studies Quarterly* 59, no. 4: 186–92.

AFRICAN AMERICAN GAY MEN

Mourning and Artistic Resistance in a Time of Pandemic

Keith Clark

Evidence of Being: The Black Gay Cultural Renaissance and the Politics of Violence
Darius Bost
Chicago: University of Chicago Press, 2019. xi + 181 pp.

In the introduction to his absorbing study of Black gay men's artistry and activism in the seventies, eighties, and nineties, critic Darius Bost expounds upon its title: "By naming this proliferation of black gay cultural production a renaissance, I hope to demonstrate the significance of collectivity to black gay aesthetics, cultural production, and politics, and to black gay men's everyday struggles against the various formations of violence targeting them" (6). Informed by Bost's claim and expanding it to our contemporary cultural moment, I would adduce that the last five to ten years have marked a continuation of the fertile creative decades Bost's study foregrounds. Consider the profusion of works by and about African American gay men in multiple genres: Raoul Peck's Oscar-nominated documentary *I Am Not Your Negro* (2016), scholar/commentator Eddie Glaude's *Begin Again: James Baldwin's America and Its Urgent Lessons for Our Own* (2020), and Barry Jenkins's 2018 acclaimed film adaptation of *If Beale Street Could Talk*—all avouching James Baldwin's inestimable impact on the American consciousness long after his 1987 death; 2020 Pulitzer winners Jericho Brown (poetry) and Michael R. Jackson (drama); the publication of heralded novels by Robert Jones (*The Prophets*) and Bryan Washington (*Memorial*), as well as memoirs by such authors as Rashod Ollison, Darnell Moore, Saeed Jones, and Brian Broome; and perhaps the most monumental and widely lauded work, Jenkins's Academy Award–garnering film *Moonlight* (2016). We might even include the meteoric rise of recording artist Lil Nas X (Montero Lamar Hill), so unabashedly Black and gay and mainstream that he's graced the stage of SNL. Thus, while the term *renaissance* might seem a bit belabored given its fulsome applications and misapplications (think here of such shibboleths as "respectability politics" or "intersectionality"), it nevertheless seems apposite given the proliferation of Black gay men's voices in so many mediums.

Bost's *Evidence of Being: The Black Gay Cultural Renaissance and the Politics of Violence* is a signal achievement, part of a burgeoning body of African American LGBTQ-centered studies by scholars such as GerShun Avilez, Jeffrey McCune, Kevin Munford, C. Riley Snorton, and Calvin Warren. Concentrating on New York City and Washington, DC, as the twin epicenters of Black gay men's culture in myriad forms, Bost excavates and explores voices and lives that may be foreign to even the most well-versed students of gay African American history. The breadth and scope of Bost's subjects—from African American literature scholar, novelist, and poet Melvin Dixon; the performance troupe "Cinque" and writers for/publishers of *Blacklight* and *Black/Out* magazines; to the NYC-based "Other Countries" writing/performance collective and even a memorial service for a prominent member of this group—explode boundaries separating popular, academic, literary, mainstream, and vernacular cultures and forms. And while the book is grounded in foundational Black LGBTQ scholarship by such seminal thinkers as Marlon Ross, Sharon Holland, Phillip Brian Harper, Robert Reid-Pharr, Cathy Cohen, and E. Patrick Johnson, Bost distinctively builds on it in articulating innovative critical and theoretical methodologies for gay Black men outside the orbit of hegemonic white gay popular and academic spheres, as well as sexually parochial Black institutions.

In the book's introduction, "On Black Gay Being," Bost puts forth his critical/theoretical framework, briefly expounding on the ontological challenges that render Black gay male subjectivity alternatively vexing, perilous, provisional, and elusive. While emphatically distinguishing his scholarly apparatus from Afropessimism, Bost avers that his study "illuminates how black trauma (rooted in slavery and its afterlife) and queer trauma (rooted in homophobia, transphobia, and AIDS) converged during this historical moment to doubly mark the black gay body as a site of social and corporeal death" (4). Contrapuntally, a cavalcade of gay men engaged in manifold artistic expressive endeavors—creative writing, literary scholarship, performance art, and political activism—to assert nuanced iterations of Black gay subjectivity amid multiple assaults on their personhood. As Bost argues, this violence occurred on multiple fronts—primarily but not limited to the state in the form of abject neglect during the AIDS plague, as well as "pick-up" murders in Washington, DC, and Black heteropatriarchal institutions such as the church and its fervent denunciation of its gay brethren generally and those with AIDS specifically. Given this inimical reality in which same-gender-loving men were buffeted by unrelenting attacks and the trauma left in their wake, Bost ultimately "turn[s] to black gay literature and culture as evidence for reimagining black gay personhood as a site of possibility, imbued with the potential of creating a more livable black gay social life" (4). The introduction also establishes the primary subjects of Bost's critical exploration: Melvin Dixon and his notion of "double cremation," which encapsulates Black gay men's imperceptibility vis-à-vis the dominant Anglocentric queer culture and the coaxial pruning of gayness from the hetero-orthodox African American "family tree"; the network of bars, social clubs, performance spaces, and AIDS organizations in New York and Washington; the writings of the renegade performance artist/poet-essayist/activist Essex Hemphill as well as unpublished works by lesser-known writers; and visual images in the forms of photographs and journal covers. Bost clearly enunciates his methodological modus operandi: "I privilege the archival recovery of authors and texts marginalized in black studies and queer studies that allows for readings of loss and abjection alongside political longing and subjective possibilities" (17).

The first chapter, "The Contradictions of Grief: Violence and Value in *Blacklight* Magazine," probes a flashpoint from the DC Black gay scene in the seventies and eighties: a series of "trick murders" in which gay men were slain by younger men from whom they hoped to procure sex. Conjunctively, Bost explores the varied responses to these crimes by the mainstream press (*Washington Post*), the white gay press (*Washington Blade*), local niche publications such as the Black gay periodical *Blacklight*, and denizens of the relatively insular local Black gay social club scene. Bost mines not only relatively obscure written resources but also accounts from his interviews with such figures as *Blacklight* publisher Sidney Brinkley, the venerable activist Courtney Williams, and other, primarily middle- and upper-class men affiliated with a vibrant if *sub rosa* gay men's social club culture who witnessed firsthand the harrowing events that enveloped and demoralized the community. The conclusions Bost draws are, regrettably, unsurprising—the mainstream press's titillating reporting on the "deviant" Black gay men's demi-monde and the attendant hypersexualizing of murder victims and perpetrators; the white gay press's ambivalence given the victims' race. I do take issue with Bost's admonition of Brinkley for his admittedly serrated description of "rough trade" as "usually dirty, foul-mouthed, under-educated, sexually repressed, emotionally immature and angry" (32). Bost extrapolates from this an overarching condemnation of tragic figures such as Ronald Gibson (aka, "Star"), a transvestite sex worker who was shot to death in an area where men solicited sex with "drag queens": "Laying claim to the value of black gay men murdered by hustlers inadvertently participates in the processes of Othering that mark as normative the violence done to drag queen prostitutes like Ronald Gibson/Star. In turn, this devaluation of their [Gibson/Star's] death reflects broader social divisions in the emerging black gay cultural landscape in Washington, DC" (32). While such class-based hierarchies are inevitable in a city as economically disparate as the nation's capital, Bost's reading of Brinkley's denunciation of "rough trade" as somehow analogous to those who would Other and victim-blame sex workers such as Gibson seems incongruous. There is a marked difference between predatory young men who may or may not be sex workers (i.e., "hustlers," "rough trade") preying on perennially imperiled Black gay men (class distinctions notwithstanding) and transvestite sex workers often driven to the streets for economic survival.

Buttressing his analysis of the community's reactions to these crimes and the psychic personal and collective trauma they induced, Bost offers compelling, scrupulous readings of the prolific if underappreciated Hemphill, specifically his elegiac poems on death, grief, and longing. Especially commendable is Bost's discussion of the largely unknown performance ensemble "Cinque," which consisted of Hemphill and dancers/singers Larry Duckette and Wayson Jones (the text includes a rare photo of the group). Bost recuperates and reprints their unpublished poem/performance piece "The Brass Rail," which he then explicates as a "site of ecstasy and fear, of communal eroticism and the shared threat of terror" (43). The study's opening chapter is a microcosm of the entire study: the range of materials explored and included—print journalism, poetry, unpublished work, performance pieces, interviews—makes it a primer for those interested in or unaware of DC's dynamic if underacknowledged Black gay cultural life and times.

Chapter 2, "Loneliness: Black Gay Longing in the Works of Essex Hemphill," continues in the vein of the previous one, dissecting Hemphill's essays and poems as, concurrently, lamentations for Black gay men suffering in the throes of AIDS; odes for a sort of existential loneliness more pronounced for men doubly othered; and declarations for what the poet-activist called a "functioning self," one that reconciles a heretofore fractured self rendered so by racism and homophobia. Bost punctiliously chronicles Hemphill's protracted struggle with two antiphonal but stentorian forces: (1) mainstream white queer culture, for whom Black gay men were either invisible or *hyper-visibly* objectified—the latter reified in photographer Robert Mapplethorpe's disembodied images of faceless Black men's torsos and sex organs, and (2) Hemphill's native racial community, an inhospitable homespace from which he feels alienated because of its long-standing abjuration of same-sex desire. Bost approaches Hemphill's fraught life and work with sensitivity without becoming maudlin or indulgent. In addition, this chapter contains a brief but engrossing discussion of Hemphill's contemporary Joseph Beam, a journalist and gay rights activist who compiled and edited the landmark volume *In the Life: A Black Gay Anthology* (1986) (Bost's recuperation of Beam dovetails nicely with Kevin Mumford's extensive exploration of him in his 2016 book, *Not Straight, Not White: Black Gay Men from the March on Washington to the AIDS Crisis*). Bost adroitly interlards Hemphill's writing about Beam—whom Hemphill considered "my brother" —with the tragic circumstances of Beam's death and Hemphill's own life and words in theorizing Black gay individual and collective loneliness. Bost trenchantly argues that their mutual personal despair was especially ironic given that both were widely known for their outspoken public stances on gay rights and AIDS. In Bost's estimation, public memorials such as the AIDS quilt could do little to mitigate the multitudinous forces arrayed against Black gay being and beings. His remark about the silence and mystery surrounding Beam's death applies to Hemphill as well: "The public efforts of black gay artists could not always alleviate their individual psychic pain" (58).

Chapter 3, "Postmortem Politics: The Other Countries Collective and Black Gay Mourning," is perhaps the book's most consequential, for its comprehensive and elucidating discussion of a neglected but pioneering Black gay men's writing coterie. With its origins in the "Blackheart" collective in New York City, "Other Countries" was founded by members of the original group in 1986. Bost makes the salient point that such clusters of writers of color remain largely elided in the annals of LGBTQ literary histories, while white collectives such the Violet Quill have been heralded and widely researched. The chapter's historiographic value cannot be understated, evinced in its thorough chronicling and unpacking of the group's evolution from a "new writers' workshop" to a space fostering artistic comradery, social contact, and different forms of intimacy—a welcome alternative to the often alienating and claustrophobic milieu of bars and clubs. While Bost does not gloss over its internecine conflicts, he deftly integrates interviews with former members, psychological and theoretical scholarship on mourning, excerpts from the group's public performances, and writings from its two anthologies (1988, 1993) to create a cogent treatment of Black gay creative culture in the midst of the AIDS pandemic. While its genesis was literary, especially compelling is Bost's discussion of the group's public performances, the venues ranging from esoteric (the Studio Museum in New York) to au currant (Tracks nightclub in Washington). The discussion of the funeral of Other Countries' member Donald Woods exemplifies these men's assertions of agency in grimly oppressive conditions. Bost quotes his interview with writer Marvin K. White, who attended Woods's memorial service. Woods's family expunged any references to the writer-activist's sexuality and AIDS-related death in a sort of straight-washing in the service of heteronormative "respectability." However, the solemn event metamorphosed into what White deemed "Our Black Gay Stonewall" when another OC member, Assotto Saint, brazenly disrupted the service and proclaimed that Woods was "out, was gay, and had died of AIDS, not a heart attack" (89). Bost provides a nuanced discussion of the politics of public mourning rituals and how institutions such as the Black church and family during the 1980s promulgated "a fictive boundary between black homosexuality and heterosexuality, as well as maintaining the fiction of the black family and the black church as solely heterosexual institutions" (90). While I would not dispute this claim, I think Bost might have better contextualized these execrable fallacies—noting, for instance, that African American institutions by and large often mimic their more powerful white counterparts; thus, politicians and clerics such as Jesse Helms, Jerry Falwell, Sr., and New York's Cardinal John O'Connor were mounting a ruthless assault on homosexuality generally and AIDS victims specifically in the halls of government buildings and in their "sacred, apolitical" edifices. This by no means mitigates the suffering Woods and Hemphill et al. experienced within their home communities, but it does situate lamentable events such as Woods's straight-washing within the larger eighties' context of antigayness, AIDS-phobia, and antiblackness. Still, Bost offers a convincing counter-hermeneutics with respect to Black gay men's creative impulses and productions, public personae, performances, and modes of mourning, remembering, and resisting.

The final chapter concentrates on the diaries and other writings of Melvin Dixon (1950–92), another premature casualty to a pestilence that snuffed out incalculable numbers of Black gay luminaries in so many fields. At once information laden and haunting, this chapter provides a wrenching account of a true renaissance man who recalls artistically ambitious gay forebears Richard Bruce Nugent and James Baldwin. Dixon felt agonizingly that "perhaps I just don't understand how to be human" by virtue of a gay identity that chafed relationships within his biological family (Bost notes that Dixon steadfastly believed that his father never loved him) as well as the larger non-consanguineous African American family; and a Black identity that rendered him subaltern in both the dominant heterocentric Euro-American culture and its smaller but inveterately prejudiced gay counterpart. Despite these multiple levels of abjection, Dixon was inarguably a "black gay genius" (to borrow from the title of a 2014 anthology), Baldwin-esque in his erudition and fluency in multiple expressive forms: literary criticism, poetry, short stories, and novels. While again employing his considerable close reading skills in using Dixon's fiction as a prism through which to interpret his life, Bost's recuperation and interpretation of Dixon's diary entries is truly enthralling. Like the blues, the pain that Bost channels through these diaries is both personal and collective, apropos given that Dixon witnessed firsthand such tectonic events as the Civil Rights and Black Power Movements, the Women's Movement, Stonewall, and AIDS. Indeed, his brief forty-two-year life, spanning the fifties, sixties, seventies, eighties, and nineties, was lived at the junction of these seismic occurrences. One of the more forceful claims Bost makes in this chapter relates to the disciplinary enterprise of LGBTQ studies, a point that speaks to an enduring deficit in terms of race and scope: "I would include Dixon and other black gay writers among those marginalized by the rise of queer theory" (118). While Bost's scholarship is firmly grounded in queer theory, it is not subsumed by it, nor does he embrace it wholesale and uncritically. In fact, his willingness to engage practitioners who use such academic frameworks to devalue Black gay men whose writings they deem wanting vis-à-vis recondite theories and paradigms is one of the book's many strong suits. The chapter ends with a poignant coda, with Bost situating himself as a personal and professional kindred spirit to the gone-too-soon griot Dixon, reflecting on his own vexed positionality in a world that may be a soupçon less racist and homophobic than the one that menaced Dixon but where "being black and gay" still "registers as a revolutionary act" (126).

Notwithstanding the rare instance where I might have challenged a contention or solicited a bit more contextualizing, *Evidence of Being: The Black Gay Cultural Renaissance and the Politics of Violence* makes a major contribution to the blossoming field of African American LGBTQ studies. In addition to its thoroughly and proficiently executed chapters, the monograph includes an invaluable appendix, composed of "Notable Individuals, Organizations, and Publications," each entry fully annotated. A work that is richly interdisciplinary, *Evidence of Being* is essential reading for students and scholars interested in a fertile era of Black same-gender-loving men writing, performing, and resisting as though their very lives depended on it. I hope that this exceptional study will be the springboard for Bost's next project, perhaps a biography of the oft-neglected Dixon or some other facet of African American LGBTQ culture and history heretofore beyond the radar of mainstream queer studies.

Keith Clark is professor of English and African and African American studies at George Mason University.

DOI 10.1215/10642684-9608217

HEMISPHERIC THINKING AND QUEER KIN

Nicolás Ramos Flores

Argentine Intimacies: Queer Kinship in an Age of Splendor, 1890–1910
Joseph M. Pierce
Albany: State University of New York Press, 2019. 336 pp.

In *Argentine Intimacies: Queer Kinship in an Age of Splendor, 1890–1910* (2019) Joseph M. Pierce analyzes how the family structure inherently sits outside normative heteropatriarchal structures that it claims to establish. By analyzing cultural productions—literary texts, family albums, private writings, and critical essays—from the aristocratic Bunge siblings, Pierce develops the notion of a "queer kinship," which orients the body through structural norms that not only conform to but also challenge and point toward new sorts of kinship "that may not yet exist" (16). Through a broad cultural analysis, Pierce asserts that the family structure is, at its core, already queered because of its various relational contradictions. It is in view of this tension that Pierce develops the book's five chapters, proposing a productive intersection of queer studies and Latin American studies that moves away from essentialist paradigms.

Chapter 1 thinks through how the literary writing of the eldest sibling, Carlos Octavio Bunge, queers the family novel as an idealized national project through desires. Pierce goes beyond reading Carlos Octavio's work at face value, arguing that his writings are "queerly productive in refashioning what desire means, how it means, and under what circumstances this multifaceted desire becomes legible" (89). Pierce underscores how the family structure is used to reify heteropatriarchal relationships through literature. Carlos Octavio's novel *La novela de la sangre* shows both the contradictions and the futurity of the family, portraying the existential angst that Argentina experienced at the turn of the last century. At times the chapter dwells too long on minute details of book production in Argentina and Carlos Octavio's life that distract from the broader points Pierce is making.

The second chapter looks closely at the diaries of Delfina and Julia Bunge, Carlos Octavio's younger sisters, spanning from 1897 to 1952 and 1903 to 1911, respectively. Pierce asserts the diary as a queer genre in the way that it breaks traditional literary structures in form, speaker, and audience. Pierce uses the diaries to consider the ways these women think about their social context, thus theorizing queerness through this writing form. Pierce dissects each sister's subjectivity as an understanding of Argentina's attitudes toward sexuality, kinship, and gender during this era. These diaries have a particular way of pointing to the *porvenir* through Delfina's and Julia's self-reflection in the diaries and the future reader that Delfina gestures toward in her rewriting and editing. The diaries become palimpsestic through the various edits, commentary, and intertextuality and through the women's relationships with each other, their family, and society.

Moving away from written texts, the third chapter explores the Bunge family's photo albums through personal portraits and family pictures that simultaneously challenge and reify the heteronormative family structure. Pierce methodically weaves together analysis of individual pictures and family portraits, positing that the intimate family gaze can be read to link nostalgia for the past with the possibility of the future. Pierce makes it clear that the photographs themselves are not queered; instead, his scholarly analysis contextually queers our understanding of them. The albums, where "representation, cultural nationalism, and modernity intersect," are "an intimate disciplinary site, as well as a site of disciplining intimacy, gender, race, and class" (139). It is in this chapter that Pierce's analysis shines the most. Similar to his exploration of the diaries, he offers a unique examination that points to the possible future this family could have lived, using the futurity of his theoretical framework in his analysis.

Pierce then shifts from analyzing family albums to looking at Carlos Octavio Bunge's textbook *Nuestra patria: Libro de lectura para la educación nacional* and Julia and Delfina's children's book *El Arca de Noé*. Pierce considers how education was used as a national building project that centered not on securing material gains for the country but rather on fostering affection for the nation and social growth. These texts are queer because the "pedagogical texts shed light on struggle between a nostalgic yearning for an idyllic (aristocratic) past, and a programmatic future in which queerness holds a central, though seldom recognized position" (191). In both, Pierce argues, the intimate familial space is used to convey a national socialization that rejects queered standards. Private love is linked to public love of the nation.

In the final chapter, Pierce analyzes critical essays via Carlos Octavio's *Nuestra América: Ensayos de la psicología social*, Alejandro Bunge's *Una nueva patria*, and Delfina Bunge's *Las mujeres y la vocación*. The three essays show both the family's elite status and its attempts to replicate the very problematic structures that led to Argentina's national malaise by conceiving idealized futures that inherently replicate extant structures. Race, gender, and religion are dissected in these texts to provide a multifaceted portrayal of Argentinian national constructs that are unique to the country. While Pierce acknowledges the limited engagement with other Latin American thinkers, this chapter would have been enhanced by a deeper connection to the works by theorists such as Cuba's José Martí or Mexico's José Vasconcelos to give a broader contextualization of national constructs of the time. Additionally, Alejandro Bunge (Carlos Octavio, Delfina, and Julia's brother) receives little attention in the book and feels more like an appendage to this chapter than a central figure in the family.

Finally, the epilogue provides a critical, nuanced contemplation of the coloniality of US-based queer studies and its application in Latin American studies. Pierce explains the importance of queer studies in Latin America, but he cautions against universal application of such endeavors and asks queer studies to critique its own coloniality when studying Latin American subjects. He states, "This is not a field statement so much as a reflection on the possibilities of queer studies as it engages with multiple contexts" (268). Pierce again points to decolonial possibilities in this analysis, underscoring the need for these intellectual endeavors.

The book is an expansive project that provides an insightful and thorough analysis that breaks with heteropatriarchal understandings of family structures in Latin America. While the analysis is incisive and at times poetic, it is often lost in the breadth of texts studied and contextual details. I wish Pierce had focused on only one or two cultural products. Furthermore, a deeper consideration of the broader region regarding both intellectual history and queer studies would have been a fruitful addition. Even so, Pierce provides a critical interrogation between U.S.-based queer studies and Latin American studies that will allow scholars in the two fields to think in more hemispheric terms.

Nicolás Ramos Flores is an assistant professor of Spanish at Colby College in Waterville, Maine.

DOI 10.1215/10642684-9608231

GETTING THE HELL OVER MANHATTAN

Jen Jack Gieseking

When Brooklyn Was Queer
Hugh Ryan
New York: St. Martin's Press, 2019. 308 pp.

When reading Hugh Ryan's *When Brooklyn Was Queer*, the reader may feel certain (as I did) that Ryan is perched next to you on a stool at a gay bar, whispering stories of queer trysts, losses, and triumphs in your ear as you ironically down Manhattans. Ryan captivatingly weaves together a vibrant history of queer waterfronts, "peg houses," communes, and scandals, which is a history also erased by highways, violence, pathologization, and morality committees. While some may be chagrined that there is yet another book on queer New York City, there are actually few extant scholarly volumes on the city's queer history, and fewer still that deemphasize a Carrie Bradshaw view of the world, i.e., queer history beyond Manhattan. Inserting new history into academic discourse, while also rereading and amplifying long adored queer people, places, and experiences for a public audience, *When Brooklyn Was Queer* is a profound mix of rigorous historical scholarship and delicious readability that will be of use and interest to queer scholars and queer youth alike.

The text is split into seven chronological chapters. After a prologue and introduction, the book opens in 1855 with Walt Whitman walking near the waterfront to pick up the first published copies of *Leaves of Grass*; the next chapter begins with the opening of the Brooklyn Bridge in 1883, binding Brooklyn to Manhattan forevermore. Ryan then structures chapters by decades (1910s, 1920s, 1930s) as he traces shifting gender and sexual mores to articulate changing notions of queerness. He splits the last two chapters between 1940 and 1945, to focus on the WWII era, and the increasingly restrictive and menacing 1945–1969 period of "great erasure," concluding with the Stonewall Riot. Ryan's chapters detail the rise of when, where, and how queer people could find one another and themselves across Brooklyn, and how they shaped the city and world we know now.

Many of the queers and queer places Ryan discusses are artists and art venues such as theaters or poets' and novelists' communal homes. These queers' art and lives were often fodder for tabloids, a vast source of archival records. Some subjects appear in multiple chapters—gay diarist and Kinsey informant Thomas Painter, lesbian activist and archivist Mabel Hampton, transgender voluntary medical subject and sex worker Loop-the-Loop, and (sexuality undefined) poet and essayist Marianne Moore—thereby affecting a sense of how queer lives seep beyond any formal periodization. Ryan's notion of queer, too, is admirably leaky and inclusive. His 114-year history situates the modern reader in shifting identities and frameworks, ranging from inverts to homosexuals, drag queens to drag kings, bisexuals to asexuals, transgender people to cross-dressers, and everyone in between and beyond, whether for one-night hookups or lifelong partnerships.

The contributions of *When Brooklyn Was Queer* are manifold. First, Ryan's political economic reading of the city is grounded in everyday lives of queer Brooklynites, whose queerness shapes and is shaped by expanding materialist locales of transportation infrastructures, working-class neighborhoods, and waterfront redevelopment. Reading urban planning through the lens of gender and sexuality renders further insights into how development worked alongside and against "deviance." Second, the text includes close readings of eugenic-saturated policing, laws, policies, and morality campaigns, along with medical developments, that shaped the notion of what homosexuals are in Brooklyn and, in so doing, how queerness works differently across city geographies and time. Some buildings, streets, and neighborhoods were mentioned so often that they become saucy characters unto themselves: the now obliterated cruising lane of Sands Street (damn you again, Robert Moses), the now knocked down, queer communal home "February House" at 7 Middagh Street (residence to Carson McCullers, Gypsy Rose Lee, and W. H. Auden, among others), and that space at the end of the Brooklyn world where everyone was welcome to play, Coney Island. There is even a record of what may be one of the first Brooklyn gayborhoods, which emerged as gay men bought and coordinated the decoration of their homes on State Street in the early 1960s (238). Finally, Ryan has written a smart, witty, and easy-to-read queer history that upsets notions of queer history as a "march of incremental progress" (223), thereby furthering the access and range of queer history for public, classroom, and academic audiences.

The most significant weaknesses of the book have to do with race foremost and gender second. Ryan cautiously explains that while he begins *When Brooklyn was Queer* with Whitman, it is the power of white gay men to retain records primarily about themselves. Some would argue it's best not to reassert the limits of the archive; yet, there are always moments in each chapter that erupt with possibilities for further intersectional insight that never come. Calling out archival absences and limits per chapter would have served the reader well. Ryan sometimes attends to but does not resound the fact that white privilege shapes most of his subjects' ability to create and, sometimes, sustain queer spaces and lives. Most potently, Ryan ends his third chapter, "Criminal Perverts, 1910–20," by noting that "fears about 'race mixing' and queer people were intimately connected, flip sides of the same eugenic coin" (98). If this sentence had framed the chapter rather than come at its conclusion, the deep and total ties among gender, sexuality, and race would have saturated the chapter as they saturate queer worlds.

Still, Ryan's Brooklyn allows the reader to take in this forever edge and "edgy" borough/county to recall its unique and important past: "If we imagine each of the queer lives this book will discuss as a single thread, Brooklyn is the place where they all momentarily knot together before shooting out again in every direction" (37). *When Brooklyn Was Queer* can be added to the thankfully evergrowing list of queer public histories that take us in hundreds of new directions we never knew existed but have craved all along.

Jen Jack Gieseking is associate professor of geography at the University of Kentucky.

DOI 10.1215/10642684-9608245

TOWARD A BLACK–QUEER CRITICAL RHETORICISM

Octavio R. González

None Like Us: Blackness, Belonging, Aesthetic Life
Stephen Best
Durham, NC: Duke University Press, 2018. 208 pp.

An ambitious book forged with the tarnished tools of queer theory and affective historiography—or "unhistoricism" (10), after Valerie Traub (2013)—Stephen Best's *None Like Us* is a manifesto. "My goal," he begins, "is to encourage a frank reappraisal" of the "*assumed conjuncture* between belonging and a history of subjection" (1; emphasis added). Best's title and animating concept originate in David Walker's 1830 *Appeal to the Coloured Citizens of the World*.[1] The "assumed conjuncture," which Best leads back to Harlem Renaissance historian and activist Arturo Schomburg, is between Black archival recovery and existential reparation. "A collective is born of this inquiry into the past," Best assures (12). But he challenges the "forensic logic" (or "forensic imagination") of *melancholy historicism*, Best's term for the critical disposition evident in the archival turn (13, 21). Melancholy historicism, he argues, "connects the collective's formation to thinking about the past" in a way that is pseudo-redemptive but ultimately self-satisfying (12). "Schomburg's recovery imperative is the manifestation of a command we have *all* obeyed since Hegel's regrettable move to exclude Africans from narratives of historical progress," he adds (12). And that "command" entails returning "to the scene of the crime" in archives of the transatlantic slave trade (21).

In Best's view, the forensic logic governing the recovery imperative makes a category mistake. It compels critics to "regard the recovery of archival evidence of black historical being, on the one hand, and recovery in 'the ontological and political sense of reparation . . . recuperation, or the repossession of a full humanity and freedom, after its ultimate theft or obliteration' [Lowe 2015: 85], on the other, *as belonging to the same order of thought*" (12–13; original emphasis).

Interestingly, Best further claims, in a chiasmus emblematic of his "rhetorical" turn, that "black studies" is "burdened by a contrary malady" to queer studies: "the omnipresence of history in our politics" (24, 2). By contrast, queer studies, Best notes, is now "reassessing . . . the optimistic hopes and visions of utopia to which queers find themselves attached" (1, 2). The cold war between antisocial queer theory and the "anti-anti-utopianism" of queer-of-color critique, exemplified by José Esteban Muñoz's *Cruising Utopia* (2009), inspires Best's union of both (Muñoz 2006: 826). (Indeed, the intersectional and antisocial are not so far apart as we used to think.[2]) Yet the chiasmus between queer and Black studies begs the question, how can you tell the dancer from the dance?

Best's manifesto urges us to abandon the crime-scene investigations of melancholy historicism to embrace what I'd call *critical rhetoricism*, a Black–queer formalism: a return to rhetorical figures and aesthetic patterns of thought that enable us to imagine a different relation to our bloody past. The coauthor of surface reading, which launched a thousand method wars, Best again seeks to reorient critical disposition: a rhetoricism to join the new formalisms.

None Like Us is grounded in the project of explaining why this break is needed. "Black studies," he argues, "confronts the . . . difficult task of disarticulating itself . . . from the historical accretions of slavery, race, and racism, or from a particular *commitment* to the idea that the slave past provides a ready prism for understanding . . . the black political present" (2).

Superficially reminiscent of Kenneth Warren's controversial 2012 study *What Was African American Literature?*, *None Like Us* extends beyond Jim Crow America to Walker and the origin of the Black Atlantic. Best argues against melancholic attachment to that origin as necessarily originary. He argues against critics' virtue-signaling self-investiture, proposing ethical "self-divestiture" instead (22); instead of heroic recovery, critical "self-abnegation" (22); instead of reconstruction, a "disintegrative impulse" (23). The writers and artists Best studies refigure Black narratives beyond a tragic recuperation of belonging. For recognition is not redistribution; following Wendy Brown (1995, 1999) and others, Best shows the "limits of the historiographical project rooted in affective attachment to past suffering," limits he insists have "been evident for some time" (55, 38). In short, his "uneasy" survey of the Black/Americanist field challenges us to stop watching reruns of *CSI: Crime Scene Investigation*.

If not melancholic, is Best's vision Afropessimist? Yes and no: "My objective is to remove the question of antiblackness"—the ontology of Afropessimism—"to the registers of rhetoric and relation" (137n18). Yet, Best's ambiguous response doesn't resolve the issue. It implies an Afropessimism simply different in register. Indeed, and ironically, *None Like Us* sublates Afropessimism. Best invokes not archives of injury but rhetorical gestures ("litotes and metalepses") (23, 24). He traces an aesthetic of "the intransmissible," "gossamer writing," and "thinking like a work of art," the title of part 1 (25, 27). Best seeks not to transcend or obliviate history, but to move Black studies past a melancholy relation to it through a negative aesthetic imagination.

In tandem, conjoining antisocial and intersectional queer theory, Best admits being "in search for selfhood that occurs in disaffiliation rather than solidarity" (22). Why? Because what "'we' share"—"whether queer or black," he remarks parenthetically (why not both?)—is "the open secret of 'our' impossibility" (19, 22). The impasse of a "we" defined as an "impossibility" requires new critical paradigms to conjure a Black present (or presence) beyond the scene of the original (or ongoing?) crime.

Best admits being once invested in a *Law & Order* paradigm, a "tort historicism that views slavery as a site of wrongful injury" (38). But his book suggests a unique way to reckon with the past. How? By being "inspired to craft a historicism that is not melancholic but accepts the past's turning away as an ethical condition of my desire for it" (20). In so doing, Best draws a fine distinction between *antirelational* and *antisocial*. His registers of "rhetoric and relation" are antisocial *and* collectivist. Best writes "in the interest of the pleasures of a shared sense of alienation understood, in the first instance, as an unfitness for the world and history as it is" (3). Heather Love (2007: 40), in *Feeling Backward*, argues that despite queer historians' desire to touch the past, the past might not want to be touched. *Noli me tangere* (Don't touch me), she writes, is "an apt motto for queer historical experience." *None Like Us* illustrates that it's just as fitting for Black queer historical—and critical—experience.

The queer art of formalism is alive and well.[3] *None Like Us* brings together antisocial queer theory and Black/Americanist studies in a dance inspired by "the pleasures" of a "sense of kinship shadowed by severance" (6). Again, "with a bit of reverb": "There are pleasures to be found in a shared sense of alienation, a shared queerness, emerging from a shared blackness . . . still understood . . . as an unfitness for the world and history as it is" (21, 7–8). What the conceptual, historical, and personal nuances are, regarding "a shared queerness, *emerging* from"—rather than dancing with—"a shared blackness," I leave for the reader to decide.

Octavio R. González is associate professor of English and creative writing at Wellesley College.

Notes

1. Best's epigraph cites Walker's preamble: "The result of my observations has warranted the full and unshaken conviction, that we, (coloured people of these United States,) are the most degraded, wretched, and abject set of beings that ever lived since the world began; and I pray God that *none like us* ever may live again until time shall be no more" (emphasis added).
2. The antisocial intersectional is a budding field within queer-of-color critique: cf. Kadji Amin's (2017) *Disturbing Attachments*; Amber Jamilla Musser's (2018: 3) concept of "brown jouissance," a sensation "that brings together pleasure and pain"; my study of queer/intersectional novelists in González 2020; and Best's *None Like Us* itself.
3. See González 2017.

References

Amin, Kadji. *Disturbing Attachments: Genet, Modern Pederasty, and Queer History*. Durham, NC: Duke University Press, 2017.

Brown, Wendy. 1995. *States of Injury: Power and Freedom in Late Modernity*. Princeton, NJ: Princeton University Press.

Brown, Wendy. 1999. "Resisting Left Melancholy." *boundary 2* 26, no. 3: 19–27.

González, Octavio R. 2017. "Queer Formalism as 'Queer Form.'" *ASAP/Journal* 2, no. 2: 274–75.

González, Octavio R. 2020. *Misfit Modernism: Queer Forms of Double Exile in the Twentieth-Century Novel.* University Park: Penn State University Press.

Love, Heather. 2007. *Feeling Backward: Loss and the Politics of Queer History.* Cambridge, MA: Harvard University Press.

Lowe, Lisa. 2015. "History Hesitant." *Social Text* 125: 85–108.

Muñoz, José Esteban. 2006. "Thinking beyond Antirelationality and Antiutopianism in Queer Critique." *PMLA* 121, no. 3: 825–26.

Muñoz, José Esteban. 2009. *Cruising Utopia: The Then and There of Queer Futurity.* New York: New York University Press.

Musser, Amber Jamilla. 2018. *Sensual Excess: Queer Femininity and Brown Jouissance.* New York: New York University Press.

Traub, Valerie. 2013. "The New Unhistoricism in Queer Studies." *PMLA* 128, no. 1: 21–39.

DOI 10.1215/10642684-9608259

REHASHED LIBERALISM, THE ACCUSATION OF RADICAL PURITY, AND THE ALIBI OF THE "PERSONAL"

Neville Hoad

Queer Palestine and the Empire of Critique
Sa'ed Atshan
Stanford, CA: Stanford University Press, xxii + 274 pp.

In five chapters, Sa'ed Atshan explores the question of queer Palestinian identities in complicated and contested local, national, and global frames. He argues in the first chapter that the queer Palestinian movement in Israel/Palestine "is mostly submerged and latent as a result of Israeli subjugation of Palestinians and Palestinian patriarchy and homophobia" (29), and through ethnography attempts to give voice to the queer Palestinians he argues are excluded from NGO participation and media representations. Chapter 2, titled "Global Solidarity and the Politics of Pinkwashing," elaborates "the split among queer Palestinian solidarity communities between those who name both Zionism and homophobia as systems of oppression that queer Palestinians face and those who prioritize Zionism and see recognition of homophobia as reinforcing a central feature of pinkwashing rhetoric" (75). How this split plays out in transnational activism and boycott politics from gay pride parades to the Boycott, Sanctions, Divestment (BDS) movement is the subject of the third chapter. The fourth chapter considers media and film representations in search of a space "for a multiplicity of voices that capture the heterogeneity of queer Palestinian experiences, subjectivities, and ideologies" (145). The final chapter "examines two theoretical frameworks elaborated by Western-based scholars—the gay international by Joseph Massad and homonationalism by Jasbir Puar—as they have been applied to the global queer Palestinian solidarity movement" to claim that these academic critiques have had "debilitating effects" on the Queer Palestine movement (185).

First, a note on method: in contrast to scholarly works on similar topics, *Queer Palestine and the Empire of Critique* is an unapologetic and unabashedly personal book. The author, who previously taught at Swarthmore College and is now an associate professor of anthropology at Emory University, presents himself as a native anthropologist, and the book is enlivened by many personal anecdotes. One, of course, cannot argue against someone's personal experience and I won't, but I can note the ways such experience is deployed to inoculate against critique. *Queer Palestine and the Empire of Critique* is framed by an autoethnography in the tropes of a coming-out narrative: "During my last night at home that summer as I looked around into the caring eyes of my family members, I imagined them withdrawing their love for me if they discovered my secret. The thought of living in exile as a result of familial homophobia was too much to bear" (xi). The preface ends with the following sentence: "And although I certainly cannot speak for all queer Palestinians, I invite readers to join me in reflecting on my deeply personal journey" (xiv). While it is obviously not possible to cite one's personal experience, it is standard academic practice to cite ethnographic interviews. Very frequently, however, ethnographic information appears in the book without citation and with minimal context: "panicked Facebook messages" from "Tamer," "even more alarming messages" from "Salma." Basil's story stands entirely without explanation or reference (36–38). No citation appears for the following clinching claim: "As one queer Palestinian activist shared with me: 'Massad's criticism of our work is like a cloud that always hovers above me. How do I prove a negative? I am tired'" (189). Where, when, and how did that exchange take place? This lack of citations is endemic.

The book attempts to articulate the author's personal history and anecdotes of conversations with the complex story of a shifting set of NGOs, cultural productions, global solidarities, funding flows, and boycotts that inter alia constitute the phenomena, historical experience, and social movements that could be held under the sign of "Queer Palestine." The book argues throughout that Zionism and anti-Zionism join hands with Palestinian homophobia/patriarchy in the mildly tautological neologism of *ethnoheteronormativity* (the last three terms are largely used interchangeably) to stall the emergence of a queer Palestinian movement/subjectivity. This stalling is caused by what the book calls "the radical purists." There is historical data in these accounts—despite the author's startling refusal to cite Arabic language sources, beyond his inadequately cited ethnographic subjects—that could have led to an interesting and urgent analysis of sexuality and political agency under conditions of present neoliberalism.

Instead, across the chapters, a polemic emerges repeatedly. Strong and often unsubstantiated attacks on some leading anti-imperialist leftist scholars and the activist organization Al-Qaws are made throughout because they are "the radical purists." The definition of the term *radical purist* is often vague, even as it appears on nearly a quarter of the book's pages, but here is the charge: "The political currents of radical purism have subsequently helped transform the critique of empire into an 'empire of critique' in which queer Palestinians . . . find themselves under numerous overlapping regimes of surveillance, suspicion and control" (13). Initially, this rhetorical sleight of hand—the transforming of "the critique of empire" into "the empire of critique" —reveals a serious confusion around matters of scale and power: academic critiques of Zionism become equivalent to the violences of settler-colonialism, the analytic purchase of terms like the *Gay International*, *homonationalism*, or *pinkwashing* as detrimental to the interests and well-being of queer Palestinians as Zionism and/or the homophobia/patriarchy/ethnoheteronormativity ensemble.

Then, this conjuring and targeting of "an empire of critique" through the accusation of radical purism becomes analogous to something like red-baiting, especially since the scholars the US-based Atshan makes exemplary of his phantasmatic empire of critique, the "Western-based" Joseph Massad and Jasbir Puar, most notably, have themselves already been subjected to a number of smear campaigns, personal and professional attacks by a range of political and institutional actors not exactly on the side of queers or Palestinians. That this "empire of critique" is characterized by the trope of "radical purism" makes those designations symptomatic of the book's moment of writing in the wider US political context. Accusations of "radical purism" come straight from the playbook of liberal/centrist/reformist establishments—think the DNC on Bernie Sanders—and the invocation of this pragmatist shibboleth is entirely congruent with the general thrust of *Queer Palestine and the Empire of Critique*. Ultimately, what the book offers in the language of tolerance, multiplicity, and heterogeneity is a return to the kinds of sexual liberalism that Massad and Puar and others have already critiqued. Yet, the book wants to claim that such a fallback into sexual liberalism would be an advance on those scholars' positions.

These bad professors build their "empire of critique" through what Atshan terms *discursive disenfranchisement*. Strong disagreement is reframed as silencing. Why should the rigorous attempt to ensure that the study and building of minoritarian and third world sexuality and gender movements is not simply *personal*—and the demand that scholars and activists take seriously questions of imperial power, the extractive political economies of racial capitalism, and the material constraints and conditions of agency—be experienced as paralyzing, let alone disenfranchising?

Of course, no critic is above criticism, and the domains of activism and scholarship are not coterminous, but Atshan's reading habits are similar to his citational ones in relation to those he wishes to criticize. He tends to paraphrase and cherry-pick his interlocutors to make them say what he wants them to say. For example, Atshan wants to accuse Massad of essentialism, so he accuses him of producing an "authentic" Arab sexuality (194). *Authentic* is not a word that appears either in the 2002 *Public Culture* Massad essay ("Re-Orienting Desire: The Gay International and the Arab World") nominally under discussion here, or in the expanded version of that essay in *Desiring Arabs* (2007), or in *Islam in Liberalism* (2015), and Massad's work generally abjures the culturalist and empiricist logics underpinning any idea of authenticity. It's not there; it can only be imputed. And then there is this extraordinary sentence: "Massad does not recognize how international aid in Israel/Palestine, as my own forthcoming research has revealed, can both facilitate Israeli settler-colonial processes and provide Palestinians with tools to resist those processes" (190). Forthcoming research has of yet revealed nothing, because it is still forthcoming, and if it is actually forthcoming, a citation would be useful. Moreover, if you already know what the findings will be, the research starts looking like confirmation bias. These kinds of rushed and incoherent claims indicate to this reviewer more of a desire to besmirch, discredit, and dismiss one's interlocutors than an attempt at serious scholarly engagement with them.

Neville Hoad is associate professor of English and women's and gender studies and the codirector of the Bernard and Audre Rapoport Center for Human Rights and Justice at the University of Texas at Austin.

DOI 10.1215/10642684-9608273

About the Contributors

Marquis Bey (they/them, or any pronouns) is currently assistant professor of African American studies and English, affiliated faculty in Gender and Sexuality Studies, and core faculty member of Critical Theory, at Northwestern University. Bey is the author, most recently, of *Black Trans Feminism* (2022). They are currently revising a manuscript titled "Cistem Failure: Essays on Blackness and Cisgender," forthcoming in 2022.

Caia Maria de Araújo Coelho is a Brazilian travesti transfeminist. The author founded the website *Transadvocate Brasil* and is a member of the board of directors of the nongovernmental organization Natrape, which claims human rights for trans people. She researches in the fields of cinema, decolonial studies, and queer abolitionism.

Stephen Dillon is associate professor of critical race and queer studies in the School of Critical Social Inquiry at Hampshire College. He is the author *Fugitive Life: The Queer Politics of the Prison State* (2018).

Nadja Eisenberg-Guyot is a PhD candidate in cultural anthropology at the CUNY Graduate Center and an abolitionist organizer in New York City. Their work argues that so-called alternatives to incarceration programs, like court-coerced drug rehabilitation, are not alternatives to criminalization. In this way, rehabilitation is part of a reformist project to stabilize white supremacy in the face of abolitionist challenges.

Travis M. Foster is an associate professor of English and academic director of the Gender and Women's Studies program at Villanova University. He is the author of *Genre and White Supremacy in the Postemancipation United States* (2019); the coeditor of "American Women's Writing and the Genealogy of Queer Thought," a special issue of *Legacy* (2020); and the editor of *The Cambridge Companion to American Literature and the Body* (forthcoming 2022). His current project is tentatively titled "Womanish: Variant Femininities of the American Nineteenth Century."

Jesse A. Goldberg is a 2021–22 research fellow in the Humanities Institute at Penn State University and will be joining the English department at New Mexico Highlands University as assistant professor of American literature in 2022–23. Their academic writing has been published or is forthcoming in the journals *ASAP/*

Journal, College Literature, Public Culture, Callaloo, MELUS, and *CLA Journal,* as well as the edited volumes *Teaching Literature and Writing in Prisons; The Routledge Guide to Alternative Futurisms; Against a Sharp White Background: Infrastructures of African American Print;* and *Toni Morrison on Mothers and Motherhood.*

Jaden Janak is a PhD candidate and Donald D. Harrington Fellow in African and African Diaspora Studies at the University of Texas at Austin. Their research focuses on prison abolitionist organizing in the twentieth and twenty-first centuries. Jaden teaches at Lockhart Correctional Facility and is involved with local and national abolitionist collectives. Their work can be seen in *Communication and Critical/Cultural Studies* and accessed via their website jadenjanak.com.

Alexandre Nogueira Martins holds an MA in sociology and a BA in social sciences from the University of São Paulo (USP). The author's research focuses mainly on social movements, neoliberalism, carceral politics, decoloniality, and queer abolitionism.

Alison Rose Reed is associate professor of English at Old Dominion University. Her book, *Love and Abolition: The Social Life of Black Queer Performance,* is forthcoming in 2022. With Felice Blake and Paula Ioanide, she coedited *Antiracism Inc.: Why the Way We Talk about Racial Justice Matters* (2019). In California she organized against prison expansion projects and in Virginia she cofounded Humanities Behind Bars, an abolitionist network of radical group-based study and mutual aid.

S.M. Rodriguez is an antiviolence scholar-activist who works against the criminalization and marginalization of LGBTI people of African descent. They are assistant professor of gender, rights and human rights at the London School of Economics and Political Science and the author of *The Economies of Queer Inclusion: Transnational Organizing for LGBTI Rights in Uganda* (2019). They lived and organized in Brooklyn, New York, served as a core member of Safe OUTside the System, and volunteered on the board of directors of the Audre Lorde Project in New York City, USA.

Kitty Jayne Rotolo is an elder trans woman, an activist, and a personal friend of both the legendary Ms. Marsha P. Johnson as well as Ms. Sylvia Rivera. Ms. Rotolo is a community elder, trans activist, and former member of the House of Field.

She is currently incarcerated by the New York State Department of Corrections and Community Supervision (NYSDOCCS) and has been, off and on, for the past twenty-six years.

Lorenzo Triburgo is a Brooklyn-based artist employing performance, photography, video, and audio to elevate transqueer subjectivity and cast a critical lens on notions of the "natural." Triburgo has exhibited and lectured in cities throughout the United States, Europe, and Asia and has artworks in the permanent collections of the Museum of Contemporary Photography (Chicago, IL) and Portland Art Museum (Portland, OR). Triburgo is a full-time instructor at Oregon State University's College of Liberal Arts online campus who teaches critical theory, photography, and gender studies with a focus on expanding liberatory learning practices in online environments.

Sarah Van Dyck is an industrial-organizational (I/O) psychologist who specializes in mixed methods research, blending and translating qualitative audio, visual, and narrative sources with quantitative data. Her work centers on gender and identity at work, occupational health psychology and disparities in underrepresented populations, and LGBTQIA research in applied settings. She holds a BA in sociology/anthropology from Lewis and Clark College and an MA in I/O psychology from Portland State University, where she is currently an ABD doctoral candidate in applied psychology. Sarah lives and works in Brooklyn, New York.

DOI 10.1215/10642684-9618679

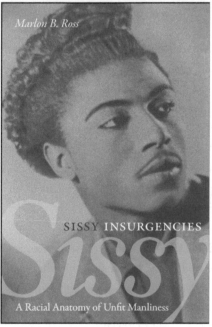

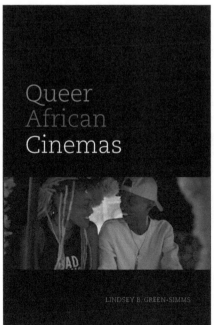

Reframing Todd Haynes

Feminism's Indelible Mark

THERESA L. GELLER and JULIA LEYDA, editors

a Camera Obscura book

"I love Reframing Todd Haynes. *It was an extraordinary experience to fall down the rabbit hole with this book and revisit the films I thought I knew so well! Each chapter brought something fresh and provocative to Todd's work. I highly recommend it."*
— **CHRISTINE VACHON**

Queer African Cinemas

LINDSEY B. GREEN-SIMMS

a Camera Obscura book

"Lindsey B. Green-Simms's compelling insights prod us to think about resistance as multilayered, incomplete, and even messy in ways that reveal how the vulnerabilities of queer life exist alongside multiple modes of survival, care, and aspirational imaginaries. Queer African Cinemas *is engaging, generative, and remarkably persuasive."* — **GRACE A. MUSILA**

dukeupress.edu

DUKE UNIVERSITY PRESS

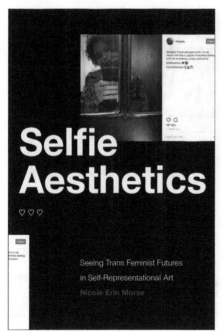

Selfie Aesthetics

Seeing Trans Feminist Futures in Self-Representational Art

NICOLE ERIN MORSE

"By giving nuanced, close attention to selfies as texts and political gestures and speech, Nicole Erin Morse intervenes in the common understanding of them as flat expressions of narcissism.... With its sustained investigation of trans feminine aesthetic digital practices, this compelling book will appeal to audiences in art history, queer theory, trans studies, media studies, and cultural studies." — **CÁEL M. KEEGAN**

Lesbian Potentiality and Feminist Media in the 1970s

ROX SAMER

a Camera Obscura book

"Rox Samer reworks the genealogy of contemporary feminist, queer, and trans cultural politics in this fascinating foray into the futures envisioned by speculative lesbian literature and media half a century ago. It's brilliant, generative, and timely." — **SUSAN STRYKER**

Gay Liberation after May '68
GUY HOCQUENGHEM

Theory Q

"An immense gift to queer theory, Gay Liberation after May '68 *promises to bring a new generation of English-language readers to Guy Hocquenghem, who can use this text as a blueprint for activism to interrupt and hopefully dismantle the gross structural inequities that shape our present world."* — **BENJAMIN KAHAN**

Queer Companions
Religion, Public Intimacy, and Saintly Affects in Pakistan
OMAR KASMANI

"Omar Kasmani offers us an exquisitely written ethnography on the queerness of religion, region, and belonging. Queer Companions *pulls us in, moving us toward more radical modes of the social life of the intimate."* — **ANJALI ARONDEKAR**

Intimate Eating
Racialized Spaces and Radical Futures
ANITA MANNUR

"Anita Mannur's extraordinary analyses of cooking and eating in photography, film, television, novels, blogs, and performance art creates new forms of the public in unexpected places.... Intimate Eating *is powerful reading for Asian American studies, queer and feminist of color studies, and food studies: I want to eat every meal with this book."* — **BAKIRATHI MANI**

dukeupress.edu

DUKE UNIVERSITY PRESS

Keep up to date on new scholarship

Issue alerts are a great way to stay current on all the cutting-edge scholarship from your favorite Duke University Press journals. This free service delivers tables of contents directly to your inbox, informing you of the latest groundbreaking work as soon as it is published.

To sign up for issue alerts:

1. Visit **dukeu.press/register** and register for an account. You do not need to provide a customer number.

2. After registering, visit **dukeu.press/alerts**.

3. Go to "Latest Issue Alerts" and click on "Add Alerts."

4. Select as many publications as you would like from the pop-up window and click "Add Alerts."

read.dukeupress.edu/journals

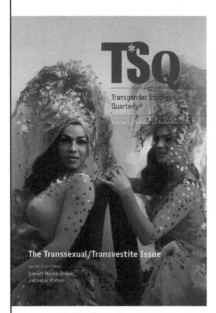